Hymen's Praeludia, Or, Love's Master-piece: Being That So-much-admir'd Romance, Intitled, Cleopatra, In Twelve Parts

Gaultier Coste De La Calprenède

HYMEN'S PRÆLUDIA:

OR,

Love's Master-Piece.

Being that So-much-admir'd

ROMANCE,

INTITLED,

CLEOPATRA.

In Twelve Parts.

Written Originally in FRENCH, and now Elegantly render'd into ENGLISH,

By ROBERT LOVEDAY.

EVAND.
Quid magis optaret CLEOPATRA *Parentibus orta*
Conspicuis, Comiti quàm placuisse Thori?

VOL. I.

LONDON:

Printed and sold by J. WATSON, in *Wardrobe-Court, Great Carter-Lane.* M.DCC.XXXVI.

La Calprenède, Hautière de
Coste, seigneur de,

To the Right Honourable

His Ever HONOURED LADY,

THE

Lady *CLINTON*.

MADAM,

T fuch Times as Your filent Authority gave me leave to want better Employment, this Trifle (that now begs to live a Shrub under the fecure Shade of Your Patronage) was finn'd into *English*; and though, not to confefs the Prefumption, be to add to it, yet its being born in Your Honour's Service, bids me hope it lefs

A 2　　　　　Rude

Rudeneſs, thus to throw itſelf at Your Feet, than to diſclaim the Privilege of being Yours.

MADAM, I am not ignorant (if You deſcend to the Peruſal of this Humble Toy) that You muſt force Your ſublime Thoughts (which uſually fly at fair Quarries) to a Stooping: But as the Sun, (who is the cleareſt Emblem of Your Virtues) when mounted to his Meridian, does not diſdain to look downwards; ſo if You vouchſafe to let fall the Beams of a Smile upon this Piece, and bid it live, how unkindly others may uſe it, ſhall never be placed among the Fears of,

MADAM,

Your Honour's moſt Humble,
And ever Obedient Servant,
LOVEDAY.

TO THE
READER.

EADER, *thou haſt here my Recreations; if they have the luck to be thine, I have my End, and we are both pleaſed: Thou wilt here find Hiſtory enamelled with Fiction, and Truth Dreſt like a* MAY-Lady, *who thro' the gay Diſguiſe of her Flowry Ornaments, does often ſhew her own Simplicity. If thou be'ſt an Hiſtorian, thou wilt trace his Ingenious Pen through* Tacitus, Florus, Suetonius, *and others that wrote* Auguſtus's *Life, and find with*

what

what skilful Method he hath cul-led such Flowers from each of their Gardens, as were fittest to beautify his Garland. It was the same Hand that wrote the much cried up Caſſandra ; and the beſt Judgments agree, now that this is perfeƈted as happily as begun, it need not yield that any other Precedency but of Time (in all things elſe it claims Ad-vantage.) But I keep thee too long at the Door.

Farewel.

R. L.

To

To his Deferving Friend Mr. LOVEDAY, upon his
Tranflation of *CLEOPATRA*.

SOME ufe to praife before they do
 perufe,
And make a common Hackney of their
 Mufe.
I love my Friend, yet do I love to
 look,
Before I pafs my Verdict on his Book.
'Tis Merit wins Encomiaftick Strains,
While Sycophants, who proftitute their Brains,
Profefs a fervile practick Art of Praife,
And crown weak Artifts with Apollo's Bays.
I would be loth my Genius fhould be fuch,
" This pure Elixir'd Grain will bide the Touch."
I dare maintain't; where Language, Method, Wit,
Approve his Judgment that commendeth it.
Nor is it greater Glory to a State,
To invent a Piece, than aptly to tranflate;
Wherein my Friend has fuch Exactnefs fhown,
His Native-Drefs has made the Work his own:
I am no Partialift; it is a Crime
That fuits with Tim-ifts, it is none of mine:
It was a Maxim from a Sybil's Mouth,
Who thwarts it, is Apoftata to Truth. [creafe,
" Where Nature grounds, and Art improves In-
" That only Hand compleats Love's Mafter-Piece.

        Nomen

Nomen amoris habens, & amare Charactere co-
   Ingenui vatis nomen omenque tenes.   (gens,
Nomen amans, & amantis opus fint pignora palmis
   Digna peregrinis, ut rediere tuis.

Arbores multi renovant Coloni,
Quo magis cultu redeant opimi;
Hoc agit *Loveday* renovans libelli
                Ora faceti.————

Cœtus ut fancti pariunt modeftos,
Et novæ veftes faciunt venuftos,
Mille te dignum tenuere teftes
            Meffe laboris.————

               R. BRAITHWAIT.

Upon this choice Work, *Love's Mafter-Piece*, expofed to light by Mr. LOVEDAY.

AS Pearl 'mong Gems, fo 'mong the Paffions
        Love
Excels, and in a higher Orb doth move.
Her Sifters Faith and Hope attend us here,
While through the Elements our Courfe we fteer;
But Love foars with the Soul beyond the Sky,
As imp'd in Her to all Eternity;
But what was here frail Fancy that did burn
Sometimes, and freeze foon after, there fhall turn
To an Angelick Nature, ever free
From all fuch Fits of Mutability;
  This Author doth this Paffion fo difplay,
And in fuch high Idæas, that he may
Stand to be Chair-Man, and to fit above
The choiceft Mafters in the School of Love.

              JAMES HOWEL.

              Thoughts

Thoughts on this Translation of *Love's Master-Piece.*

GReek Heliodorus *with* Mellifluous *Stile,*
In th' Ethiopick *Story did compile*
Idæas, *which might regularly move*
To conjugal *Affections, and pure Love.*
Loveday, *thy* Gallick *Author doth advance*
Such *with new Art and Splendors to his* France;
And thou (*whose vertuous Knowledge did compile*
Them in best *Language of thy Native* Isle)
As he to modern France, *thou to old* Greece,
For us framed of Stile the Master-Piece.

JOHN CHAPPERLINE.

Upon his teaching *CLEOPATRA* English.

I'Ve Read *some Books on this side; some beyond.*
The Alps, *where greatest Rarities are found;*
But, to speak Truth, 'mongst *all did never find*
A Version *that so richly cloath'd the Mind*
Of th' Author, *nor more gallantly advance*
Our English *Language above that of* France.
All Tongues must have their Height, and Fall. In
Rome
Tully *made* Latin perfect, *but its Doom*
Soon followed his; Loveday *has done the same*
For English, *whose Beauty will Renown his Name.*
The greatest Fear is, none can tread his Path,
So that his Lines will be its EPITAPH.

R. W.

To

To my very Honoured Friend, Mr. ROBERT LOVEDAY, upon his Matchless *Verſion*, entitled, *Love's Maſter-Piece.*

THE rareſt Plants, and Flow'rs ſometimes im-
   prove,
Their Growth and Beauty, by a kind Remove:
Sidney's the Phoſphor, thou the ſplendent Sun,
Deſerv'ſt the Laurel of our Engliſh Tongue.
The Garland's thine, O give me leave to ſay,
I like thy Dawn, but better LOVE thy DAY!

       MA. BROWN, Doc. Med.

To his Dear Brother, Mr. ROBERT LOVEDAY, upon his Tranſlation of *CLEOPATRA.*

COuld I with Pencil copy ſo,
 As thou with Pen haſt drawn this Piece,
The famed Maſters I ſhould out-do
 Of both the Empires, Rome and Greece:
And what the old Samian ſaid, prove true in this,
As Souls, ſo Arts, their Tranſmigration is.

This Grain adds nothing to thy Store,
 And want of Skill bad me not Write;
Yet Love ſaid, Do, though it be poor,
 'Twill borrow Luſtre from his Light:
A Piece of Gum that from a free Heart comes,
May ſhew true Love, as well as Hecatombs.

       A. LOVEDAY.

        To

To my much Efteemed Friend, and Dear Brother, Mr. ROBERT LOVEDAY, upon his happy
Labours of tranflating *C L E O P A T R A*.

WEre yet alive the Cleopatra *Fair*,
 Candace, Elifa, *or Grand Cæfar's Heir*,
With th' Heroes of thofe Times, they'd all allow,
They ne'er fuch Luftre did receive as now:
What ever other Authors written have,
Had Buried lain in dark Oblivion's Grave,
Or been deprived of the greateft Glory,
That all acknowledge due to fuch a Story;
But that thy Pen renew'd and imp't the Wings,
To their illuftrious Fame, repeating Things
In quainter and concifer Terms than they.
 Spurn then at Envy's Plots, contemn all them
 That ftrove to rob the World of fuch a Gem;
 Or pay th'Oppofers Thanks, fince th' others Pain
 Serves as a Foil to that Politer Strain.

J. WRIGHT.

To my very much Honoured Friend, Mr. Ro-
BERT LOVEDAY, upon his Matchlefs *Verfion,*
entitled, *Love's Mafter-Piece.*

SIR, *there is nothing that offends me fo*
 (Next to my Sins) as thefe your Lines muft go
For a Tranflation; which no lefs exceed
The French, *than fertile* Nile *the Barren* Tweed:
Which (when the Delphick Sword *of Him that*
  reigns
Hath Conquer'd France, *made the fteep Mountains*
  Plains,

And

And laid both Dialects in common,) shall
Be thought no Copy, but th' Original:
For where the Author only doth abound
With graceful Words, here th' are with Fancy
                    crown'd:
What he wrapt up in Clouds of grosser Air,
Your LOVE distills in Phrase Polite and Fair.
Where he confounds us with an irksome Night,
Your DAY Reviveth by his gladsome Light.
Chaucer *and* Gowr *our Language but Refin'd,*
You (Sir) true Chymist *like, have it calcin'd:*
Hew'd out the Barbarous Knots, and made it run
As smooth as doth the Chariot of the Sun;
Whil'st French *is but the Foil, to let us see*
The Lustre of our Tongue's Prosperity.
   And this choice Work more fitly stiled is,
   (Not only LOVE's, *but)* LOVEDAY's
      Master-Piece.

G. WHARTON.

Hymen's

Hymen's Præludia :

OR,

Love's Master-Piece.

The First BOOK.

ARGUMENT.

Prince Tyridates *rescues Queen* Candace *from the
Jaws of* Neptune, *invites her to his solitary
Residence, and there gives the Relation of his
Life. His Extraction, Education, and strange
Escape from the inhuman Cruelty of his Brother* Phraates; *and after the Murther of his Father and all his Brethren. The secret and open
Practices of his Brother's Malice pursue him
through the Courts of* Armenia, Media, *and*
Bithynia, *where he runs the hazard of his Life.
by the Treachery of King* Pharnaces. *He flies
into* Judea, *is received and treated honourably
by* Herod : *Relates his Cruelties, falls in love
with Queen* Mariamne, *and* Salome, Herod's
Sister, with him. He commands in the War

against Malichus *the* Arabian, *gives him many brave Defeats, and at laſt, by a total Over-throw, drives him out of* Judea; *returning, finds* Hircanus *murther'd. He gains* Sohemus *to let him viſit her, diſcovers his Affection, which ſhe virtuouſly rejects.* Herod's *proſper-ous Return from his* Rhodian *Voyage to* Au-guſtus. *He enlarges* Mariamne. Salome *ar-tiſtially inſinuates her Love to* Tyridates, *but is civilly refus'd, which half converts it into* Spight. Tyridates *often renews his Re-ſearch of* Mariamne, *and is often confuted and repul-ſed by her Wiſdom and Vertue, which refines his Affection.*

T HE Shades of Night had not yet given place to the firſt Bluſhes of the Day, when the ſad *Tyridates*, waken'd by his cruel Inquietudes, and not able to wait the approach-ing Light, left his ſolitary Man-ſion, to breathe his languiſhing Body and amorous Thoughts upon the Shore of *Alexandria*. The Eſtate of his Mind, with that of his Fortune, furniſh'd him with Matter ample enough to entertain the Hours, and upon this Em-ployment he ſtill beſtow'd the better Part of his Day; his Griefs were the moſt lively, and his Misfortunes the moſt violent that ever Soul was capable of repreſenting: And yet he fancy'd ſo much Glory in thoſe Sufferings, that (cruelly as they uſed him) he could neither hate nor deſire the End of a Miſery, to which he had conſecrated the reſt of his deplorable Life. He had given ſome Moments to theſe ſad Conſiderations, when lifting his Eyes from the Earth, where they had long been fix'd, and ſending a Look toward the Sea,

they

they were encountered with an Object capable to arrest them.

It was a great Fire, which raising itself from the Waves, seem'd to climb Heaven, with no other Design, than to seek a Refuge in its proper Centre, from the Enemies it fled; the Flames in somes Places, mix'd with thick Smoke, roll'd themselves in great Flashes towards the Stars, and shot their Sparks upwards so fiercely, that they seem'd to contest for Splendor with those Lights, where-with the Firmament was then embroider'd. *Tyridates* judg'd, with much Likelihood, that the Flames could not rise from the Ocean's Bosom, unless sustain'd in some burning Vessel, which made his generous and compassionate Inclination deplore their Miss-hap that were involv'd in that Combustion, and, wanting Power to give other Succours, he sent the Assistance of some Vows to Heaven for their Deliverance.

' Ah! devouring Flames! *cry'd he*, you yet act
' your Part with less Power and Cruelty than mine:
' If you be not suddenly quench'd, the Materials will
' soon fail that feed your Fury: But my Fire finds
' in my Soul an eternal Punishment, no hope of
' Relief from a contrary Element, nor End of such
' a Substance as may ever burn without consu-
' ming.' With these were mingled many Sighs, that rose in Throngs from his Breast; and in the mean time beholding the Fire with a serious Eye, he spy'd it grow pale at the Day's Arrival, which soon after disrobed the Sea and Earth of all their Sables. And thus his Sight was no sooner set at liberty, but surpriz'd again by a second Spectacle, which touch'd him more feelingly than the first, he spy'd some Persons that had indeed escaped the Fire, and were now disputing for Life with the liquid Element, and striving with all their

Strength

Strength to gain the Shore, which they saw already near them. This little Number was compos'd of two Women, who ty'd themselves with fast Embraces to a Plank that sustain'd them, and a Man that swam behind, and with all his Power push'd it towards the Shore, as if he had only tender'd his own Life to employ it in the Preservation of theirs: Yet he was grown so weary, as the Hope of making good his Assistance began to languish; for though the Distance between the Ship and Shore was not so great but a Man might swim it in a Calm, yet the Pains he had taken in thrusting forward the Ladies Plank, added to what themselves had suffered by Water's Coldness, the tossing of the Billows, a Toil too rude to agree with their Delicacy, had render'd them so feeble, as all their Force was left was not able to reach the Shore. Oh! what Beauties were there expos'd to *Thetis*'s Mercy! How proud the Waves were grown of the Privilege they had gotten, to court and kiss one of the fairest Bodies that ever Nature fram'd! and, to render their Courtship less dangerous, they seem'd to lay by a Part of their ordinary Fury, yet retained enough to make their Embraces fatal, if the Gods had not sent Relief.

Tyridates well discerning what kind of Pity the Object crav'd, staid not to weigh his Resolution, but, spurr'd by that generous Disposition, that taught him freely to expose his Life for the Safety of the Miserable, clad as he was, he threw himself into the Sea, being only covered with a thin light Habit, that could not hinder his Design, and swimming with a mighty Force, he had soon reached them, just as they were reduced to the extremest Need of Succour; and bidding the Man employ what Strength was left him for his proper Safety,

Safety, he tender'd the same Service to the Women, which till then they had not receiv'd of him, with such Success, and drove their Plank so strongly forward, as in a short time they approached near enough the Shore to find a Bottom, and stay themselves upon their Feet; then leisurely removing their Bodies, and propping each with an Arm, he led them gently to the Shore, whither presently after came their Man, just as *Tyridates* was preparing to repeat the Danger in his Behalf.

The principal of these Ladies resembled *Venus* newly sprung from *Thetis*' Womb, or something more fair, if possible; and though *Tyridates* was prepossess'd by one of the World's rarest Beauties, yet he could not behold her's without Astonishment, and some Inclination to Idolatry; he had, doubtless, taken her for some Sea-Goddess, if he had not seen the Waves use her too rudely to be her Subject: And he would have believed her a Celestial Deity, if the Extremity wherein he beheld her some Moments before had not persuaded him that he lent his Succours to a mortal Beauty: Indeed her Complexion had not so pure and delicate a White as the World could shew, though it much surpass'd common Beauties; but in revenge of this, her Eyes, to whose Blackness nothing but her Hair was comparable, shot such penetrating Rays, all the Features of her Face formed to so rare a Proportion; her Neck, then half uncovered, so well seconded the Charms of her Visage, and her Shape, much over-topping the common Stature of Women, accompanied with a Gesture so graceful and majestick, every Part helping to make the Composure admirable, that no Eye could view it, and not carry War to the

Heart,

Heart, and give the Soul a hot Alarm of extraordinary Motion.

Tyridates had not then the Leisure singly to consider all these Marvels; and she that possess'd 'em had no sooner gain'd the Shore, but she let herself fall upon the Sand, too much oppress'd with Weariness to sustain it, or command Force enough to pay her Thanks, or almost one single Regard to her Deliverer; her Woman had the same Title to repose, and was likewise fallen at her Lady's Feet; but the Man, though he had undergone excessive Toil, had too stout a Constitution to sink under what he had suffer'd, or lose the Memory and Power to render a fit Acknowledgment to his Preserver; at whose Feet he threw himself, and embracing his Knees with much Affection, ' Whatever you are, *said he*, I will speak the Resentments I ought to have for the Life I owe you, if they were fit to be mentioned with what you have for another: But, Sir, the whole World is my Fellow-Debtor to your Generosity, for the Safety of one of the most considerable Persons.'

Tyridates helping him up, and inviting him to sit a while, and endeavour to dismiss the Weariness his Travel had contracted, told him, ' That he would hold that for the happiest Day the angry Gods had ever sent him, if he had done any thing in relation to his or that Person's Preservation, upon whose precious Life he had set so rich a Value.' To these they both added some other Expressions of Civility, when the beauteous Lady, Time having restored Part of her Spirits, rose from the Seat her Feebleness had chosen, and casting her Eyes round, staid them upon *Tyridates*, whom she knew had preserved her. His Face was none of those that might be seen without Surprizal, for the World had very few that could

could shew more Signs of an Illustrious Birth:
such a pleasing manly Sweetness was stamp'd in
all his Features, that the Fair unknown found
enough in his noble Looks to claim Respect, and
judging him worthy her Civility, she accosted him
with a Gesture replete with Grace and Majesty.

' I owe my Life, *said she*, but am not troubled
' to be redeuable to a Man that carries in his Face
' so many Marks of a Birth and Vertue sublime
' and illustrious.' *Tyridates*, who by the Beams
of that admirable Beauty, and the Stranger's advantageous Character, had already understood what
was due to her, rose from his Seat, and returned
her these Words with much Submission. ' Ma-
' dam, You honour me with a high Opinion,
' borrow'd from erroneous Conjectures; yet, 'tis
' true, my Extraction is none of the meanest; but,
' with much Regret, I confess, I owe that to the
' Glory of my Ancestors, which I despair to make
' good by my proper Vertue.' This Fair unknown
had certainly endeavour'd to confute *Tyridates's*
Modesty, if he had not oppos'd it, by representing
the Inconvenience she suffered in her wet Habits,
and the Hazard her Health might run if she continued in that Condition; to remedy which, ' Ma-
' dam, *said he*, I am a Stranger as well as you,
' and the rather so, because the Miseries of my
' Life have enjoined me to fly all sorts of Society;
' they are those which will not suffer me to offer
' a Retreat worthy of you, which at some other
' Time, and in another Country, I might possibly
' command; I have only here a little House, some
' five or six hundred Paces hence, seated in the
' most savage and solitary Place that I could chuse;
' there are some Chambers commodious enough,
' and Beds in them, where you may repose your-
' selves till your Clothes be dry. Your Entertain-

B 4   ' ment

'ment will not be fo fplendid as the City may
'afford, but you fhall have lefs Noife and Trouble,
'where you fhall fee no Perfon that will not be
'difpofed to ferve you.'　'Your Offers are full
'of Noblenefs, *reply'd the Fair Stranger*; but
'before I accept them, if you pleafe, I would
'gladly learn what City this is, and in what
'Country we now are.'　'You do now behold,
'*faid Tyridates*, the Walls of proud *Alexandria*,
'the Metropolis of the great Kingdom of *Ægypt*,
'made illuftrious both by her Founder, and the
'fuccefﬁve Refidence of fo many mighty Kings ;
'but, it feems, at prefent fhe fadly fuffers the
'Change of her Condition ; for, having been the
'Royal Seat of the *Ptolemy's*, *Anthony's*, and
'*Cleopatra's*, fhe is now reduc'd, not without
'the Reluctance of fome Difdain, to be the Man-
'ﬁon, and bow to the Command of a Governor.'
While *Tyridates* utter'd this, the Man which was
fav'd from the Wreck began to renew his Acquaintance with the Shore, and Walls of *Alex-*
andria, and beheld them with Aftonifhment ;
from thence, turning his Eyes upon the Stranger's
Face, he perceived her change Colour, and underftanding fome Sighs, which the Words of *Tyri-*
dates had forced from her Breaft, but ftriving to
recover her Temper, fhe intreated *Tyridates* to
inftruct her further.　'It is *Cornelius Gallus*,
'*faid be*, that now commands *Alexandria*, to-
'gether with all *Ægypt*; for the Emperor *Au-*
'*guftus*, who gave him this Government, after
'the deplorable Death of the unfortunate *Anthony*,
'and the great Queen *Cleopatra*, who, in this
'unhappy City, about nine Years fince, loft both
'Life and Empire ; but fure you muft know this
'Story, for it is not likely the Earth hath any
'Part which the Fame of that fatal Quarrel, that

'de-

' decided the World's Command, has not vifited.'
' I have heard of it, *reply'd the Stranger with a*
' *faint Voice*, but by the Difcourfe you have
' made me, I fee myfelf reduced to make ufe of
' your Bounty, and accept of the Retreat which
' you profer.'   ' Let us go then, *faid fhe, offer-*
' *ing him her Hand*, when you pleafe ; and the
' Dangers I have newly efcap'd among treacher-
' ous Men, cannot hurt the Confidence my Opi-
' nion hath of your Vertue.'   At thefe Words fhe
began to fet forward ; and on either fide ftaying
her Arm on him and the Man that was preferved
with her, fhe overcame that fhort Way, not without much Trouble, caus'd by her former Wearinefs, together with the Coldnefs, and Weight of
her wet Apparel.

. The Houfe whither *Tyridates* conducted her,
and where he then made his own abode, was
feated amongft divers points of a *Rock*, which
over-look'd one fide of it ; on that quarter where
the High-way lay, it was conceal'd from the
Eye, by a Wood mingled with Rocks : but on
that fide which regarded the Sea, they might
have a full free view from the Windows, as far as
the fight would reach.   The fair Lady, with her
Retinue, was no fooner arriv'd there, but *Tyri-*
dates (having given Command to fome Servants,
fpeedily to make a well furnifh'd Chamber fit
to receive them) led them thither, and there re-
fpectively took his leave, that they might freely
enjoy the privacy of laying off their Robes : They
went to bed, the Miftrefs commanding her Servant to lie with her, being a privilege fhe had
often granted her in their former Travels : *Tyri-*
dates chang'd Cloaths, and fent a Servant with a
dry Sute to the Stranger, whofe Countenance gave

him a good Character, and spake his Age about
fifty Years.

After they had all bestow'd some hours upon repose, Dinner was serv'd up to the Ladies in their
Bed, and *Tyridates* having din'd in another Chamber with his unknown Guest, desired him to ask
the Ladies at what hours he might visit them, and
not be importunate: the *fair Stranger* having sent
her answer that she was ready to receive him, he
entred the Chamber, where she treated him with
much civility; she was then so well recovered,
that all the Beauty which pain and fear had put
to flight, was come back again to its usual lustre,
which *Tyridates* took some time to admire; for,
though his Heart was captive to another, yet it
could not hinder him from giving her the Palm,
from all that ever his Eye acknowledged fair:
The Lady had no less satisfaction from his brave
looks; and this mutual esteem gave to each an
almost equal desire of a further discovery: The
respect which the Lady's Face had imprinted in
Tyridates, would not suffer him to own his Curiosity; but she was so hardy to profess hers, and
after she had invited him to a Seat near the Bed,
and beheld him with a more pleasing Aspect than
she had yet exprest; ' I should be very ungrateful,
' *said she*, if I had any design to hide my conditi-
' on from a person to whom I am indebted for
' my life; and though there be many Reasons
' weighty enough to disswade the discovery of
' my Name, Birth, and Fortunes, in a Country
' that has deserv'd to be suspected; yet I should
' easily consent to trust the secret of my Life to
' the remembrance of what I owe you, and the
' opinion I have of your Vertue, if my desire to
' know you better did not want some satisfaction:
' Pardon this Curiosity to my Sex and Appre-
' hension,

' henfion, and think it not ftrange that I am
' willing to underftand his Name and Condition,
' whofe Face and Behaviour have already fpoke
' fo much to his advantage: If you do not find
' caufe to fufpect me, deny not my defire, and
' in exchange I fhall give you the Relation of di-
' vers paffages, which, with the confidence I re-
' pofe in you, may be judged important.'

Tyridates took fome Moments to reply to thefe
words; but a while after (lifting his Eyes from
the Earth, and fixing them upon the Face of his
fair Gueft) ' You defire that of me, faid be,
' which can never be paid for with a lefs price
' than what you offer; and I fhould be very,
' hardly drawn to reveal the fecret of my life to
' any that could challenge lefs refpect and obedi-
' ence than yourfelf; it were frivolous to conceal,
' that to the confeffion of my Name is faften'd
' the manifeft danger of my life; for, that is
' fallen to fo low a Value in my Confideration,
' that it cannot oblige me to hide it from you;
' but if I give this Relation faithfully, I muft dif-
' clofe things which were never yet declared to
' any, and which I was refolved to continue fe-
' cret, fo long as my Breaft could hold them;
' yet I fhall forget all thefe Confiderations, and
' (arm'd with the hope of your promis'd Ex-
' change) try to fubdue all the Difficulties that
' withftand my Obedience.'

Inftead of rebating, thefe Words enflamed the
Lady's Defire, yet fhe referved fo much Difcretion, to tell him, ' That fhe fhould be forry to
' importune the Recital of fo weighty a Secret:'
But Tyridates replyed, ' He had already cleared
' all the Obftacles that refifted his Inclination to
' obey her;' and (having kept filence fome Moments

ments to prepare Attention) he began his Story in this manner.

The History of TYRIDATES.

THE Discourse I am now beginning, is nought else but a Web of Miseries, interwoven with a few memorable Events; it would afflict your Patience if I did not resolve to abridge it, and (slightly touching the rest) only enlarge myself upon those Adventures that are most important.

My Name is *Tyridates*, I am of the Illustrious Blood of the *Arsacides*, Son of *Orodes* King of the *Parthians*, (under whom the *Roman* Power receiv'd so great a Shock by the loss of *Crassus* and his Army) and Brother to the cruel *Phraates*, who now possesseth that great Empire, which our Ancestors have commanded, since the grand *Arsaces* founded that proud Monarchy of whom we are descended from *Father* to *Son*, in a direct Masculine Line.

At the Knowledge of *Tyridates*'s Quality, his fair Guest regarded him with a graceful Eye, and (interrupting the beginning of his Discourse) ' I took my Conjecture, *said she*, from many
' Signs I observed, that your Birth was not com-
' mon, and am well pleased to find my Opinion
' not erroneous; and lest you should believe her
' a mean Person, that hath engaged so great a
' Prince to this long Narration, I shall let you
' know (before I give a more ample Relation of
' my Life) that I was born a Princess, and am
' lawful Queen to one of the most Puissant and
' Rich Empires of the World.' At these Words *Tyridates* rose from his Chair, and making an Obeisance as low as the Verge of her Robe, demanded Pardon for the Faults his Ignorance had

com-

committed; the fair Queen made him the same Excuses, and when they had allow'd some time for this Discourse, *Tyridates* being returned (by the Queen's Intreaty) to his Seat, thus pursu'd his Story.

I was born under an unfortunate Planet, and those which consulted the Stars at my Nativity, did all find me menaced by most malicious Influence, especially the Mathematician *Thrasillus*, who, before his Youth had done blooming, had acquir'd a great Reputation in that Science, and does at this Day pass for one of the World's living Wonders; he saw me in *Armenia*, which I visited in one of my unfortunate Voyages; after he had perused some Lines in my Hand and Face, and been inform'd of the Day and Hour of my Birth, he foretold my Miseries should not end but with my Life, that neither should long continue, that I was threatned with a Death, which should be neither violent nor natural, but participating something of both. In my first Childhood I was nourished in the King my Father's Court, with a great Number of Brothers, of which I was the youngest, *Pacorus* and *Phreates* being sixteen or eighteen Years elder than I. I was not eight Years old, when my Brothers the Princes *Pacorus* and *Labienus* broke into the Territories of *Asia* that obeyed the *Roman* People, defeated *Saxa*, and, swell'd with their lucky Success, ravaged *Cilicia*, with a Part of *Syria*; it may be you have heard of the Progress they have made in so short a time: But the End was much different, for the following Year they were defeated and unluckily slain by the *Roman* Army, commanded by *Ventidius*, Lieutenant to *Antonius*.

After the Death of *Pacorus*, the Prince *Phraates* my Brother, not much short of his Age, being already

ready married, succeeded to the Helm of the
Parthian Affairs; for the King our Father, beginning to stoop under his Years; desired the comforts
of a calm Age, and to be releas'd of the Troubles which his Youth had sustain'd. At my tenth
Year, the King sent me to a little City upon our
Frontier, where usually the *Parthian Royal Infants*
were educated, and there the Prince *Pacorus* had
learn'd Part of his Exercises: I took some Pains
at mine, with a Success fruitful enough to content
my Tutors; and after I had there imployed about
four Years time, and began to think of being
called home to my Father's Court, I understood
it had been lately dyed with Blood, and that *Blood
Royal*, newly drawn from my poor murthered
Brothers: This Act hath been too well known to
all the World for the Honour of *Arsacides*, whose
Name to all Ages will stand blotted with eternal
Obloquy; the cruel and ambitious *Phrnates*, unworthy of the Race and Memory of *Arsaces*, desirous to make sure of that *Authority*, which he
feared his Brothers might one Day find means to
disturb, caused them to be barbarously slain; and
the aged King our Father, for making his Grief
appear in his just Complaints, and declaiming
against his detestable Inhumanity, in some Terms
that displeased, provoked him to compleat the
Horror of this Age, and the Infamy of *Royal
Dignity*, by the Addition of *Parricide*, thus pu-
nishing no other Crime in his murder'd Father,
than the giving Life to that Cut-throat of him and
all his Off-spring.

I had shar'd the same Fate with my Brethren,
if he that was dispatch'd with the bloody Commission to the City where I was, had not been
touched with the Sense of *Vertue*, and a Respect
due to the *Extraction of Kings*. Instead of exe-
cuting

cuting *Phraates*'s Command, he sav'd me from his
Cruelty; and having informed me in few Words
of my Brothers deplorable Murther, for that of
the *King my Father* was not yet perpetrated, with
the Charge he had given him; ' But *Arsones*,
' *said he*, will sooner choose a thousand Ways
' to perish, than consent to dip his Hands in his
' Master's Blood; let us save ourselves, *Young*
' *Prince*, and evade the dire Design of that savage
' *Monster* that would destroy us.' I intirely resigned myself up to his Conduct, and being followed by my Governor, with five or six Servants
that were willing to run my Fortune, I got to
Horse; and though I had scarce attained to four-
teen Years, I exposed myself to the hardship of
a painful Journey, uncertain to save a Life, which
I never yet could own with Comfort.

Thus I first grew miserable, and began at an
early Age to inure myself to Banishment; and
thus I have learn'd to hope no better than to
finish my Disgrace and my Days together.

Arsanes first conducted me to the Court of *Armenia*, where the King, keeping no very friendly
Correspondence with *Phraates*, and not willing in
his Behalf, to violate the Right of Nations, receiv'd
me into his Protection. In that Court I enjoyed
some Tranquillity. Besides what the King allowed
me, *Arsanes* had brought a Quantity of Jewels,
valued at above a thousand Talents, which the
King my Father, to whom he disclos'd the Design
he had to save me, had given him at his Departure: But Fortune soon shew'd how much my
Repose displeased her, by the Calamities that befel the good King that had gave me shelter, who
most unfortunately fell with all his Family into
the Hands of *Anthony*, her Enemy, and was led
bound to Queen *Cleopatra*, who some time after

with

with most barbarous Inhumanity, caus'd his Head to be struck off. This Disaster, which doubtless you have heard, being important enough to spread over the whole Earth, sent me to seek another *Sanctuary*; which *Arsanes* would needs have to be the Court of *Media*, betwixt whose King, and the King *Orodes* there was some Alliance; there I found the Retreat I desired, and staid two or three Years. In that time there happened the Ruine of *Anthony* and *Cleopatra*, the Establishment of *Augustus Cesar* in the *Roman* Empire; and many other Revolutions, in which the whole World was concerned.

The cruel *Phraates* often sent to demand me of the *Medean King*, but could never dispose him to put me into his Hands; yet after he had made many Incursions upon his Territories, he at last obtain'd his Promise to protect me no longer. At *Praaspa*, the capital City of *Media*, I receiv'd his Orders to retire, colour'd with divers excusive Reasons, which laid the Blame upon Necessity. From whence I went into *Bithynia*, where I was receiv'd by the old King *Pharnaces*, who for two Years time treated me with Humanity enough: But at last the Baseness of his Nature shew'd itself: And indeed, what Faith could I hope for from a disloyal Wretch, that in favour of the *Romans*, had betray'd his own Father, the great *Mithridates*, and inhumanely constrain'd him rather to give himself Death by his own Hands, than fall into his? This perfidious Man, suffering himself to be gained by *Phraates*'s Promises, (who spightfully pursu'd my unhappy wandring Life with an inflexible Cruelty) at last promised either to poyson me, or deliver me up. These Practices were not carried so secretly, but *Arsanes* began to scent them; and detesting such barba-

barbarous Infidelity, after he had given me notice, we made ufe of the Night to fave ourfelves,
and got out of the Confines of his Kingdom, with
our beft Diligence.

After this we long wander'd from Place to Place,
till at laft we arrived in *Judea*, which then groan-
ed under the Scepter of *Herod*, who was formerly
fupported by *Anthony*, and is now favoured by
Auguftus.   And thus I have paffed my difaftrous
Youth, wandering from Province to Province,
and begging Shelter from Court to Court, for
this wretched Life, which was never worth the
Pains I took to preferve it.

I have hitherto epitomiz'd the recital of my
Voyages, which had I drawn at large, muft needs
have tir'd your Attention; but now my Difcourfe muft take a larger Scope to relate the Accidents befel me in *Judea*, fince they are the Authors which compos'd my prefent Condition.   I
had plenty of Reafons to feek a Sanctuary with
Herod; for he was the greateft Enemy *Phraates*
had, and had indeed receiv'd fuch fenfible Affronts from that Patricide, which were all frefh
in his Memory, that he fought all Ways to breathe
his Revenge.   A little before my Arrival at his
Court, *Phraates* had not only fupported his Enemy *Antigonus*, and lent him force to make War
upon him, but had invaded his Dominions, fpoil-
ed his Provinces that were contiguous to *Parthia*,
and took *Hircanus* and *Phafolus* Prifoners; the
latter of which, rather than remain in that Tyrant's Power, chofe to beat out his own Brains
againft a Rock.   Befides thefe, he had done him
other Injuries, which though *Herod*, being then
perplext with other Affairs, had little Power to
repay, yet he laid them up in his Memory, with
a Refentment fo violent, as he would willingly
have

have given a large Part of his Dominion, for an Occasion to requite his Mischiefs. Of this he gave a clear Proof in the Reception he made me, which was imputed by one that understood his Humours, rather to the Reasons I have given, than any natural Inclination to Goodness.

Indeed, he did heap extraordinary Favours upon me, allow'd me large Pensions for Subsistence; and not only promised me Protection from my Brother, but Forces to make War upon him, and take Vengeance for his cruel Persecutions. I receiv'd those Offers with a becoming Acknowledgment; the whole Court, by his Command, treating me with much Respect: And thus I began to live with Tranquillity enough; I say, I began: But alas! the Repose was not long-liv'd; for if my Body enjoy'd a peaceable Retreat, my Soul was encountred with a cruel War, or rather fell into the hardest Captivity that ever Soul resented. Ah! how much better had it been, that I had abandon'd myself a willing Prey to *Phraates*'s greedy Cruelty, than expos'd myself to such rending Torments as have since cost it so many Groans! How justly might I say, to avoid the least of Evils, at least the shortest liv'd, I have thrown myself headlong upon the greatest of all Calamities; I would say the bitterest, if the Glory to suffer so did not poise the Misery? In fine, *Tyridates* was doom'd to die by a brighter Weapon than any *Phraates* had; and receiving the Wound that conducts him to his Tomb, he took it with a Respect so profound, as judged it a Sin to murmur.

Herod had espoused the Princess *Mariamne*, sprung from the glorious Blood of the *Asmoneans* and *Maccabes*, Grand-child to the two Kings, *Hircanus* and *Aristobulus*; indeed, a Scien truly worthy

worthy of so illustrious a Stock, from which Herod following Antipater's Steps, by the help of
the Romans, had usurped the Judean Crown: 'Tis
possible you have heard what Ways he took to
arrive at that Height; how his Father Antipater,
after he had divided the two Brothers, Hircanus
and Aristobulus, at last made use of the Roman
Power to ruine both; and whilst Aristobulus sigh-
ed in his Chains at Rome, after he had served for
an Ornament to Pompey's Triumph, he took Advantage of Hircanus's Weakness to invade the Sovereign Authority, and make way for his Son
Herod, after the Destruction of all the lawful
Heirs, to mount the Throne. He had then newly made an End of the miserable Reliques of the
Family; Alexander, the eldest Son of Aristobulus, being escaped out of Prison at Rome, and
having got some Forces together, was unluckily
surpriz'd and slain by his Enemies, and the unfortunate Antigonus, his Brother, the same that
fled for Refuge to Phraates, and the last King of
the Asmonean Race, being fallen into their Hands,
had his Head cut off by the barbarous Command
of Anthony, who, being Herod's Friend, believed
he could not otherwise assure him the Crown.

Though Mariamne had a just Resentment
against this Cut-throat of her Family, yet she was
forced to marry him in Obedience to the Princess
Alexandra her Mother, and old Hircanus her
Grand-father, who being escaped out of Parthia,
where he was Prisoner with Phaselus, liv'd at Jerusalem in the Condition of a private Man, and
in that Womanish Softness, that made him tamely sit down with the loss of a Crown both from
him and his: And thus the old Man's Weakness,
and the Woman's Ambition, sacrific'd her to their
Interests: But they could never bow her Soul to
love

love that Husband, whose Disproportion of Manners, and Inequality of Birth, with the bloody Outrages he had committed in butchering her Kindred, and the Usurpation of a Crown, which in right belong'd to young *Aristobulus* her Brother, induc'd her to regard with Aversion and Disdain: Yet she had liv'd in a most admirable Moderation with him, and with an Excess of Vertue done Violence upon her Inclinations, by enduring him, whom Heaven and her Parents had given her for a Husband, till by one horrid Act of Cruelty, she defac'd all that a forc'd Obedience had character'd; it was the Death of the Prince *Aristobulus*, Brother to this fair Queen, whose Vertue and excellent Qualities contriv'd his Destruction; for *Herod*, the subtilest of Men, growing jealous of the People's Inclination to this amiable Youth, that was now eighteen Years of Age, caus'd him to be cruelly strangled in a Bath. There was never beheld a more goodly and accomplish'd thing than this young Prince: no Wonder then if his Sister express'd her Resentments in a sharper Tone for so dear a loss; yet *Herod* clear'd himself of it before *Anthony*, but in such a manner, as all the World still thought him guilty, and *Alexandra* and her Daughter beheld him as the poor Prince's Hangman.

The Court and Family of *Herod* were in this Condition when I came thither, and I soon knew all the Reasons why the fair Queen detested her savage Husband; it was then my Eyes lost me all my Repose, by lifting themselves to that Divine Princess.

The Beauty of *Mariamne* was not, like common ones, to be seen without a dangerous Wonder; the Eye of Man never saw any thing more perfect, and till this Day I believ'd none but

young

young *Cleopatra* capable of Comparison; he that was sent by *Anthony* to make Discovery of the World's choicest Beauties, publish'd her a Piece that surpass'd Humanity; and, to speak my Opinion freely, Madam, yourself excepted, and that young Princess, Daughter to the great and unfortunate *Cleopatra*, I think the World cannot shew another that may equal her.

These Words chang'd the Queen's Modesty with a Blush; and, interrupting *Tyridates*, 'I have 'not Vanity enough, *said she*, to believe that what 'you call my Beauty can challenge an Equality with 'the Queen *Mariamne*'s; I am better acquainted 'with her Face than you imagine, for I have 'view'd at our Court the Portrait both of her and 'her Brother, the Prince *Aristobulus*, and indeed 'acknowledged them for the exactest Pieces that 'ever the Hand of Nature drew.' 'It is true, '*reply'd Tyridates*, the Princess *Alexandra*, ra-'vish'd, as well as others, with the Beauties of 'her Children, had caus'd their Pictures to be 'drawn, and sent to divers Parts of the World: 'But, Madam, had it been in the Power of Art to 'represent her Soul, as well as her Body, your 'Eyes had yet been entertain'd with better Won-'ders. All that Report ever spake of the most 'sublime and refined Vertue, will but serve to ex-'press an imperfect Ray of *Mariamne*'s Worth; 'and in those great and frequent Occasions that 'call'd her to the Tryal, she gave Proofs of it, 'that could not be seen and not admir'd: Her 'Constancy shined in her Afflictions, her Pa-'tience in the Persecution which she suffer'd, with-'out the least repining; and that prodigious Force 'of Spirit taught her to endure a Husband, whom 'she had so much reason to hate; and one so 'contrary to all her Inclinations, fix'd her like an

'un-

' unshaken Rock, beat off all the Batteries of her
' malignant Fortune, and took all those Outrages,
' in which another Spirit would have found one
' Reason for Revenge, with a Temper that never
' so much as bow'd itself to the least Thought
' that might unbeseem the Grandeur of her Cou-
' rage.'

And since *Mariamne* was thus, was it possible
for *Tyridates* not to love her, having a Heart susceptible of Love's Impression, and a Soul capable
to comprehend the divine Qualities of *Mariamne*?
Was it possible to defend itself by the Consideration of Vertue from such a Puissance, when Vertue herself came and help'd to give the Passion
Birth? Nor did it ever inspire me with a Thought
that might justly offend her; I lov'd *Mariamne*
with no Intent to improve my Hopes by the Abuse
of her Vertue, but because Love had no stronger
Arms than what that lent him, to make himself
Master of my Soul; and I lov'd *Mariamne*, because it was impossible to see, to know, and not
to love her: Yet I endeavour'd to put my Heart
in a Posture of Resistance, and to the Birth of my
Affection often oppos'd all the Difficulties I could
encounter in my Intentions; the Danger I threw
myself into, and the Remembrance of that which I
ow'd to my Protector: But all these Considerations
were too feeble to defend me; one Look, one
Word from *Mariamne*, would in a Moment destroy all the Fortifications against her, that had
been three Months a rearing: Then I began to
arm the Glory against the Difficulties I had to vanquish, the Peril I slighted by undervaluing my
Life, and excus'd myself to *Herod* with the Violence *Mariamne* did me, my Affection not being
an Effect of my Will: And further, Madam, I
confess I suffer'd a Hope to flatter me of being let
                                                    into

into the Queen's Bosom, by that just Aversion
which the King had given her; for, as I understood it, the Love of a Wife to her Husband,
founded either upon Inclination, Merit, or Obligation, is the best Weapon she can take up to oppose
the Pursuits of a Lover; and the Queen having such
strong Reasons to dispense with all those Ties, had
now no other Defence than for herself, singly consider'd, no Fear of Remorse left for a Husband,
who had but too much merited all the Revenge
she was capable of taking: And from that Time
I began to call in these Apprehensions, my Passion
grew able to corrupt the most virtuous Inclination,
to render me ingrateful to my Benefactor, and to
induce me now no more to regard him as my Protector from *Phraates*, but as he that murder'd the
Brother, the Father, and Grandfather of *Mariamne*: Then Jealousy began to join with my Affection, and I could not reflect upon the Advantages
he possess'd, without deeply sighing; and a thousand times crying out, that the Favours of that
fair Queen were more lawfully due to him, who
was willing to buy them with his best Services and
dearest Blood, than the Man who had paid nothing for them but Indignities and Injuries: When
Love first enter'd my Heart it used me gently, bi-
ling those cruel Ideas of Torment he hath since
afflicted; but now it hath taken an entire Possession, and doth exercise an Authority, which leaves
no Liberty to act by any other Motion than his
own; all my Thoughts, all my Discourse, all my
Actions had no other Subject but *Mariamne*; nay,
my very Sleep, whose proper Office it is, by be-
numbing the Senses, to charm all our Cares, would
not quiet mine, still representing to the Eyes of
my Soul, when the other were clos'd, the divine
Perfections of *Mariamne*.

This

This continual fixing my Spirits, robb'd me of all Repose, and produced Effects that were soon observ'd both in my Face and Behaviour; and though the Care I took to hide it kept the true Cause undiscover'd, yet it could not hinder the whole Court from taking notice of my deep Melancholy, accompany'd with an unnatural Paleness, a Change of my Humour, and an Alteration of my Health.

Arsanes and my Governor, from whom I never before kept any thing conceal'd, in this were Strangers to my Thoughts; and I preserv'd the Disguise with my best Care, rather out of Respect to my Passion, and the Cause of it, than any Doubt of their Affection or Fidelity.

In the mean time, my Access was so easy, that I daily saw the Queen; for the Hopes which *Herod* cherish'd, by my Means to revenge himself of the King of *Parthia*, had made him sweeten his Savage Humour, on purpose to endear me with a kind Entertainment. A thousand times was my Tongue ready before that adorable Princess, not openly to declare my Passion, for I had not the daring to take such a Liberty before a Vertue that made me tremble; but at least, to let her know that no Man had a more passionate Interest in her Fortune, or could pay down his Life with greater Joy than myself, to purchase Solace for her Affections: But still Fear arrested my Intentions, and I have shak'd at the thought of my Design, like a timorous Soldier at the Sight of an Enemy, or his Approaches to an Assault; yet I expres'd part of that in Looks, which my Tongue would fain have said at large; and then if she chanced to cast her Eyes upon mine, and take them in the Fact, they lost all their Assurance, and were either too feeble to receive the Beams she shot, without Astonishment,

ment, or (confounded with the Surprifal) threw themfelves at the Feet of this divine Princefs, and feem'd, by that fubmifs Action, to ask Pardon for the Fault.

The Queen had foon difcover'd the Truth, if fhe had not been prevented by fo many cruel Cares, that would not permit her to faften an obferving Thought upon any of my particular Actions. I was one Day with the Princefs *Alexandra* her Mother, and as I kept a Complaifance full of Refpect in my Behaviour to them, by the help of an Opinion which they had conceived to my Advantage, they began to repofe much Confidence in me: *Alexandra* being of a boiling Spirit, and a Temper which wanted much of the Sweetnefs and Patience the Queen her Daughter was endued with, abandon'd herfelf to the Refentment, which was yet frefh for the Death of *Ariftobulus*, exclaimed againft the Cruelty of *Herod* in moft violent Terms, and deplor'd her own and her Daughter's Condition in Words full of Paffion and Tranfport. From the Injuries fhe receiv'd in her Son's Death, and the Ruin of her Kindred, her bitter Complaints paffed to the deadly Jealoufy of *Herod*, and the fatal Effects it had like to have wrought, by the Order he had given to his Uncle *Jofeph*, which (at the Brink of his going to appear before *Anthony* at *Laodicea*) commanded him to kill *Mariamne*, in cafe that Voyage proved fatal to him. *Alexandra* went on with Vehemence, in recounting divers other Effects of her Son-in-law's Cruelty; and during all the Difcourfe, the Queen never fo much as open'd her Mouth, but only to let go fome redoubled Sighs, and made her Tears keep company with her Mother's Words, which gave frefh Luftre to her Beauty. Oh Gods! what new deep Wounds did the Sight of that lovely Sor-

row give me! how possible it was to behold my
divine Queen in that Estate, without suffering all
her Sorrows! I had now no longer Power to dissemble; and losing all Remembrance of my present Condition, and the Danger whereinto I threw
myself headlong, by provoking *Herod* against
me, I blindly abandon'd myself to the Motions
of my Passion; and casting my Eyes, moist as the
Queen's, upon her's, that were letting fall their
dejected Looks to the Earth, ' Good Gods! *cry'd I,*
' *sighing,* is it possible you should submit the most
' accomplish'd Piece that e'er you made to so much
' Affliction, and must I owe Safety to a Man whose
' Actions have given me so much Horror!' I presently repented that I had suffer'd these Words to
escape me, fearing I had declared myself too far;
but after I perceived I was understood by none
but the Princesses, and that they appeared un-
moved, I recover'd my Assurance; and a little after, the Princess *Alexandra* being retir'd to the
other End of the Chamber to confer with some
Persons, and seeing myself alone with the Queen
by her Bed's Side, I made a strong Assault upon
my Fear, to recover my Discourse; and beholding
the Tears that still crept upon her fair Cheeks,
' Would to Heaven, Madam, *said I,* that all the
' Blood I have could stay the Recourse of those
' precious Tears you spill. Ah! with what Joy
' should I resign it, how gladly sacrifice my Life
' for the Repose of your's!

These Words, wholly compassionate as they
were, were ascribed by the Queen to nought but
the Compassion I took of her Misfortunes; yet
they called her from the Contemplation of her
Miseries, which had seized her Thoughts, and
raising up her Eyes to mine, with a Look full of
a sweet Acknowledgment: ' I should be sorry,
' *said*

' *said she*, to buy the Quiet of my Life with the
' Danger of your's; and I have yet more Right
' to my own Miseries, than to your Afflictions;
' we are both perfecuted, you by a Brother, and
' I by a Husband: Your Resentments I cannot
' disapprove, but I can admit none that are un-
' lawful against my Husband; and if his Actions
' do frame our Calamities, 'tis fit I should believe
' that Heaven makes use of them to chastize our
' Crimes. By them it hath let fall its Wrath up-
' on the Head of our deplorable Family, and
' therefore if any Complaint breaks from me, it
' makes its Way through the Weakness of my
' Nature, and must be owned for the Child of
' Justice.' ' O miraculous Vertue! *cry'd I, in-
' terrupting her*, it is requisite I should redouble
' my Griefs, to see you plunged in such deep Ca-
' lamity.' ' My Misfortunes are not insupport-
' able, *reply'd the Queen*, if you would find the
' way to understand them right; and if you know
' the God which I adore, you would likewise
' know the Consolation I taste in my Sufferings,
' which now you cannot apprehend: If he hath
' given me *Herod* for a Punishment, as well as a
' Husband, I ought to receive him from his Hands
' as both: And if he ordains me to pardon the
' Injuries done by the most cruel and remote Ene-
' mies, sure he would have me forget those with
' an entire Resignation I received from him, to
' whom he hath pleased to tie me in a Knot so
' sacred.' ' It is that, Madam, *answer'd I*, that
' makes me hold my Condition unfortunate, that
' Heaven hath raised you up an Enemy and a
' Persecutor, against whom I cannot offer you
' my Sword and Life, without offending your
' Vertue; that your high-raised Reflections can-
' not be combated by a Man that reveres you;

' nor

' nor can I cenfure the Confideration you keep
' for the King your Husband, fince in his Arms
' I found my Refuge, nor do him any ill Office
' without Ingratitude: But if the Intereft which
' I take in your Wrongs, the Admiration I have
' of your Vertue, and Refentments much more
' preffing and particular, make me find in your
' Afflictions a Subject---------' At thefe Words I
ftopped, and confidering how the infenfibleTranf-
port of my Paffion had carried me into Terms of
Difcovery, I ftaid in an abrupt Silence, without
conducting my Words to any Period.

The Queen obferving my ftrange breaking off,
look'd upon me, and doubtlefs either expected
what was behind to clofe my Difcourfe, or would
have asked the Caufe of my fudden Silence; when
the Princefs her Mother came back again to my
Refcue from the Perplexity wherein my Imprudence had engaged me: Yet I think we had fpent
more Time in this Entertainment, if the Arrival
of fome Ladies had not interrupted us; the Principal of which was *Salome*, the Sifter of *Herod*.
It was not Amity that brought her to vifit the
Princeffes, for fhe hated them mortally; but having a dexterous and artificial Spirit, fhe made it
bow to her Interefts; and knowing the Power
Mariamne had, as unfortunate as fhe was, in the
King's Affections, fhe forc'd herfelf to appear officious, and cover'd her malicious Thoughts with a
black Diffimulation. The Ill-will fhe already
bore to the Queen, was augmented by a Mif-
chance, which I muft now recount; for, fince
you have ordained me to give you the Truth of
my Fortune, ftript of all Difguife, I am forc'd to
tell you, Madam, though the Relation may offend Modefty, that my mifhap, and no other
Caufe, made me belov'd of *Salome*. I had already
oþ-

obferv'd her Affection by divers Signs, but was
eafily perfwaded to flight my Difcovery, either by
a juft Anticipation which chain'd me to another,
the meaneft Part of whom was infinitely above all
that *Salome* could boaft lovely, or by an imperfect Knowledge I had already got of her dangerous Humour; however, I was content to anfwer
her extraordinary Careffes, with fuch a Civility,
as I believ'd was due to the Sifter of *Herod*; and
if I received them at firft with any Satisfactions,
from that Time wherein my Life grew confiderable, becaufe I had given it to the Queen, and had
begun to feek all that Sweetnefs I could fancy in
her only, I had fcarcely allow'd one fingle Regard, either to the Face or Actions of *Salome*.

For that Day fhe cut off my further Difcourfe
with the Queen, but I had Liberty enough to renew it in thofe that fucceeded; the Court was
not then very large, every Man fearing to provoke
Herod's jealous and fufpicious Spirit; but in all
the Converfe I had with her, Fear ftill fetter'd my
Tongue, and I had not the Confidence to difclofe
my Thoughts further than what my Eyes, or fome-
times a fudden Change of Colour could exprefs.
In the mean time, *Herod* (either through Generofity, or thofe Reafons I render'd) ftill permitted
me thofe Liberties, when Fortune prefented an Occafion to improve my Credit with him.

Malichus, who commanded the *Arabians*, an
ancient Enemy to *Herod*, with a powerful Army
invaded the Frontiers of *Judea*, committing a
thoufand Acts of Hoftility; it was fince believ'd
he kept Intelligence with old *Hircanus*, who, as I
told you, liv'd at *Hierufalem* in the Condition of a
private Man, without any Craft or Cognizance of
Affairs, and with the Princefs *Alexandra*: however it was, *Herod* uniting his difperfed Forces
C 3

with

with exceeding Diligence, had soon gather'd a
confiderable Army; and not being able to go in
Perfon, becaufe of fome Troubles he fufpected at
Home, befides his intended Voyage to go vifit
Auguftus Cæfar, then at *Rhodes*, he put his Brother
Pheroras in the Head of it. I was afham'd that
I had employ'd all my Youth in running away
from Death; and defiring Leave of the King that I
might accompany his Brother in that Expedition,
he not only confented, but gave me the Command of all the Cavalry: I parted very well pleafed with the Employment, and endeavour'd to
fweeten the Grief I took to leave *Mariamne*, with
a Hope to merit her Efteem by fome Action of
Valour. I will not trouble you with the Particulars of this War, and fhall only content myfelf to tell you, that by an Excefs of good Fortune, I acquired a Reputation large enough; in
the Engagements made with my Troops, I defeated
the Enemy in divers Encounters, which I had
ftill the Hap to fignalize by fome perfonal Action.
In one Combat, which was obftinately difputed
with a Squadron of our Troops, I kill'd the
Brother of *Malichus* with my own Hand, and a
few Days after, having furpriz'd half the Enemy's
Army at a Pafs upon a River, I charg'd it with
4000 Horfe I had then with me, with fo ftrange
a Succefs, that we kill'd above 8000 *Arabians* upon the Place, and routed the reft with fuch a
grand Confufion, that they left all their Baggage
to our Soldiers.

By this and the precedent Encounters, I had
acquired as much Credit in the Army as I could
well defire; and *Herod* receiving the News, conceiv'd an Opinion of me fo advantageous, as within a fhort time after, having call'd home his Brother *Pheroras* to the Government of the State,

during

during his Voyage to *Augustus*, he desired me to accept the Command of the Army in Chief, rather chusing to repose so weighty a Trust in me, though young, and a Stranger, than in any of his old and more experienced Captains. After the Departure of *Phereras*, I had the sole Command; and Fortune, that had favour'd my Beginnings, did so well second her Kindness in what follow'd, that at last I entirely chased the *Arabians* out of *Judea*, after they had lost above 10000 Lives in divers Encounters. Thus, when all was pacified upon the Frontiers, and we had no more Enemies to combat, after the Garrisons were fortified, I returned towards *Jerusalem*, less satisfied with the Applause was prepar'd me for my good Success, than with the Hope of being suddenly restor'd to the Sight of *Mariamne*; and to see her at such a time, when I believ'd the Service I had done her Country, had purchased some Esteem in her Thoughts.

But, oh Gods! how surpriz'd was I at a sad Report I met with upon the Way, which told me that *Herod* was departed from *Rhodes*, with design to gain the same Credit with *Augustus* that he had with *Anthony*; but before his Departure, he caus'd old *Hircanus* to be strangled, out of Suspicion that he kept Intelligence with *Malichus*, and that great Princess his Grand-Child, with her Mother, to be shut up in a Castle, or rather a close Prison near the City, under the Guard of *Sohemus* and *Joseph*, with express Order to restrain their Liberty, and forbid them all Converse till he came back again. This News not only moderated the Contentment I took in my Return, and the successful Event of my Expedition, but possess'd my Spirit with Astonishment, Horror, and Compassion. I was amaz'd at the Cruelty of *Herod*, who

hold-

holding his Life and Scepter of *Hircanus*'s Goodness, though he was then fourscore, had not the Patience to stay till Nature would relinquish him to his Tomb; the Horror of this Act, and the sad Pity I had for the Affliction and Captivity of *Mariamne*, bruis'd my Soul with a Grief so weighty, as I was ready to give over all Resistance.

Arsanes, and my Governor *Polites*, seeing my Sorrows swell to such a Proportion, as they thought too big for my Interests in *Herod*'s House, earnestly entreated me to undisguise the Cause of it. At first I resisted; but in fine, considering the little Reason I had to disturb them, after they had given such clear Proofs of their Affection, I abandon'd my Secret to their Discretion, and avowed my violent Passion for *Mariamne*. This Confession surprized them, though well knowing what Charms the Queen possessed, and after they had in vain represented all the Reason they could make to extinguish my Flame, they disposed themselves to serve me at the Peril of their Lives. I was a little comforted with the Protestations they made me, and began to judge their Advice not unserviceable for the Conduct of my Desires. I finish'd the rest of my Journey, with such a setled Melancholy, that the Reception I had from *Pheroras* and the rest of the *Jews*, was incapable to moderate it; What, said I, when I was alone, or had only my two Confidants about me, is *Mariamne*, to whom all should resign their Liberties, become a Captive? and can the Gods permit the most perfect Piece that ever they put their Hands to, to be given up to the Cruelties of such an Inhumane? *Mariamne* now weeps the loss of a Grand-father with that of her Liberty; and the feeble *Tyridates* weeps too like her, without offering other Succours than a few womanish Tears; he keeps his Arms across,

actors, while the Monsters tear his Heart in the
Person of *Mariamne*; add then how weak the
Reasons are that will not let him arm himself a-
gainst the Hangman! A Tyger! a thousand times
more cruel than *Phraates*: No longer my Protector, but my Persecutor, my Enemy. Savage Monster! too, too unworthy of those dear Advantages
thou possessest, trust no further to that Obligation which till now hath tied me to thy Interests,
and believe it, I am more injur'd by thee in *Mariamne*'s wrongs, than oblig'd for my shelter; for
her I will draw my Sword against thee and all
the World; nor can it be Ingratitude to defend
Vertue from the Oppression of Tyranny.

These were the Thoughts I convers'd with, for
this last Effect of *Herod*'s Inhumanity had so galled my Spirit, that it forsook all the Considerations I had for him; and now I made no scruple,
for the Service or Revenge of *Mariamne*, to do him
the worst of Mischiefs; *Arsanes*, to whom I
shew'd these Thoughts naked, begg'd of me to cover them, since their publishing might procure my
Ruine without the least Advantage to *Mariamne*;
in the mean Time I told him it was impossible
for me to live and not see her, that I was resolved to try all the Ways, though never so dangerous, to compass it. *Arsanes* long oppofed this Intention: But, seeing no Possibility of Dissuasion,
resolved to seek some Means to serve me in it.

He was very well known to *Sohemus*; besides,
I call'd to mind that I had done him a Courtesy
with *Herod*, in a Business wherein he stood in
great need of my Favour: This gave *Arsanes* a Belief, it might make way for the obtaining Part of
my Desires, and indeed we found a greater Facility than we durst hope: For *Mariamne*, against
the Power of whose Charms there was no Resi-

C 5   stance,

ftance, had so perfectly gain'd *Sohemus*'s Heart, as
he had no Passion more powerful than a Desire to
please her, and would not have scrupled to hazard Fortune and Life itself to serve her; he was
very willing to have set her at liberty, and have
follow'd her Fortune, if his Companion in the
Charge had not been suspicious it would betray
him to the Rage of *Herod*. At the first Proposition, *Arsanes* made him let me see the Queen; he
shewed much Willingness to oblige me, only
scrupled the Difficulty of gaining his Companion's
Consent to my Satisfaction, and therefore thought
it unsafe to hazard the Proposition. *Arsanes* gave
the Desire I had to see the Queen no other Title,
than Pity of her Miseries, and so made my Passion
pass for an Effect of Generosity.

Sohemus demanded the rest of that Day to seek
Expedients to content me, and on the Morrow
came and told me he was resolved to satisfy me,
though he foresaw some Danger threatned the Enterprize. *Arsanes* intreated him not to impart our
Design to the Queen, for fear, *said he*, she should
oppose it with some timorous Consideration; but
he found it more difficult to make that Request
prevail with *Sohemus*, than any he had yet mentioned, so entirely was that honest Spirit at the
Queen's Devotion; but at last, clearing his Doubts
with a Belief that I would bring no other Intention, than to serve her, and that I would not have
sought an Occasion so perilous to make my Visit,
if I were not assured my Sight would not be unwelcome. They resolved then, that the following
Evening I should be ready at a certain Place near
the Castle, where *Sohemus* had appointed, and
there he promised him, about two Hours within
Evening, to come and conduct me to the Queen's
Presence: He made choice of that Hour, because
the

the Queen had then her Chamber free, and was not importun'd with *Joseph's* Visits, who, at that time, was usually retir'd to his own. Besides, my Face was so well known to all the Court, that no Disguise, without the Aid of Darkness, could have conceal'd it.

There was much hazard in this Enterprize, as well for what might then have befallen me, as for the Fatal consequences, if *Herod* should ever light upon the Discovery: Yet I not only slighted all that Fear could alledge, but waited the wished Hour with an impatience that took all those that preceeded it for tedious Years. At last it came, and when the Night had spread all her Sables, I left *Hierusalem*, only followed by *Arsanes* and my Governor, and having not above a hundred Furlongs to ride, I soon arrived at the Place desired.

Sohemus kept his Word, it being that Day his turn to Command the Castle, and therefore free for him to go in and out when he pleas'd; he came to find me, only attended by one of his Guard, which was a young Man, in whom he repos'd an entire Confidence. Besides, he chose him from all the rest, because his Age and Shape did not much disagree with mine. The Plot was, I should put on his Cloaths, and he stay with *Arsanes* in mine, that those that saw me enter with *Sohemus*, might take me for the same Man that went out with him, my Face being hidden from those in the Night's black Masque. When I had got on the Guard-*Casaque*, he led me to a Gate of the Castle, flanked with high Towers, and surrounded with a deep Ditch, and commanding the Bridge (by a Signal given) to be let down, he conducted me into the Court without a Torch, having left an express Order with those that guard-

, ed

ed the Gate, not to light any thing; who seeing me enter with him, never examin'd my Face, or regarded whether I was their Companion or not; yet he would not lead me by the great Stairs, nor carry me through the Guard-Hall, but conducting me up a little pair of Stairs, and so through a Gallery, where there stood a Centinel, which he made a shew to come on purpose to relieve, and put me in his Place, he led me to the Door of the Anti-Chamber.

By this time I confess all my Courage had almost forsook me; for though no Danger could ever instruct me what was meant by the fear of Death, yet I trembled to think I might displease the Queen by this bold Intrusion; and then unseasonably reflecting on what was past, I almost repented the Enterprize, and was divers times about to stay *Sohemus*, and so return back without seeing the Queen.

At the Name of *Sohemus*, the Door of the Anti-Chamber was presently open'd; and because of the Inclination he had always exprest to the Queen's Interests, he had a free Access to her at all Hours. When we entred her Chamber, she was upon her Knees by the Bed's-side, praying with an ardent Devotion to the God she ador'd, and the Princess her Mother was newly retir'd to her Cabinet. The Noise we made coming in, made her turn her Head that Way; and having spy'd us, she asked *Sohemus* if he had any thing to say. I did not give *Sohemus* time to answer, but approaching with a troubled Posture, I fell upon my Knees before her, and taking one of her fair Hands, joyned it to my Lips with an ardour so vehement, as bereaved me of the use of Speech. The Queen (finding this Action too familiar, and too passionate for a Guard) at first repulst me with

some

some Disdain; but afterwards suspecting a Part of the Truth, and beholding my Face with a serious Eye, by the help of those Lights which were set by her Bed's-side, she knew me. It was no mean Astonishment wherewith this Sight surpriz'd her, and recoiling some Paces back, after she had withdrawn her Hand from mine: ' Ah! ' *Tyridates*, *said she*, what mean you? to what ' a Danger have you expos'd yourself? Danger, ' *Madam*, *replied I*, Ah! that the Gods would ' confront me with a thousand times more, that ' I might find Occasion to shew you how mean ' a thing I think my Life in Relation to your Ser- ' vice. My Calamities (*replied the Queen, en-* ' *gaging me to rise*) are too much in debt to your ' Compassion: But I cannot yet quit the fear you ' have given me, and the Knowledge I have of ' *Herod*'s Humour, makes me Wish from my ' Soul, you had not tempted this Peril to see me. ' I beseech you, *Madam*, *said I*, do not keep ' those Fears for me; for believe it, while this ' Condition lasts, to which your Misfortunes have ' reduc'd me, I shall neither fear *Herod*'s Hatred, ' nor desire his Amity. I have a long time con- ' sider'd him as a King, of whom I hold my Life, ' but must now know him for a Man, that hath ' used that Life a thousand times more cruelly ' than Death itself would have done, from which ' the Retreat he gave me hath possibly defended ' me. Till now the Obligation disputed with the ' Outrage, and in the Person of *Mariamne*'s ' Persecutor, I found my Protector; but at last, ' *Madam*, the Resentments of what I owe him, ' have quitted what they held within me to such ' as have a juster Title; and these last injuries ' which he printed in your Grand-father's Mur- ' ther, and your own cruel Captivity, have strangled

' all

' all thofe Confiderations, which till now my
' Heart fuffered to fpeak in his behalf, and have
' brought me to ask Orders at your Feet, which
' I vow to execute without Condition or Referva-
' tion. Be not loath then, *Madam*, to ordain me
' all that may be done in your Quarrel; and if
' you pleafe, believe that I will not only fhut my
' Eyes upon all forts of Confiderations, but tram-
' ple upon all Difficulties that fhall offer to with-
' ftand me, when once fortified with the Honour
' of your Commands.

While I fpake in this manner, the Queen regarded me attentively, and though fhe knew the
malicious Heart of her Husband, and remembred
how often fhe had been deceiv'd by fuch as acted
the Part of officious Perfons, and made ufe of
fome fuch Terms as mine to found her Intentions, with Defign to carry the Report to the King,
I was fo happy as not to be fufpected of fo bafe
an Ambufh; and of this fhe affur'd me by
thefe Words: ' I have too good an Opinion of
' you, *faid fhe*, and can too well diftinguifh the
' Princes of *Arfaces*'s Blood from cheap and bafe
' Perfons, to fufpect the Diffimulation wherewith
' divers others have betrayed me.

' I know your Words parted from a true Com-
' paffion, and fuch generous Motions as are fa-
' miliar with Perfons of your Extraction: Befides,
' you have given Proofs of too great a Vertue, to
' leave me the Shadow of fuch a Thought; and
' (to witnefs the Confidence I have in you) I will
' open my Heart to you with a moft entire Free-
' dom. It is true, though Heaven hath given
' me *Herod* for a Husband, I cannot love him,
' and indeed I fhould be rather infenfible than
' conftant or loyal, if the Death of my Grand-
' father *Ariftobulus*, of my Father *Alexander*,
' of

' of my Uncle *Antigonus*, of my Brother *Ari-*
' *ſtobulus*, and this laſt of my Grand-father *Hir-*
' *canus*, ſhould be remembred without ſtirring
' my Soul againſt him that murthered them, and
' deſtroyed the royal Houſe of the *Aſmoneans*;
' beſides theſe known Injuries, I have received
' ſome more Particular, but not leſs Senſible.
' There comes not a Day wherein I do not look
' for a Knife at my Throat, and this bloody
' Man, at his Departure for *Rhodes*, hath given
' the ſame Command to *Sohemus*, that he did be-
' fore to his Uncle *Joſeph*, to kill me if the
' Voyage proved unfortunate. I have now free-
' ly repreſented my deplorable condition with *He-*
' *rod*, but I muſt tell you (with the ſame Truth)
' that (as much Monſter as he is) he is yet my
' Husband; that my Apprehenſions of his Inju-
' ries, are not more prevalent than the Rules of
' my Duty, and that I am not permitted to de-
' ſire a Revenge againſt him, which Heaven hath
' reſerved for its own Appointment. If my Mi-
' ſeries come once to be pitied by our Sovereign
' Maſter, he will find Power to releaſe me of
' them ; and if it be his Pleaſure they ſhould ſtill
' continue, I ſhall endeavour ſo to ſuffer for the
' Love of him, as I may be render'd more wor-
' thy of his Love. Behold, *Tyridates*, the State
' of my Condition, with the Temper of my
' Thoughts, I am deeply in your Score, for the
' Propriety you claim in my Misfortunes : But let
' me now beg you will give it over, leſt the Dan-
' gerous Pity ſhould at laſt prove fatal to its
' Owner. Ah! might it pleaſe the Gods, (*cried*
' *I, wholly tranſported*) that your Evils might
' be brought off, with the cruelleſt Death that
' *Herod* is capable of inventing, with what glad
' Heart ſhould I run to embrace thoſe glorious
TOR-

' Torments, which poffibly might procure me
' fome fmall Acknowledgment in yours! How
' fair would be my Deftiny to pay down my Life
' for this adorable Princefs, to whom all Lives,
' all Hearts ought to be facrificed!' Thefe Words,
with the Paffion that helped to pronounce them,
open'd the Queen's Eyes, and fhewed her, by a
prompt Reflection on what was paft, that Tranfports fo violent could not fpring from a naked
Pity; this Difcovery call'd up a Blufh into her
Face, and having filently beheld me with an Action that betrayed fome Trouble: ' Tyridates,
' *faid fhe*, do you well confider what you fay?
She let fall thefe Words in fo fevere an Accent,
that it ftruck fuch a Terror into me, as I loft all
my Affurance; and, inftead of anfwering, fell to
confider how imprudently I had opened my Breaft;
but I had kept too much Paffion to keep the reft
ftill difguifed; and in this Uproar of Thoughts,
(tofs'd with Love, Grief, and Defpair) I let myfelf fall at the Queen's Feet, embracing and kif-
fing them a thoufand times over, without fo much
Power as could utter one Word; by this Action
clearly confirming the Sufpicion my Words had
given her. Oh Gods! how fenfibly fhe was
touched! how violent were her firft Apprehenfions to proceed from fo fweet a Soul! She took a
long Time to weigh the Refolution was fitteft to
be taken, and I, in the mean Time, the Advantage of her Silence and Immobility, to rally my
fcattered Spirits. ' Madam, *faid I, (keeping my*
' *Hold at her Feet, without daring to lift up*
' *my Eyes to her Vifage*) if my Tongue have be-
' trayed my Soul, and, contrary to my Intent,
' difplay'd a Paffion which my whole Life fhould
' have preferved a Secret, ordain me all the Pains
' that are due to it; and I vow by all the Gods,
'   ' to

'to suffer them without a Murmur; to you I
'will not justifie a Passion, which otherwise
'might call to its own Purity to defend it. I
'will not tell you 'tis impossible to look upon you,
'and not incur the Fault I have committed, nor
'that the Silence of divers Years, have given
'some Proofs of my Respect. No, I am Crimi-
'nal if I have contracted your Anger, and am
'worthy of the most cruel Punishments, if I have
'been capable to displease you.' I had gone further, if the now-resolved Queen had not staid my
Progress, and repulsing me with one Hand, while
she carried the other to her Face to hide some
Changes there: ' Tyridates, *said she*, you are yet
'more culpable than you believe, and if you had
'known me well, you would never have granted
'yourself the Licence to give me the Displeasure
'I have now received. I will not noise your
'Folly, because I know *Herod*'s Humour, which
'doubtless would destroy you for it; and as I
'pardon him the bloody Injuries he hath so often
'done me, so I forgive the Offence you have so
'lately committed.

At these Words she rose from her Chair, and
calling *Sohemus*, who was discoursing with her
Maids in the Anti-Chamber, commanded him to
conduct me presently back, and so resolving to
hear me no more, she retir'd into her Mother's
Cabinet. Oh Gods! in what an Estate was I,
when I saw myself thus deserted! in what a strange
Fashion I followed *Sohemus*, when he led me out
of the Castle the same Way we enter'd it? I had
scarce the Power to embrace him at our Parting,
or to give him thanks for the Courtesie he had
done me. I found my Men, got to Horse, and
return'd to *Hierusalem* with a Melancholy darker
than the Night's blackest Shades, and with a Countenance

tenance which I think little differ'd from that of a condemn'd Man.

I would scarce hear the Comforts *Arsanes* offered me, to whom I had recounted my Disaster, but passed the rest of the Night in the most cruel Inquietudes that ever tore a Soul; I could not remember the incensed Looks of my Divine Princess, without calling in the same Fear that seiz'd me at the first Effects of her Anger; nor think of the Displeasure I had given her, without letting myself sink almost under the Sorrow I resented; all the Words she spake came flocking to my Memory; but it galled me me to think she should put my Offence in the same Ballance with *Herod*'s Villainies. Ah unjust *Mariamne*! said I, how unskilful you are in discerning Injuries! Could you have judged aright, you would have found little Cause to associate the Cruelties of *Herod* with the Oversights of *Tyridates*. *Herod* hath wrested the Crown from your Family, *Herod* still blushes with the Blood of your nearest Kindred; *Herod* gives daily Orders for your own Death, and *Tyridates* gives you his Heart, his Soul, and himself entire. Sure this Offence is not of a Nature so heinous, as those you have receiv'd of that Miscreant, and methinks you need not the same Patience to endure them; but why, said I, repenting my Words, why do I justify my Crime? Is it not true that I am Faulty, since my Rashness hath merited *Mariamne*'s Anger? I ought to consider her as a Divinity sublim'd above the Reach of human Thoughts; I should tremble before her Vertue; and if it were impossible to see her without falling in Love with so much Beauty both of Soul and Body, yet I should have suffer'd those glorious Pains without Publishing, and not have improved my Misfortune by my indiscreet and rash Discovery.
                                                      In

In such thoughts as these I passed the night, and divers other days that followed it, in which space I often saw *Salome*, *Pheroras*, with the chief of the *Judean* Court, who strove among themselves, who should treat me with most Caresses for the service I had done their Country; but neither their company nor their kindness could ease the evils which my Love inflicted, nor sweeten the sorrow I took for the choler and captivity of *Mariamne*: But about that time there came News to *Jerusalem*, that *Herod* was triumphantly return'd from *Augustus*; that by an Artificial Oration full of an affected generosity, he had so gain'd upon the spirit of that great Emperour, as it procur'd him a specious entertainment, and got him little less in his amity, than he had before in the affections of *Anthony*. Those that had an interest in his good success, were more overjoy'd at the news, in which (a few days after) they were confirm'd, when they saw him arrive with a proud train at his heels, and read in his erected looks the satisfaction he receiv'd in that Voyage.

There was made him a magnificent reception, and (I mingling my self with those that went to meet him) he receiv'd me with extraordinary caresses, call'd me the valiant Defender of *Judea*, and promised a grateful remembrance of the services I had rendred to his Crown. But alas! how little was I sensible of his Offers and Civilities! And though indeed I could not but confess he had put me in his debt, yet the love of *Mariamne*, and the resentment of her wrongs stifled all his obligations. The same day he arrived, he restor'd her liberty, and burning with love, could not forbear to visit her in the same place which had been her Prison, where he spent the night with her, and the next day brought her

back

back with him to the City, with many open professions of a moſt ardent affection.

I underſtood by *Sohemus*, that at that interview he had made her a moſt paſſionate Diſcourſe, and after he had excus'd the death of *Hircanus* with a neceſſity that conſtrain'd him, ſo to prevent the deſign he had to ruine him, he deeply proteſted, that the abridgment of her freedom, was only meant to ſecure her perſon from the attempts of ſuch, whoſe diſaffection in his abſence might hazard her ſafety, and to diſarm the deſigns of ſome perſons that were likely to make uſe of hers and her Mother's preſence (whoſe turbulent ſpirit he was well acquainted with) to authorize ſedition, and ſtir up troubles in the State.

The wiſe Queen receiv'd this Diſcourſe with a becoming temper; and, if ſhe could not entirely hide her diſtaſtes, ſhe diſſembled part of them, left they ſhould prove as fatal to *Sohemus*, as they had been to *Joſeph*. The Court was then more glorious than ever; the King highly pleas'd with the ſucceſs of his Affairs, and (having nothing elſe to ſubdue that might keep him from getting above the reach of Fortune, but the ſpirit of *Mariamne*) he ſought all ſorts of occaſions to divertize her; but if the Queen (whoſe griefs were gone too deep to be ſweetned with the vain ſhadow of pleaſure) took little notice of it, I was not leſs incapable than ſhe, of taking any jollity; and my remembrance kept the deep graven Characters of my Love and her Anger ſo freſh in my Soul, as all the ſplendor and pomp of *Herod*'s Court wanted power to charm them. I ſtill ſaw her every day, becauſe ſhe forbad it not; but I ſcarce durſt open my mouth in her preſence, ſcarce lift up my Eyes to her face, inſtructing all my actions to inform how deeply the fear to diſ-

pleaſe

please her was engraven in my heart ; yet neither her looks, nor her actions exprest any sign of
aversion : indeed she had a Soul too beautiful,
too sweet an inclination to loath a man, who had
only offended with Affection, since she had
much ado to return hatred where it was deserv'd
by such bloody Injuries : but believing she could
not hear my Love plead farther, without offending Virtue, she avoided all occasions of Dif-
course as much as possible; and though she still
spake to me with much affability, yet she never
did so but in company, and so contriv'd it, that
we never exchang'd words without a witness.
Though this behaviour of hers could not give me
an entire satisfaction, yet it left me no cause of
complaint; and the knowledge I had of her admirable Virtue, having extinguisht with my hopes,
a part of those flames her Beauty had kindled, I
learn'd to think my Passion sufficiently rewarded
by the esteem she had of me. Indeed there was
never any person lov'd with less interest ; and with
truth I may say, I lov'd *Mariamne* for her self
alone, nor in all the process of my Passion did I
ever consider *Tyridates*.

In this manner I liv'd a whole year ; and though
my Eyes did all the messages of my love, yet she
might easily read in all my actions, that it had lost
no ardour ; and that my sufferings were therefore
more cruel, because they stood in awe of respect.

At last my perseverance, link'd with discretion
(which she knew by a thousand marks) touched
her with compassion; I say compassion, for Love
could never be admitted : And what she did since
in my favour, did all proceed from a motion so
purely generous, as the most perfect Virtue was
engaged to commend it; nor could it be censured
by any without injustice. Her heart which was
neither

neither ftone nor brafs, fuffer'd itfelf to be foftned
with pity; but it was never capable of an impreffion not conform'd to the fevere rules of her
duty: fhe could not fee a Prince languifhing fo
many years, a Prince dying for her, but dying
in a fafhion fo refpectful and obliging, and dying
without complaining of the caufe of his death, or
of death itfelf, and not give fome proofs that Nature made her fenfible: But fhe would rather have
fuffer'd him to die; nay, died her felf, than let
in the leaft thought to her foul of pitying him, to
the prejudice of her Virtue: I was fo happy in
the conduct of my paffion, and had carried fo
much caution in all my actions, that *Herod* (the
moft jealous and diftruftful of all men) had not
yet the leaft fufpicion of me; and this difcretion
was not undervalued by the Queen.

I was one day in her company with the King,
Pheroras, *Salome*, and fome other of the chief Courtiers in the Palace-garden, where we had walked a long time, and where I had done my beft
to evade the purfuits of *Salome*, who had then
been trying (having too much courage to give
me her naked Paffion) to make me fpy it in her
Actions, and underftand it by a thoufand ambi-
guous Difcourfes; when the King, who had walked all this time with the Queen alone, being
oblig'd by fome important Affairs to retire, he
called me to him, and giving me the Queen's
hand, which till then himfelf had held: 'I leave
' you to Prince *Tyridates*, *faid he*, and I cannot
' put that which I tender more dear than my felf
' into better hands than his: Try, if you pleafe,
' to divert her from her deep Melancholy.' To
thefe words I return'd no other Anfwer, but an
action full of reverence and refpect; and, confidering how my condition ftood with the Queen, I

durft

durſt not adventure to take her hand, till ſhe tender'd it her ſelf, with a countenance that did put on
a World of ſweetneſs : And thus I helped her to
walk, without daring either to open my mouth, or
to look upon her. Her behaviour was a long time
like mine; but at laſt ſhe broke ſilence, and took
this opportunity to declare what her heart had for
me. ' *Tyridates*, *ſaid ſhe*, if the King knew
' your Intentions, he would not put me into your
' Hands with ſo much Confidence ; and ſince they
' were known to me, I ought to have hinder'd
' it ; I could eaſily have done ſo, if my Will had
' conſented ; and probably I had too, if I had
' not believ'd I might permit your Converſe, and
' acquaint you with my Thoughts, without in-
' tereſting what I owe to him or myſelf. Know
' then, *Tyridates*, that the firſt Notice I had of
' your Malady, gave me ſome Reſentment againſt
' you, but the Progreſs of it, Compaſſion ; I have
' truly pitied the Eſtate you are in, and cannot,
' without Grief, ſee a Prince (to whom Heaven
' hath given ſuch excellent Qualities) paſs his
' Life in a Condition ſo miſerable. But, in fine,
' *Tyridates*, what are your Pretences ? and if you
' have judged me worthy of your Eſteem, what
' can you hope for of me ? Think you I can li-
' cenſe in your Favour the leaſt Act that may ſa-
' tisfy your Paſſion ? I ſay the leaſt ; for, did I
' believe you could harbour a Thought to my
' Diſhonour, I would look upon you as a Mon-
' ſter, as a mortal Enemy : Do you think the
' little Content I have with *Herod*, and the Re-
' membrance of the Wrongs he hath done me,
' can turn my Affections upon another, becauſe leſs
' worthy of my Averſion ? Is it upon this Thought
' you build your Hopes ? If ſo, *Tyridates*, diſ-
' abuſe yourſelf; and believe, that if Heaven hath
' made

' made me miferable, by fubmitting me to this
' cruel Man, I will never confent to merit my
' Misfortunes by my Actions; though my for-
' lorn Hap hath married me to him, it fhall ne-
' ver match me to his Crimes: I would not be
' fo ungrateful to the Goodnefs of Heaven, that is
' ever fending Comfort to my Miferies; nor fo
' unworthy of your Eftimation. For my fake,
' *Tyridates,* confider thefe Truths, fince they are
' reprefented with as much Mildi.efs, as much
' Affection as I can keep for you with Reafon's
' Leave: Call up the Greatnefs of your Courage,
' to give a brave Affault upon yourfelf, and pro-
' pofe this ruinous Paffion to your Thoughts as
' an Enemy you ought to fear, as an Enemy that
' would deftroy you, and probably me too, unlefs
' you vanquifh it.' The Queen ended with thefe
Words, which I heard with Admiration; and during the Difcourfe, having rallied out Part of the
Confidence Fear had fcatter'd, I made it ferve
me to anfwer thefe Terms.

. ' I am unworthy, Madam, of this Favour you
' have given me; and fince I have merited your Dif-
' pleafure, 'tis fit I fhould perifh for the Expia-
' tion, rather than referve myfelf for fuch a Pity
' as you lately mention'd; nor fhould my Tongue
' ever hazard a fecond Purchafe of your Indigna-
' tion, if that generous Bounty, which keeps com-
' pany with the reft of your admirable Vertues,
' did not allow me liberty to juftify my Thoughts
' before you. I will adventure then to tell you,
' That Love, as I apprehend it, can neither be
' odious nor confiderable to the Perfon beloved,
' but by the Effects it produceth, fince of itfelf it
' is obliging and advantageous, even to the Crea-
' tures leaft capable of Apprehenfion; if my Paf-
' fion had hatched any Defire within me contrary

' to

‘ to your Virtue, you might deteſt it as a Crimi-
‘ nal, as an Enemy that would poiſon the Purity
‘ of your Soul.   But if it ſhall never inſpire any
‘ other than ſuch as ſhall inſtruct me to revere
‘ thoſe admirable Qualities the Gods have given
‘ you, to intereſt myſelf in your Fortune, and ſa-
‘ crifice myſelf for your Intereſts, where will you
‘ find a juſt Occaſion to condemn it? Is it a Crime
‘ for *Tyridates* to do the Homage of a pure Ve-
‘ neration, to the divine Beauties and Perfections
‘ of *Mariamne?* Is it a Crime for *Tyridates* to
‘ give up all his Thoughts, and dedicate his whole
‘ Time to this Imployment? And is it a Crime
‘ for *Tyridates*, to long for an Occaſion, with
‘ the Price of his Blood and Life, to buy Repoſe
‘ for *Mariamne?* Madam, If I have other
‘ Thoughts, other Deſires than theſe, puniſh me
‘ with all the Rigour your firſt Reſentments in-
‘ ſpir’d you with; and let the Divine Powers joyn
‘ with yours, to compleat me the moſt Miſera-
‘ ble of all Men: But if you find in my Affecti-
‘ on all the Innocence you require, in the Gods
‘ Name, Madam, give me leave to carry it to
‘ my Tomb; it is a Neceſſity which will never
‘ endure to be diſpens’d with, a Favour which I
‘ conjure you by the Remembrance of all that you
‘ hold moſt dear, to grant me: And if the Place
‘ were clear’d of Witneſſes, that I might be per-
‘ mitted to ask it at your Feet, I would never
‘ riſe from thence till I had obtain’d it.’

   Theſe Words, and the Vehemence wherewith
I pronounced them, wrought upon the generous
and tender Spirit of the Queen, and ſtirred up
ſuch Thoughts, as took her ſome Time before ſhe
could get them out into an anſwer; at length ſhe
diſpos’d herſelf to it; and as ſhe was beginning,
we found ourſelves at the End of an Alley, where

VOL. I.   D   turn-

turning to continue our Walk, we fpy'd *Salome*
and the reft of the Company fo near us, as the
Queen faw fhe fhould not have Time to difcharge
her Heart, and feeing her Company ftaid to let
us pafs, before we quitted the Place, fhe thus replied: ' *Tyridates*, if your Thoughts be fuch as
' you fay, I can find no juft Caufe of Offence:
' But were they yet more innocent, I muft coun-
' fel you, and do with all my Soul crave of you,
' if it be poffible, to difcard them from your
' Heart, fince they cannot be but ruinous to your
' Repofe and mine.

She faid no more, and whether it were that
fhe was willing to purfue this difcourfe no further,
or that fhe fufpected the malicious Spirit of *Salome*
might probably raife a bad Comment upon our
Privacy, fhe join'd with the reft of the Company,
and would feparate no more.

From this Day I dated a happy Change in my
Condition, and believed my Eftate much more advantageous than formerly. The Queen, though
fhe difapproved my Refearch, and faw the Continuance of it with Difpleafure, yet fhe endured it
with a moft noble Patience, that would neither
fuffer her to banifh, nor hate a Prince who ado-
red her with a Devotion fo pure and unbyafs'd,
as nothing in it could be found fit to cenfure;
and never hoping to advance farther in her Favour, I learn'd to ftay my Content upon what I
had. This began to reftore my Spirits, and re-
cal my Colour; and if my Face ftill fhew'd fome
Difcontent, it had a Root in the Queen's Miferies,
and not mine.

The Condition of this great Princefs was deplorable; and though the King loved her with an
almoft enraged Paffion, fuch was her Averfion to
all the endearing Paffages of his Love, as fhe took

them

them for so many Effects of Heaven's Indignation; and though her vertuous Resolution held her to the severe Rules of her Duty, her great Courage could not be pliable to such Caresses as she believ'd not due to the Destroyer of her Family, and a Man yet crimson'd with the Blood of her nearest Kindred. These Disdains sometimes raised such Tempests in the King, as he was often ready to pour them upon her, as the last Effects of his Fury; but then would Love step in to check Anger, and, taking the Reins from those raging Transports, which he had suffer'd to get uppermost, render'd him more soft and submiss than ever; and sent him to seek that with Prayers and Tears, which he could not obtain with all his Menaces.

We were one Day in the King's Chamber, whither he had invited the Queen: And they standing together at a Window; after some discourse which we heard not, he proffer'd to kiss her: But the Queen, whether she thought such Condescension injurious to Modesty in so great a Company, or in effect, follow'd the Motions of a just Hatred, recoil'd some steps back, and turned away her Head with disdain enough. The King was so gall'd with this Action, especially appearing before so many Witnesses, as all the Power he could make was not capable to hide his Passion; and beholding the Queen with Eyes sparkling with Rage, and a Countenance on which Fury had spread itself: ' You are unworthy, *said he*, both ' of the Honour was offer'd you, and all those ' that went before it: Go, get you out of my ' Chamber; and if you do not remember the De- ' stiny of your Fathers, remember that I promise ' to make you know him for your King, whom ' you now scorn to acknowledge for your Hus- ' band.' The Queen return'd no other answer to •

these

these cruel Words than a disdainful Look, which more provok'd him; and saluting the Company, without Change of Countenance, quitted the Chamber to retire to her own. The King's Choler (which had often produc'd horrid Effects) made the whole Company tremble, only in me it miss'd that Influence; for, all the Prudence and Discretion I could make, had much ado to hinder my Discontent from breaking loose, and it was the Consideration I had for the Queen, and not myself that bridled it: Yet not in such a Manner, but when I saw the Queen retire, I hasted after, and offer'd my Hand to lead her to her Lodging: But, as her Spirit was less distemper'd than mine, and had therefore more judgment at the Stern, to apprehend how much the Civility I proferr'd might displease *Herod*, and deeply endanger me, she refus'd it; and having no time to explain her Thoughts, she only made me a Sign with her Eye to retire. I came back again to the King with much Regret, whom I had indeed displeas'd with this Action, but it was otherwise taken from me, than it would have been from any one of his own Subjects: He thunder'd still against the Queen in most bitter Terms, but seeing that (without unmasking my Inclinations) it was in vain to speak in her defence, with much constraint, I silently heard all his injurious Language: A few Days after he was appeased by the powerful Ascendant the Queen had upon his Spirit; but he quickly relapsed again; and their whole Life was nought else but that continual Disorder, which usually results from the Incompatibility of Vice and Virtue.

In the mean time, *Salome* had given so many clear Proofs of her Affection, as I cou'd scarce any longer personate an Ignorance; and though she had still the Power to forbid herself an open

Decla-

Declaration, yet she had said enough, and her
Actions had too well seconded her discourse, to
permit me to doubt it; I had sought all Ways to
escape this Discovery, and when I was perfectly
assured of the Truth, yet I dissembled it as much
as was possible. *Salome* well judged by her Actions and mine, that I knew well enough what
pinched her; and this coldness kindled in her
such a Despight, as in any Spirit but hers, would
have been capable to have quenched Affection.

We met one Day at the House of *Pheroras*,
whom I often visited, and who at that time was
indispos'd; after we had spent some time by the
Bed's side, *Salome* that longed to exchange some
particular Discourse, invited me to walk with her
into an adjoyning Gallery, pretending to shew me
some Pictures; I could not civilly avoid the Snare,
and lending her my Hand, I led her thither,
where we entertain'd some time in perusing the
Pictures, wherein were represented the most memorable Events of the *Judaick* History; there she
shewed me so many admirable Things, as might
pose the Belief of all but those of their own Religion. She pointed at some Captains, which in
the midst of their Battles, with their Prayers,
staid the Course of the Sun, and gave a prodigious Day to the Universe: Of others that opened
the Flanks of the red-Sea for their Troops to pass
through; but she chiefly insisted upon the Actions
of *David* (the greatest of their Kings) and upon
those of his Son *Solomon*, which among them
passed for a Miracle of Wisdom; and relating in
order the Life of that latter, she particularly staid
upon one Picture that represented a beautiful
Queen, that fell so in love with the Fame of
Solomon's Virtues, as she abandon'd her Realm,
and travell'd a vast Tract of Land to visit him.

Salome took Occasion to assault me with this History, having compriz'd it in a few Words: ' This Prince, *continued she*, was the wisest of ' all Men, and yet disdain'd not the Affections of ' a Prince that loved him, but requited her with ' his, to the Satisfaction of all her desires.' At these Words *Salome* (though in a little Confusion) beheld me with a fixed Eye; and by that Action oblig'd me to answer her. ' It was but just, *said* ' *I*, that a King so vertuous as you have spoken ' him, should be flexible to so fair a Queen, that ' had forsaken her Estate, to expose herself to ' the Hazard and Inconvenience of a long Voyage ' to see him; this Enterprize was so considerable ' in the Person of a great Princess, as *Solomon* ' cou'd not have been just (as you have represented ' him) had he used her ingratefully.' ' You have ' said enough to convince yourself, *said Salome*, ' and if these be your own Thoughts, you shou'd ' consider what you owe to Princesses, who ('tis true) ' have neither abandon'd Realms, nor travers'd ' Provinces to see you; but abandon'd for your ' sake a Liberty more dear than Empires, and ' trampled upon Obstacles more difficult to sur- ' mount, than the Incommodities of a Voyage.

     This Discourse, which I had always feared, put me to trouble past all dissembling; and seeing myself oblig'd to reply: ' I am too unfortunate, ' *said I*, to believe that ought can appear in the ' Miseries of my Life, but Subjects of Compassi- ' on; the Affections of Princesses will doubtless ' find Objects more worthy of themselves; and I ' am too far from imagining that a Wretch exi- ' led from his Country, persecuted by his King, ' that has no Retreat upon Earth, but what he owes ' for to the King your Brother's Bounty, shou'd ' triumph over those precious Liberties which are

     ' doubt-

‘ doubtless reserv'd for Persons more happy, and
‘ for such as by the Loss of their own, with a
‘ long Succession of faithful Service, have deserv'd
‘ them.’ ‘ Those that have bought them at a low-
‘ er Rate, *said Salome*, are more oblig'd than
‘ such as paid for them with Pains, Blood, and
‘ Years of Service; and without extream Ingra-
‘ titude, they cannot prefer those Things that have
‘ been dearly sold, to such as have been liberally
‘ given them. You are of this Number *Tyridates*;
‘ you evade the Notice of Obligations, that you
‘ may fly Occasions of Requital; you are better
‘ esteem'd in *Herod*'s Court than you desire to
‘ be, and the Misfortunes of your Life are there less
‘ consider'd than the Qualities of your Person:
‘ You know this for truth, though you force a
‘ cunning Ignorance to disguise it: You are too
‘ clear-sighted, not to perceive it by a thousand
‘ Actions, and as many Discourses, which have
‘ but too plainly declared it. But disdain closes
‘ your Eyes and Ears; and none but such a Soul
‘ as that you play the Tyrant with, but would
‘ turn edge at your Neglect, yet she hath prefer-
‘ ved many Years in the same Ardour, and with
‘ much Satisfaction would so continue her whole
‘ Life-time, if you would let her hope that such
‘ a Constancy should not go unrewarded.

　While *Salome* pronounced these Words, her Eyes
let fall their Looks upon the Earth, with all the
Signs of Shame, which she was not able to dissemble: And indeed how should she, when myself
was so ashamed in her behalf, as I had a harder
Task to hide it from her, than to find Words to
answer her ? ‘ Madam, *said I*, (*after I had a*
‘ *while kept silence*) till now my Soul hath been
‘ so chain'd to the Consideration of my Miseries,
‘ as it hath not been capable of other Thoughts;

and

' and I have found so little Appearance, nay, so
' little Reason in what you have done me the Ho-
' nour to let me know, as, it could never have
' enter'd my Imaginations. 'Tis this must answer
' for the Faults I committed, and not a Disdain,
' which never grew in my Nature; and which
' I should practise but unhandsomely. The Gods
' have not given me those advantageous Quali-
' ties to look up at a Fortune so little thought
' of; and though it should offer itself indeed in-
' to my Arms, in this wretched Condition, where-
' to my Miseries have reduced me, I think I
' should not have Power to taste it.' *Salome*
(who could no longer doubt, but that her Love
was perfectly discover'd) found my Words, and
the Action wherewith I pronounc'd them, so disobliging, that (if it had been possible) that very
Moment she would have thrown it off: However,
she would no further advance a Parley, the beginning of which taught her to hope for little
Satisfaction in the Sequel; and turning back to
Pheroras's Chamber, in a Fashion that shew'd the
Marks of Spight: ' Oh! Well, *Tyridates*, said
' *she*, your Perplexities shall no more be redoubled
' by a Discourse so disobliging; and since you are
' oppress'd with Affection, there shall be care ta-
' ken to free you of that Importunity.

As she finished these Words, we enter'd the
Chamber of *Pheroras*, which stopped my Answer;
and she was so overcome with Anger, as all the
Time we staid together, she would neither vouchsafe to speak or look upon me. Since that Day I
began to understand her Disposition, of which I
had already a very evil Opinion; and at my next
Conference with the Queen, I had not Power to
conceal *Salome*'s Folly, willing to prepossess her
Spirit by a true Relation, lest the malicious Creature

ture fhould render me fome evil Office with her.
This Relation provok'd the Queen's Vertue to exprefs more Contempt and Averfion for *Salome* than
ever : Which, after fhe had witneffed by fome
Words fhe let fall againft her, ' *Tyridates, faid*
' *fhe, fmiling,* are you fo cruel then to Ladies
' that love you ?' And a little after, putting on a
more ferious Look, ' If you open thefe Eyes to
' Reafon, which Paffion hath fhut up, you will
' foon perceive, that God doth punifh your unjuft.
' Affection with another, which yourfelf difap-
' proves; and if *Salome* (being married) cannot
' hatch fuch Defires, and not be wicked, fure I
' that am in the fame Eftate, and having a King
' to my Husband, cannot countenance your's,
' without incurring the fame Sin you condemn
' in *Salome.*' ' Ah ! Madam, *faid I,* what a
' vaft Difference is there betwixt fuffering an Af-
' fection pure and innocent, as mine, and perfe-
' cuting, with a vicious Paffion, a Perfon that
' loaths it ! And if ever my Adoration fhall oblige
' you to let fall any particular Favour upon me,
' how well may *Salome* ferve to excufe it ? And
' then how little reafon have you to confider a
' Man, which hath more Right to the Title of
' cruel Enemy than that of Husband ?' ' I have
' often told you, *reply'd the Queen,* that you
' ought not to ground any Hope upon that Con-
' fideration; nay, though I were releas'd of all
' which is due to *Herod,* yet I fhall never forget
' what I owe to myfelf.' With fuch Anfwers as
thefe, the Queen ftill gently confuted me; and in
thefe pleafing Liberties of Difcourfe were ftor'd
my beft Advantages. While this Life lafted, I
was but too happy ; for my Hopes had fuch weak
Encouragement to afpire at better Fortune, from
fuch a Vertue as *Mariamne*'s, as I did my beft to
bound my Content in what I had.

D 5,   The

The Neceſſity I had of the Aid of *Sohemus*, made me open my Heart unto him : Beſides, by ſome Preſents, I had gain'd *Philo*, the Queen's Eunuch; and *Cleople*, whom of all her Maids ſhe moſt truſted. Theſe Perſons, though the Queen knew it not, befriended me with their beſt Induſtry; and I had no hard Task to get ſome Confidence among them, becauſe I knew the whole Family deteſted the King : Yet the Queen was ignorant of my Influence upon her People; which had ſhe known, ſhe would never have ſuffer'd. She avoided all Occaſions, as much as poſſible, of being alone with me; and when ſhe could not ſhun it, ſhe kept me in ſuch Awe to diſpleaſe, as I had ſcarce the daring to open my Mouth; yet ſometimes I broke theſe Chains, and calling that Commiſeration to my Succour, which ſhe never had ready for my Miſeries, methought I taſted moſt delicious Comforts in that very Liberty of ſpeaking; but when I preſumed, upon a large Privilege, to take a Kiſs from her Hand, ſhe would take ſuch an Anger into her Looks, as carried me to the Extremities of Grief and Repentance.

In the mean time, if the Circumpeſtion which I carried in all my Actions deceived the Eyes of *Herod* and his Court, *Salome* (as the moſt intereſted, and therefore the moſt clear-ſighted of all others) finding little cauſe to attribute this Contempt of mine to any thing but Anticipation, ſet ſo much Care and Cunning a-work, as to obſerve my Looks, and ſpy out all my Actions, as at laſt ſhe began to gather Part of the Truth; but ſhe had not then Time enough to enlarge her Diſcovery, becauſe I ſoon after parted from *Jeruſalem*, and was obliged for a Time to leave the Queen, upon an Occaſion which I ſhall let you underſtand.

o

Hymen's

Hymen's Præludia:

OR,

Love's Master-Piece.

PART II. BOOK I.

ARGUMENT.

Phraates, *upon the old Quarrel, invadeth* Judea *with* 30,000 *Parthians, under the Command of his Lieutenant* Barsapharnes; *they ravage and devaſt the Country about* Samaria. Tyridates *is ſent General by* Herod, *with an Army to oppoſe them: He ſends a brave Defiance to* Barſapharnes, *which he ſtoutly accepts.* Barſapharnes *is ſlain in the Fight, and his Army totally routed.* Tyridates *returns to* Jeruſalem, *and is welcom'd by a general Applauſe.* Salome *plots his and* Mariamne's *Ruin, by kindling Jealouſy in* Herod's *Breaſt, which enrages him to a Resolution of deſtroying* Tyridates. Mariamne *gives him notice of it by a Letter.* Arſanes *ſpills the Poiſon as he was lifting it up to his Mouth.* Tyridates, *with his Servants,*

attempt-

attempting an *Escape* by *flight*, finds the *Streets* all blocked up with *Soldiers*: They endeavour to cut a *Paſſage* with their *Swords*; but, oppreſs'd by the *Multitude*, are forced to take *Sanctuary* in the *Temple*. The *Conteſtation* between Herod and the *Prieſts* about him. Socius, a Roman *Senator*, interpoſes, and threatens Herod to a *Conſent*, that Tyridates might go ſafely out of his *Territories*: He conducts him out of Jeruſalem. Tyridates returns the ſame Night in *Diſguiſe*, by Sohemus's *Aid* is admitted to the *Queen*, takes a paſſionate *Leave* of her, and quits Judea: Goes to Rome, and is honourably treated by Auguſtus. His *Melancholy* drives him from thence. He is caſt upon the *Shore* of Alexandria, and ſo finiſhes his *Story*. Eteocles (*commanded* by Candace, to acquaint her with his *Fortunes*) begins with thoſe of CLEOPATRA; her *Deſcent*, *Beauty*, and rare *Qualities*. Her *Brother* Ptolomy's vicious *Inclinations*, by the wicked *Advice* of his *Counſellors*, he deſigns her Ruin: She takes up *Arms* in her own *Defence*, is overpower'd, and beſieged by him in Peluſium. Pompey flies to him for *Refuge*, after his Pharſalian *Overthrow*, and is baſely murther'd by his *Command*. Cæſar brings his victorious *Army* into into Ægypt. Cleopatra petitions his *Protection* againſt her *Brother*; her *Condition* kindles *Pity*, and her *Perſon Affection* in Cæſar's *Heart*. He reconciles them. Ptolomy's treacherous *Intentions* to murther Cæſar; being diſcover'd, he flies to open *Arms*. The bloody *Sea Fight* betwixt them, wherein he is ſlain. Cæſar crown's Cleopatra *Queen* of Ægypt, and privately marries her.

The

HE barbarous *Phraates* seeing he could neither prevail with *Herod* to give me up into his Hands, nor put me to death, which he had often sollicited, and being otherwise his mortal Enemy, sent thirty thousand *Parthians* upon his Frontiers, under the Command of *Barsapharnes*, one of his Lieutenants, and the very same that some Years before had taken *Hircanus* and *Phaselus* Prisoners. *Barsapharnes* did all the Mischiefs in *Judea* that Hostility could exercise, and made all that stood in his way, without Distinction, feel his impartial Sword. Yet his March was not kept so secret, but (before he entered *Judea*) *Herod* (that like a most prudent and vigilant Prince, always kept store of Spies in pay) had a timely notice of it, which made him rally his Forces with such Diligence, that before the *Parthians* had made any considerable Progress, he was grown strong enough to oppose them. He would gladly have marched in Person; but Mistrust (the ordinary Companion of Tyranny) made him fear some Palpitations in the Heart of his Estate, if he absented himself, and therefore resolv'd to send one of his Lieutenants. I had too much Interest in this War, not to seek the Employment; and all the Regret I suffer'd to leave *Mariamne*, was swallow'd with the greedy Desire of Glory and Vengeance, which drew me at the Feet of *Herod*, to ask the Conduct of his Army. He was very well satisfied with what I had already done in his Service; and weighing the Propriety I had both in the Motive and Success of that War, he concluded he could not put his Forces into better Hands than mine, and therefore freely bestow'd the Command upon me.

So

So soon as my Equipage was ready, I disposed myself to part with that Place, where I left the better Part of my Soul. The Queen (who could not hate me, though my Passion still perplex'd her) was well pleased to hear the King had given me this Employment; and told me, in most obliging Terms, She had an Opinion that I would bring home a fair Increase of Honour: But when at the Even of my Departure, I desir'd she would give me a particular Audience, and permit me to take leave of her in her Chamber, without any further Witnesses but those we suspected not, she was deaf to my Prayer; and after she had begun with some sharp Words, to shew me how much the Request displeased her, ' No, *Tyridates*, (pur-' *sued she, with a milder Look*) this Conference ' is not necessary; I know already all you would ' say: Nor are you ignorant of what I have to ' answer you; cashire these unjust Desires, if it ' be possible, and believe it, if a high Esteem of ' your Virtues, and a thousand Wishes for your ' Happiness, may requite your Affections, you ' shall never have cause to call me ungrateful.

Though these Words were perfectly innocent, yet the Queen fear'd they betray'd too much Favour, and could not let them go without a Blush, wherein I read so much ravishing Sweetness, and fancied such Advantages to myself, that I found nothing in my Condition that might patronize Complaint. I did all that was possible to obtain leave to write to her: At first she return'd me a mild Refusal; but, in fine, she absolutely forbad me any further Importunity. I submitted to her without repining; and being constrain'd to take leave of her in the Presence of the King, and the chief Courtiers, I render'd the same Respects to *Salome*, who was then in the Presence; by this

Means

Means avoiding a troublesome Discourse, in which a particular Farewel might probably have engaged me. She well understood my Intention; and adding this to her former Quarrel, she could not keep her Spight from breaking into her Looks; but when I bow'd to salute her, after the *Jewish* Mode, she lifted up her Head, and thus whisper'd as low as possible: ' Signor *Tyridates*, your Carriage is fair, but somewhat dangerous.' I had no time to reply to this, and indeed it had put me into so much Disorder, that I should hardly have found out fit Words for an Answer; and this she understood so plainly by my Looks, as it powerfully served to confirm her Suspicion.

Thus I parted from *Hierusalem*; and putting myself at the Head of the Army, which attended my coming, we marched towards *Samaria*, where *Barsaphornes* had made some Progress, and already burnt some Villages, with some little Cities, that were not able to make Resistance. Madam, I suppose you willing to learn the Events of this War in a few Words; I shall endeavour therefore to contract a Narration that may sound too harsh to your tender Ears, and only tell you, that I advanced, by great Marches, towards *Barsaphornes*; and being arriv'd within two Days March of the Place where his Army was encamped, I sent to offer him Battle, and to let him know that *Tyridates* himself had brought his Head into the Field; and if he could get the Good-will of Victory, he should reap that desir'd Fruit of his Enterprize, with the entire Satisfaction of his Master.

Barsaphornes (who was espoused to the cruel Disposition of his King) gladly accepted the Battle; and (trusting in the *Parthian* Valour) quitted his Quarters to advance towards ours. Upon the second Day the Armies came in view; and both
being

being ranged with as much Care as we were capable to carry, there began a most cruel and bloody Battle. The *Parthians* were, doubtless, much better Soldiers than the *Jews*, and their Numbers full as great as ours; but the Gods favour'd the Justice of my Cause, and we so happily made good our Choice of some local Advantages, as after an obstinate Dispute, which cost us five or six thousand Lives, Victory came and lighted upon our Banners. The Hatred which the *Jews* bare to the *Parthians*, made it more bloody than I desired; and though the unnatural *Phraates* had so deeply provoked me; yet, in the Pursuit, I used all the Power I had to spare the *Parthian* Blood, and to draw those out of the Victors Hands that had not yet felt their Fury. A *Jew* presented me with the Head of *Barsapharnes*; and though the View at the same time gave me Horror and Compassion, yet I thought it fit to send it to the King of *Parthia*, instead of that which he demanded; and to let him know, by that Present, in what manner I was able to defend mine against his inhuman Pursuits. The Prisoners I sent freely home again, by this gentle Usage, obliging them to detest the Cruelty of their King: And after we had repaired the Damages the *Parthians* had made upon the Frontiers, and put the Fortresses there in a better Condition of Resistance, I triumphantly return'd to *Hierusalem*, where I was receiv'd by the People with great Acclamation, by *Herod* with extraordinary Caresses, and my fair Queen bad me welcome, with an Aspect that assur'd me the Importunity she receiv'd from my Passion, could not wipe out her Interest in my Success.

But oh! the Pride of my Content! when I learn'd from her fair Mouth, that she had admitted Fear for the hazard of my Life, what could I

do?

do? Nay, what Acknowledgment might my Thoughts be capable to fathom, that might suit with the Effects of such a Bounty? This put me in possession of the most glorious Estate that my Reason would let me wish for; and though the divine *Mariamne* was neither able nor willing to bow her Soul to any Sentiments which she judg'd unjust or criminal, yet she let me have as much Estimation and Affection, as Innocence could part with. All those (to whom either good Fortune, or a long Perseverance had given an entire Possession of what they lov'd) could not boast so dear a Satisfaction as mine; nor could I fancy so much Glory and Happiness in having the rarest Beauties of the World at my Feet, as I found in kissing the Robe of *Mariamne*; I say her Robe, for I never kissed her Hand but by surprizal; and when I took that Licence, it cost me the Pains of many Days to expiate the Boldness.

The different Effects of my Passion produced as many Varieties in her; sometimes she laughed at the Extravagancies which the Violence of it forced from me; but the Cruelty of my Sufferings still made her conclude with Pity. Indeed she would take up an earnest Anger, when any Word chanced to escape my Mouth, that she thought favour'd of Impiety; for the Severity of her Religion, which acknowledg'd but one Deity, would not permit me to attribute any thing divine unto her; but when I did, she would use all the Authority she had to command me silence.

I received her Words as I would do Oracles; for she never spake any thing but what deserv'd an entire Attention, and an eternal Memory. ' Tyridates, *said she one Day to me*, how com-
' mendable it would be in you, and how much
' you might oblige me, for my sake and your
.' own,

' own, to recover yourself of this Distemper,
' which must be fatal to one of us, and possibly
' may betray us both to Destruction: I suffer'd
' the Beginning of it with an Indulgence that can-
' not be excus'd, and 'tis that hath render'd me
' guilty both of your Misfortunes and your Faults;
' employ the same Courage wherewith you van-
' quish'd *Judea*'s Enemies, to combat this dome-
' stick Foe. I know you have Virtue enough for
' the Design, if you would use it.; try but to op-
' pose it with all the Forces of your Reason, and
' you will carry an undoubed Victory, in which
' both you and I shall find our perfect Repose
' and Satisfaction. I have yet, by the Grace of
' my God, led my Life in Innocence, and taken
' no Licence from the Provocations of *Herod*, to
' commit any Act unworthy of my Birth; do
' not desire, *Tyridates*, to blemish that in me
' which you prize highest, because 'tis undefiled:
' to drop a Blot upon my Fame, which can never
' be washed off again: If you have yet blinded
' the Eyes of *Herod*, do not dim your own with
' a hope of the same Success for the future. *Sa-*
' *lome* hath an Interest that will set Spies upon
' all your Actions, and soon discover enough to
' ruin you; and if that cruel Woman doth nei-
' ther spare the clearest Innocence, nor the nearest
' Alliance, 'tis but just you should fear her as a
' Stranger; and a Man, who, in her Opinion, is
' already culpable.

The fair Queen utter'd these Words with a
Grace wholly divine; but alas! they found little
Inclination in me to be so wrought upon; for
what Influence could she hope, upon a Spirit that
had reserv'd no Power to dispose of itself, that
could resent nothing in those sweet Words, but
what redoubled the Passion they dissuaded, and
ren-

render'd it incapable of that rigorous Complaifance fhe demanded? I fhew'd her this Weaknefs of mine in as paffionate and fubmiffive Expreffions as my Love could utter; protefted how impoffible it was to obey her, and forgot nothing that I thought might ftir her Goodnefs: I fay her Goodnefs, for upon that only I built all my Fortune.

But I had roved too much in a Calm, too long belied my unfortunate Birth, and the Science of thofe Aftrologers that condemned me to fo many Misfortunes; till then I had fo warily kept my Paffion under Hatches, as the King (though of a moft diffident Nature) had not perceiv'd it; but *Salome*, that furvey'd my Actions, with more defign than all the reft, who of herfelf was one of the fubtileft Women in the World, at firft fufpected, and in the end, by divers Marks, difcover'd the truth of it. Of this fhe gave me fome Intelligence, by the Words fhe let fall at my Departure for the Army; and though they fenfibly touch'd and taught me to carry more Care in my Behaviour for the future, to leffen her Sufpicion, yet all thofe Endeavours proved unfruitful; and the Artifice I employ'd to difguife my Affection, (which, in all likelihood, would have gotten Credit in any Soul but *Salome*'s) in her produced an Affection quite contrary, and confirm'd her in that mifchievous Belief fhe had already entertain'd: When this was once eftablifhed in her Head, Spight came, and joined fo violently with it, that in a fhort time, I think Hatred flam'd higher in her Heart than ever Love had done. The Queen fhe always mortally hated, as well out of Envy of her admirable Qualities, which had infpir'd all others with Love and Veneration, as fome Difdain fhe apprehended in that great Princefs, who indeed could not fo debafe her Spirit to fmile on

fuch

such as she deemed unworthy of Affability: Besides, her Power was too great with the King, and *Salome*, that aim'd to be uppermost in his Favour, was stung with Discontent at the Queen's Authority.

With these Considerations she mingled her Jealousy, which stirr'd up such impetuous Storms in her Breast, as made it capable of the foulest Treasons, and blackest Crimes; and if she hardly endured her Disrespect and Authority, she could not look upon her as a Rival, without resolving her Ruin, and with her to destroy that, which a few Days before her Affection had set at so high a Value.

This Change may appear strange unto you, but it was so true, that she no sooner believed me amorous of *Mariamne*, but that Love with which she had before perplexed me, was converted into such a hatred, as render'd her apt to entertain most violent Resolutions, and set her presently a hatching a Design to involve me in the Mischiefs she prepar'd for that innocent Princess; she was so well acquainted with the King her Brother's Spirit, as she knew it to be of the same Temper with her own, and therefore doubted not but to make the least Impressions she could give him, powerful enough to destroy us. By this Way, as the most assured, and the least dangerous, she resolved our Ruin, and began to labour it with all the Subtilty that her Malice could invent: She first began to observe the long Stay I made in *Judea*, notwithstanding that I might elsewhere find Sanctuaries of more Assurance, and that the Emperor *Augustus* (an Enemy to the King of *Parthia*) had invited me to *Rome*, and offered me a peaceable Retreat there, with all forts of Succours against *Phraates*. She shew'd him how it disagreed.

greed with Reason, that I should disdain such advantageous Offers, to be supported by the Masters of the Earth, if I had not some powerful Tye in *Judea*.   Then without unmasking her Design, she made him curiously to mark my Actions, desired him often to observe my Face when I enter'd the Queen's Chamber, to take notice of my Sighs, my passionate Looks, with divers Passages, in which a violent Love cannot belye itself to the Eyes of interested Persons that will carefully survey them. These Things in a short Time wrought upon *Herod's* Spirit, and (as none was more tenderly sensible and impatient in that Respect than he) I should soon have felt his Fury if he had not been restrain'd by divers Considerations.

Besides the hatred which he bare to *Phraates*, and the services I had render'd to his Crown, he consider'd me as one protected by *Augustus*, who had oft writ to him in my favour, and express'd a particular care of me : This dextrous and politick King dissembled his first resentments, only he made known to *Salome* a part of his suspicion ; and when that malicious wasp perceiv'd she had made way for her intention, and half train'd the King to her design, she neglected no time to strike the blow as she had premeditated.

' Sir, *said she one day to him*, I am constrain'd
' to declare that which (till now) the care I che-
' rished for the quiet of your Family, made me
' conceal ; but the peace of your mind being yet
' more dear to me, hath overcome all those con-
' siderations, that made me dissemble my thoughts.
' Seek no more for the cause of *Mariamne's* dis-
' dain, her aversion doth not spring from a re-
' sentment for the death of her Kindred ; for were
' she not prevented by another passion, the proofs
' of your love must needs have softned her : That

Rock

' Rock so insensible to your Caresses, is not so
' unrelenting to others; for that *Parthian* that
' that holds his safety of your Charity, does doubt-
' less love her with better luck than you; I have
' discover'd their intelligence by divers marks, and
' whatever care they took to disguise it, their passion
' hath so blinded them, that they have lost all power
' to dissemble it, and I fear at last the whole Court
' will perceive it with scandal; I strugled hard be-
' fore I could resolve with my self to reveal this
' to you, and I should have been willing at the
' price of my blood to have shunn'd the occasion
' of it without betraying you; but at last, Sir, my
' zeal for you interests, and my indignation at the
' Queen's ingratitude, have vanquished those Rea-
' sons that would enjoyn me silence.

While *Salome* spake, the King accompanied
her Discourse with many sighs, and swallow'd at
deep draughts the poison she had prepar'd him;
this first information wanted little of transporting
him to some fatal action: but, as he had shewn
much power upon himself in divers encounters,
he then mastered these first motions, and grew
desirous to discover further, before he enterpriz'd
things that might bring him such displeasing consequences. For this reason, suppressing his apprehensions as much as possible: ' Sister, *said he to*
' *Salome*, I am oblig'd to you for the advice you
' have given me, and doubt not but it parts from
' the affection you bare me; I have already had
' suspicions conform'd to your belief, but they
' were not so strongly grounded to seize wholly
' upon my judgment; besides, I have understood
' the Queen's Vertues by so many proofs, as I
' found it hard to believe that her aversion to me
' could urge her to the violation of her duty:
' Yet now I begin to lean to your opinion, and
' with

' with you to judge it almoſt impoſſible that a
' thouſand ardent proofs of my affection ſhould
' not efface the Queen's reſentments, nor ſo much
' as ſoften her rocky heart, if ſhe had not given
' it to another. I love her but too well, *con-*
' *tinu'd he with a ſigh*, too, too well I love that
' ingrateful Woman, and though ſhe unworthily
' abuſes my love, yet I cannot chooſe but love
' her.' He ſtopp'd at theſe words, walked up and
down the Chamber with an action that expreſt
his tranſport and irreſolution, wherein *Salome*
might read, that her plot had not ill ſucceeded.

Ah! *Tyridates* cry'd he, after ſome ſilence, doſt
thou thus requite the protection and refuge I have
given thee? Doſt thou not fear to find that in my
juſt anger which thou haſt avoided by my aſſiſtance? Had I deſerv'd to have felt thy indignation, couldſt thou not have galled me in a part
leſs ſenſible? And canſt thou believe that a cruel
brother is more formidable than a jealous huſband, than a paſſionate lover? He mingled theſe
words with freſh ſighs, and again took ſome turns
in the room; then turning to *Salome*, ' Siſter, *ſaid*
' *he*, before we enterprize any thing upon the ad-
' vice you have given, 'tis fit we inſtruct ourſelves
' farther; for the quality of *Tyridates*, back'd
' with the care that *Auguſtus* takes of his ſafety,
' preſcribes me much caution; if you pleaſe, con-
' tinue to improve your diſcovery of the truth,
' and on my ſide I ſhall take ſuch care, as it ſhall
' prove a very hard taſk for them ſtill to abuſe me.

This was the diſcourſe between the King and
Salome, all which a while after I learn'd from *So-*
bemus, who had been told it by an Officer of the
King's, his intimate friend, that over-heard it in
the Anti-chamber.

From

From that day thefe two malicious fpirits employed all their care to obferve my behaviour, and indeed I confefs, that (whatever circumfpection I endeavour'd to carry) many paffages flipt from me, capable to undifguife my paffion to perfons fo powerfully concern'd; my looks, fighs, and change of Countenance often betrayed me; for before I underftood the King's fufpicion, I behav'd my felf with lefs prudence than I fhould have ufed, had I diftrufted it; the Queen was yet more narrowly fifted, and as that great Princefs obferved fomething in me (if I may fpeak it with Modefty) that gave me a better Title to her Efteem than any of the *Jews*, and poffibly feeling herfelf obliged to my perfevering refpectuous Paffion, fhe compell'd herfelf to fhew fuch apprehenfions of it, as reafon told her were full of innocence, and treated me in publick with a countenance capable to confirm the King in thofe cruel impreffions *Salome* had given him.

This jealous Prince that faw not but with the troubled Eyes of his fufpicion, beheld all our actions, as if every one had the countenance of a Criminal; the effects of the Queen's goodnefs and civility were interpreted for fo many marks of her affection; and thus he was ready every moment to abandon himfelf to fuch a rage, as almoft pofed all the prudence he could make to tame it. I often marked thefe Changes both in his Looks and his Humour: and, though in the whole Courfe of his Life he had appear'd the moft dexterous Diffembler of all Men, yet his raging Jealoufy had fo weakned the Power, which ufually held the Reins of his Paffions, as he could not fo well contain himfelf, but I difcover'd much Coldnefs and Change in the Difcourfe and Entertainment he made me; indeed I fhould have apprehended

prehended all thefe Things with fuch a Spirit as his,
and doubtlefs had fo, if the powerful Love of *Mariamne* had not ftifled that in my Soul, which Nature places there for our proper Safety, and forc'd
a Neglect of all that Care I fhould have carried
about me for the Prefervation of my Life. The
Queen perceiv'd this (which fhe always fufpected)
as foon as I; and though her Confcience witneffed
to herfelf the Innocence of her Carriage, yet fhe
was defirous to avoid the Danger fhe apprehended, by treating me with a more referv'd behaviour, if poffible, than fhe had done formerly. I
ftudied a more fpecious Diffimulation, but it was
too late, the Tempeft was already rifen, and at
laft made itfelf known by moft dangerous Flafhes.

One Day, the Remembrance of which I muft
preferve as the moft remarkable of my Life, the
very fame whereon the *Jews* celebrate that which
they call the Feaft of Tabernacles, being defirous
through Curiofity (though of different Religion)
to affift at their Ceremonies, I accompany'd the
King to that famous Temple, which from the
Name of its Founder, they call the Temple of *Solomon*, and which for Riches and admirable Structure, may pafs with more juftice than that of *Diana*
at *Ephefus*, or that of *Jupiter* the *Olympian*, for
one of the World's Wonders; at firft the Ceremonies borrowed my Attention, for methought they
were very fpecious: But in fine, no longer able
to keep them off, I tranfported all my Thoughts
to *Mariamne*, and with thofe tied my Eyes to her
Face, with fo attentive a Regard; and though
Arfanes, who ftood behind me, often endeavour'd to call me to myfelf, and made me mark
in what manner the King obferv'd me, I had much
ado to retire them for a few Moments, while the
Sacrifice lafted; nor was I ignorant of the Fault I

committed, but I believe the Gods struck my Reason blind, to punish my Offence of assisting at the Sacrifices of a Religion which was Enemy to theirs: Whatever the Cause was, that was the Day wherein the King abandon'd himself to his Jealousy, though possibly he had not yet determin'd upon the Resolution he was to take. Coming back from the Temple, he went to visit the Queen's Lodging, full of furious Thoughts, his Face carried the Copy of his troubled Soul, and his Eyes sparkled Messages of Death : Yet they were no sooner encounter'd by the Queen's, but all their Storms clear'd up, and those Tempests which Rage had rais'd against her, by that marvellous Ascendant she had upon his Spirit, did homage to the Charms of her Beauty, and grew calm in a Moment ; of one terrible as a Lion, in a few Minutes he became mild and tractable ; and instead of uttering the Threats he had prepar'd, his disarmed Anger gave Place to Kindness, which render'd his Spirit pliable to Caresses and Flatteries.

He made the Queen a Discourse full of Affection, which she receiv'd with her usual Modesty. But then offering to take some Liberties with her, which he might have lawfully believ'd his due, if (by so many Cruelties inflicted upon her and hers) he had not violated the Rights, and lost all those Advantages of which Marriage had possess'd him, that courageous Princess, who could never tamely hide her Resentment in a Disguise, disdainfully repuls'd him.

Herod, that was not ignorant of the true Cause of this, though he suspected others, would not take a Denial from her first coldness ; but perceiving she resisted with an invincible Resolution, and being no Way able to obtain these Favours from her, which his desires were greedy of, he recall'd

recall'd that Choler that had so lately shook him,
and beholding her with Eyes that sparkled Fury:
' Ingrateful Woman, *said he*, do not longer
' think to abuse me by thy specious Pretences;
' but know I am not ignorant that it is the Love
' of *Tyridates*, and not the Memory of *Hircanus*,
' or *Aristobulus*, that renders thee inflexible to
' thy Husband's Kindness.

Though the Queen had ever fear'd these Things
from *Herod's* Humour, yet she could not be less
than surpriz'd at this Language, and appear'd as
if she had been struck with a Thunder-bolt; her
Tongue remain'd mute, her Visage chang'd Cho-
lour, and from the profound Astonishment which
Herod there observed, he receiv'd cruel Confirma-
tions of his jealous Thoughts. This Apprehension
redoubled his Fury, and now not doubting but
the Queen's powerful Surprisal rose from the Reproaches of her Conscience, and the Shame or Fear
she might have to see her Passion discovered, he
gave himself up to the most furious Transports
that Rage could inspire, and had much ado to
keep it from committing Outrage upon her Person; but he upbraided her with the most injurious Words that Choler could invent: ' How now
' Traitress, *said he*, must I then be robb'd by a
' Barbarian's Witchcraft, of what is only due to
' myself? And thou, that would'st fain pass for
' a demure Zealot, does it suit with the Law of
' thy God, or the Repute of the World, that
' thou findest more Sweetness in the shameful
' Embraces of an Infidel, than in the legitimate
' Affections of a Husband? Ah! disloyal Wo-
' man, unworthy of a Love, which has preserved
' thee in a Rank from whence thou hast deserved
' to fall with thy Family, a Love that hath expo-
' sed me too, to the Contempt of my People:

' Is

' Is it by thefe infamous Paffions thou makeft
' good thy claim to the *Maccabean* Blood, of
' which thou haft fo often boafted? Thinkeft
' thou thofe illuftrious *Afmoneans*, with whofe
' Glory thou haft ftill reproached me, (fhould
' they return to the World) could approve of the
' ignominious Preference thou makeft of an exi-
' led *Parthian*, to a King, whom the lateft of
' thy Anceftors gave thee for a Husband, or ra-
' ther who honoured thee with the Title of his
' Spoufe, when he might have ufed thee as his
' Subject?

He accompanied thefe Words with a Torrent
of others more cruel and injurious; during which
the fair Queen, having had time to reftore herfelf from her firft Aftonifhment, began to regard
with all the Affurance that Innocence could give
her; and, neither able to make her Spirit flexible,
to his Flatteries, nor her own Juftification, of
which fhe believed him unworthy, after that he
had given fome truce to his Invectives, ' Finifh,
' *faid fhe*, thou cruel Man, finifh thy Rage, and
' believe that after the Exercife of fo much brutifh
' Cruelty upon mine, thou may'ft give it leave
' to let fall its laft Effects upon myfelf; there on-
' ly remains the laft Part of it to be acted upon
' me; for having had (by the Murther of my
' deareft Friends, by a miferable Captivity, and
' the bloody Orders thou gaveft for my own)
' my Repofe fo often tortured, there refts no
' more but to affault my Honour, which by the
' favour of Heaven I have till now defended from
' thy horrid Perfecutions: Do, tear my Reputati-
' on, which hath maintained itfelf pure and fpot-
' lefs in my Misfortunes, and ftill perfecute the
' *Afmonean* Memory by the Shame thou prepa-
' reft for the laft of its illuftrious Blood, which
thou

' thou haft fpilt fo brutifhly: Hope not I will
' affert my Innocence; no, that Account muft
' only be render'd to him that knows it, and by
' his Goodnefs will defend it againft the Calum-
' ny of my Enemies: believe all of the unfortu-
' nate *Mariamne*, wherewith her envious Detrac-
' tors have infpir'd thee: Thy Cruelties have gi-
' ven me but too much Caufe to difpenfe with
' the Juftification which I owe to him, whom
' Heaven in its Anger gave me for a Husband;
' but do not involve fuch Perfons in my Mifery,
' as have no Part in the Crime thou impofeft;
' and if thy Rage demands a Victim to appeafe
' it, feek no other than her whom thou haft
' taught to defire Death, by rendering her Life
' calamitous.

The laft Words of the Queen tranfported *Herod* to the fartheft Degrees of Fury: And now,
more than believing the Care fhe took of my Juftification, while fhe difdained her own, could
fpring from no other Root but that of Love, he
concluded the Proof clear enough to convince her;
and not able fo far to over-rule this Belief, to
diffemble his Intention: ' Yes, perfidious Crea-
' ture, *cryed he*, I will credit all that my Eyes
' and Ears, and not the envious Detractors, have
' told me; I will credit all that will convince thee
' of the moft fhameful and blackeft of all Trea-
' fons; and in fine, believe that of thee, which
' thou wouldeft I fhould do, and difdain'ft to
' difavow: The Care thou takeft of that ingrate-
' ful Wretch, which has fo bafely betrayed me,
' to the Prejudice of thy own Safety, fhall fuffice
' for his and thy Condemnation: The Ruin of
' that thou holdeft fo dear, fhall begin the Pu-
' nifhment of thy Difloyalty, and the Choice of
' Victims due to my juft Anger fhall not be at

E 3 thy

' thy Difpofal; for before thou learneft what to
' refolve upon thyfelf, prepare to know what I
' fhall execute upon the Perfon of thy Adulterer.

At thefe Words he flung out of the Chamber,
with a Countenance fo furious, as thofe that met
him in the Paffage could not behold him without
trembling; alas! how erroneous was the Opinion he had of my Fortune? how remote was I
from that fovereign Degree of Happinefs, and how
worthy my Condition had been of Envy, had his
Sufpicions been true.

In the mean Time I was at my Lodging, wholly ignorant of what had paffed at the Palace, and
employed the reft of that Day upon my ordinary Diverfions. The Hour of Supper being come,
I was ferved after the ufual Manner, and fitting at
the Table with fome Friends of the Court, which
were come to vifit me, we had done Part of our
Repaft, when, calling for Drink, one of the King's
Cup-bearers that was accuftomed to ferve me,
prefented the Cup with a troubled Look, and dif-
compofed Countenance: I obferved this Change
in his Vifage, but made no Reflection upon it, only contented myfelf to ask him if he was not
well; and in the mean Time taking the Cup from
his Hands, I was carrying it to my Mouth, when
Arfanes enter'd the Chamber, and haftily running
up to me, juft as I touched the Cup with my
Lips, he rufhed againft my Arm fo rudely, as he
made me let fall the Cup, and fpill the Liquor,
part on the Table, and part upon my Cloaths:
This Action of *Arfanes* was fo little refpectful, that
(knowing his Difpofition) I concluded he had not
done it without fome powerful Motive: But he
ftayed not till I fhould ask the Reafon, and (defirous to hide his Intent from thofe were with
me) ' Sir, *faid he*, I befeech you to pardon the
' Offence

' Offence which my rash Haste hath made me
' commit, and be pleased to vouchsafe me the
' Liberty of your Ear for one Moment.'   This
said, he drew me by the Arm with an Action so
earnest, as I perceived he had some Advice of
Importance to communicate: I rose from the Table, making a bad Excuse to those that supp'd
with me, and followed *Arsanes* into my Cabinet,
which he first enter'd.   We were no sooner there,
' But, Sir, *said he*, nothing but a speedy Flight
' can save your Life, the Gods in good time con-
' ducted me hither to spill the Poyson prepared
' for you; but if we stay longer here, it will not
' be possible, with the same Facility, to put by
' those other Dangers that menace you; read this
' Note, which just now I receiv'd of the Queen's
' chief Eunuch, it is written with her own Hand;
' and if the Gods consent that we escape, 'tis to
' her alone you owe your safety.'   I was amaz'd
at the Words and Actions of *Arsanes*, and without reply to his Discourse, I took the Letter,
where I found these Words written by the Hand
of my divine Queen.

Mariamne *to Prince* Tyridates.

' T H E Peril to which I expose myself in wri-
' ting to you, cannot hinder an Advice which
' I owe to your Virtue, and the Proofs of your
' Affection. *Tyridates*, if it be possible save your-
' self, and stay no longer in a Place, where Poy-
' son and Sword are employ'd to give you Death.
' I read over the Billet twice or thrice, kiss'd
those amiable Characters which that adorable
Hand had traced, and after the Perusal, I was
much to seek, whether the Cruelty of *Herod*, that
sought to destroy me, after he had given me shel-

ter, or the Goodness of *Mariamne*, who took such noble Pains to preserve my Life with the Peril of her own, touch'd me deepest; I knew not to which of these Resentments my Soul was to give Preheminence, but I know well the Death that was threatned could not put on so rude a Shape as that departure, to which I saw myself condemned by the Hand of *Mariamne*.

The Grief I felt was too prodigious to be wrapt in Words. I stood a long Time silent and immoveable, which *Arsanes* (who had ballanced the Estate of my Affairs) disapproving, after he had often urged me to resolve: ' What would you I ' should do, *said I?* What Resolution can you ' with me to take in so cruel a Proposition? ' think you this Life, which through your care ' I have miserably dragg'd from Court to Court, ' is so dear to divorce me from *Mariamne?* Do ' you believe this separation more easy than that ' of my Soul from my Body? Shall I abandon ' her for ever, whom I can scarce leave for a ' Moment without dying? And to avoid one ' single Death, shall I carry a thousand in my ' Breast, through all those Places where my piti- ' less Fortune shall lead me? Ah! let us die first, ' continued I, walking a great Pace, without ' listning to the Reasons *Arsanes* pressed for de- ' parture; let us die a ready Death, since a flow ' one is much more sensible, leave the Body cold ' and pale in that Place which the Soul cannot ' abandon; and since we must die one Way, let ' us seek to die in the Eyes of *Mariamne*; and if ' that Glory be refus'd, at least give up that Spi- ' rit which neither was, nor ever shall be, but to ' her, as near her as is possible.

I pronounced these Words with an Action full of transport; and while thus my Irresolution
shook

shook me with such terrible-Inquietudes, *Arsanes*
lost all his loyal Pains about me ; but after he had
alledged divers persuasive Reasons, to which I
could not so much as lend Attention : ' Sir, *said*
' *he*, I doubt not but you dispose yourself to this
' parting with much Regret ; but if the Care of
' your own Life cannot oblige you, consider the
' Command you receiv'd from the Queen, you
' will find it so express, that if you have any Re-
' spect left for her, it is impossible to disobey it.'
' The Queen's Command, *replied I*, proceeds
' from nought but a compassionate Care she takes
' of my Life : Did she know that to die were a
' thousand Times more pleasing than to quit her
' for ever, she would doubtless permit me to
' stay here still.' *Arsanes* was about to reply,
though he could never have perswaded me, when
my Governor enter'd the Closet, and told me in
a few Words, that *Sohemus* desired to speak with
me, that favour'd by the Night's Darkness, he
had slipt into the Garden where he had attended
me, not daring to approach farther, without running à Danger too manifest, and giving the King
such Suspicions as might bereave him of the Means
to serve me.

I ran, without replying, to the Place where
Sohemus waited, without a Torch, or any Company but *Arsanes* and my Governor ; and so soon
as I came at him, ' Well, my dear Friend, *said*
' *I, embracing him*, then we must either die or
' separate ; and by the Cruelty of *Herod* and Fate,
' either Life or *Mariamne* must be quitted.'
' Yes, Sir, *reply'd* Sohemus ; and if you use not
' Diligence, 'tis possible you will have both snatch-
' ed from you.' ' That may easily be done, *said*
' *I*, and I shall feel less Pain and Repugnance
' that way, than violently to chain my Body
' where'

' where my Soul refuſes to keep it company.'
Then I repeated almoſt the ſame things I talked
to *Arſanes*; to which, when he had lent an Attention as ſerious as the Troubles that involv'd us
had left him, ' Sir, *ſaid he*, if you love the Queen,
' you ought not to conſult farther, nor enlarge
' your Explications upon her Commands, which
' cannot be but fatal to one or other ; if you ne-
' glect your own Life, you ought to conſider
' hers, and to believe, that while you are in *Judea*,
' ſhe can never be in ſafety ; 'tis not only againſt
' you that the King's Anger does lighten, 'tis ra-
' ther her that this riſing Storm doth threaten ;
' and you have no other way to keep it off her
' Head, than by removing the Cauſe of the King's
' cruel Jealouſy.

Then, in order, he briefly recounted what he
had learn'd of the Conference between the King
and Queen from the chief Eünuch, who had over-
heard it ; and thus, by urging the Queen's Safety
and Repoſe, he rang'd all that was repugnant in
me under his Obedience. Yet I could not diſpoſe
myſelf to forſake the Queen for ever, but I reſolved for ſome time to fly the Rage of *Herod* ;
and, in the mean time, to go in ſearch of ſome
Occaſions that might either reſtore my Condition
by the Knowledge he might gain of the Queen's
Innocence, or, if it were poſſible, procure to ſee
her without her Knowledge. This was my Hope
that got my Conſent to part ; but I would rather
have taken a thouſand Deaths, than given it to
take eternal Leave of *Mariamne*.

While I diſcourſed with *Sohemus*, thanked him
for his good Offices, and promiſed a perpetual
Amity, with ſuch a Share in my Fortunes, as his
own Deſires ſhould crave, (if ever the Gods thought
fit to change them) and drew Promiſes from him

to persevere in his faithful Assistance, *Arsanes* and my Governor got ready our Arms and Horses; and having caused them to be led, without Noise, by three or four *Parthian* Servitors to the Garden Gate, (that had served me from my Infancy, and followed me in all my Voyages) and having carefully pack'd up my Jewels and Money, with what else was necessary, I rewarded *Sohemus* with some Gems of great Value, and leaving others in his Hand to give to *Cleophe* and the Eunuch that had been my Confidants, I bid him adieu with Tears in my Eyes; and arming myself, in a short time I got to Horse with *Arsanes*, my Governor, and my faithful *Parthians*, without taking any *Jew* along with me, or so much as letting them know of my Departure.

I went out at the same Gate *Sohemus* enter'd, which open'd into an unfrequented Street; while I issued out at the back-side of my Lodging, the Front of it was assaulted by those that *Herod* had sent either to take or kill me; and as they had Order to environ my Lodging, I had not trod many Steps in the Streets, before I saw both Ends of it seiz'd upon by a great Number of Soldiers, that shut up the Passage on all sides. I perceiv'd I should find it a hard Task to save myself; yet I resolved to sell either my Life or Liberty as dear as possible, and turning to those that followed me : ' Are you resolved, *said I*, to de-
' fend yourselves like valiant Men, and either to
' owe your Safety to your own Bravery, or pe-
' rish with your Prince, if the Gods have so or-
' dain'd it?' They protested with one Voice, That they would die at my Feet : And being assured of their Resolution, I spurr'd in upon those, with my Sword in my Hand, that defended the Passage, and was follow'd so courageously by mine,

that

that my Enemies began to judge it not so easy a Task to take me as they imagined.

I pass'd upon the Necks of those that first opposed me; and cutting out our Way with our Swords, we bestirr'd ourselves so vigorously at the first Encounter, as (after we had thrown many of our Enemies dead at our Feet, and scatter'd the fiercest of the rest) the Passage through the Street remained free, and we advanced into another more large, through which we galloped towards the Gate that was nearest. And now we had begun to entertain some hope of escape, when passing through a Place adjoining to the Temple, we espy'd so many Troops of armed Men from all Corners approaching to us, as we judg'd it very difficult to force them.

The Light which the Torches cast, shewed me *Alexas*, the Husband of *Salome*, at the Head of the foremost; and hearing him loudly animate his Men either to take or kill me, I ran up unto him, with my advanced Sword in my Hand, which I let fall upon his Head so forcibly, that had not the Blow been warded by a Soldier, that put his Sword before it, his Life had paid for his Wife's Malice; nevertheless, the Blow was not so slight, but it threw him with a deep Wound at the Feet of his Soldiers: The *Jews* raised a loud Clamour at the Fall of *Alexas*; and, in the mean time, we charged in so successfully, as we tumbled many of them dead at our Horses Feet. Indeed we did perform Actions there worthy of some Remembrance; and 'tis probable the *Jews* had never seen such a Handful of Men in their City dispute their Lives so courageously. But in fine, our Enemy's Strength increased to such a measure, and ours grew so feeble, as we soon perceived, without some miraculous Assistance, the Ways to

Safety

Safety were all blocked up. My Governor *Politis*, who till then had accompany'd and serv'd me in all my Difgraces, with a marvellous Affection, (bravely fighting by my Side) was forced by a Multitude of Wounds to breathe his laft; his Death was fucceeded by one of my faithful *Parthians*; and fure I had not long ftaid behind him, if *Arfanes*, who is endow'd with a dextrous Wit, and that temper'd with a marvellous Prudence, bethought himfelf, in the very midft of Danger, of a way to fave us; and approaching to me, as near as poffible, ' Sir, *faid he*, I ' befeech you follow me, I have difcovered a fe- ' cure Retreat.' And at thefe Words, inftead of fpurring towards the Gate, as we did before, where the thickeft Throng of Enemies and Diffi- culty withftood us, he caufed me to face about to- wards the Temple-Gate, which was behind us; and on that fide (having but few Enemies to com- bat) we foon cleared the Paffage; and were no fooner arrived there, but we readily quitted our Horfes, and threw ourfelves into the Temple, which was then open, becaufe of the Feaft of Tabernacles, the Celebration of which lafted three whole Days.

That Temple had always been a Sanctuary for Criminals, but at that Feaft (the moft confide- rable of any the *Jews* Religion celebrates) it was fo affured a Refuge, as the *Jews* would rather have fuffered the entire Ruin of their Nation, than permitted any to be forced from the Tem- ple, that had there taken Sanctuary, whatfo- ever Crime they were convicted of. This cool'd the Heat of their Purfuits; and when they faw us entered, they ftopp'd at the Gate, and ftood with Arms a-crofs, without the leaft offer to follow us. Indeed fome there were of the moft

muti-

mutinous among them, and the most interested in the hurt of *Alexas*, and the Deaths of their Companions, that cry'd out to the Priests to put us out; that I was the King's Enemy; that it was by his Order and express Command they pursued us: But the Priests, instead of listening to their Clamour, received us with much Humanity, and protested they would rather perish than suffer the Temple's Privileges to be violated. The Dignity of the Priesthood among the *Jews* was very eminent: That of the High-Priest had heretofore been only exercised by Kings themselves; after the Kings *Hircanus* and *Aristobulus*, the Grandfather and Brother of *Mariamne*, had discharged it, and then it was in the Hands of one the nearest ally'd to the Crown. And thus we saw ourselves in that sacred Fortress, and our Enemies only content to environ it, without daring to advance one Step to force an Entrance; but as soon as Day shewed itself, the King having learn'd the Truth, after he had sent divers Messages to the Priests in vain, he came himself, wholly transported with Fury, in such a Tempest, as gave belief to those that were next him, it would hurry him to the most violent Extremities.

The Priests, inform'd of his Arrival, came to the Gate to meet him; but so soon as they saw him, in the Name of their God they forbad him to put a Foot into the Temple, if he brought any other Intention than to render that Respect which was as due from him, as from the meanest *Jew*, to that holy Place, and the Divinity within it.

Herod, though deeply in Rage, and possibly not over-zealous in the Service of his God, as he was very politick, fear'd, that being already hated, and but weakly assured of the *Jews* Fidelity, (should he venture to violate their Customs, and infringe

their

their Privileges) it might provoke some Revolt ;
besides, news was brought him, that in divers
Parts of the City, the *Pharisees*, that were the
greatest Zealots in their Religion, and the most
considerable among the People, began to murmur.
He considered that there was then cause to fear
every thing, the Feast having fill'd the City, not
only with its own Inhabitants, but with the greatest Part of all *Judea*, which the Solemnity had
summoned thither. These Considerations staid
Herod at the Gate ; but the Trouble of his Soul
express'd itself at the Eyes, and in the disjointed
Words his Rage let fall : Yet, Time having re-
conciled him to some Reason, he represented to
some Priests, that the Asylum of the Temple was
not to protect us ; that we were Infidels, and of
a contrary Religion ; that they ought the rather
to put us out, lest our Presence should prophane
the Place's Holiness. But the Priests reply'd, That
God's Asylum was equally for all Men ; that if
our Opinions did not tread the right Path, we
might there find it through the Conduct of his
Grace ; that probably having made us incur the
King's Displeasure, he had therefore called us
thither.

Herod answer'd, That I had violated the chief
Rights of Hospitality, that were as ancient as
Temples themselves ; that no Nation ought to
contain a Refuge of the Man that had directly
abused the proper Person of the King, and mortally wounded his Brother-in-law : But all the Arguments he could urge, were not strong enough
to batter the Priests Resolution ; neither his Menaces nor Promises could dispose them, either to
remit me into his Hands, or suffer him to enter
into the Temple, without thundering against him
with all their Authority; wherewith their Office
had

had invested them, which enjoin'd the Conservation of their Privileges.

The Gods can witness, that I did not love my Life so well, to bestow all the Care they made me take upon its Preservation : But I condescended much to the Entreaties of *Arsanes* and my Servants, and indeed to the Priests themselves, who would not permit me to leave the Temple, though I had desir'd it.

Whatever Resentment I had entertain'd against *Herod*, as the Persecutor of my Life, and *Mariamne*'s Repose ; yet I could not quit the thought of his first Reception, and the Shelter that he had so many Years given me against my Brother's Barbarism. This Remembrance made me desire to see and speak to him, to testify that I was neither ingrateful to his former Kindness, nor had ever injured him in the least Particular he could imagine. Upon this Score, forcing this Resistance of *Arsanes*'s Dissuasion, I approached within eight or ten Paces of the Gate, where he contested with the Priests ; and, so soon as I could be seen or heard, ' King of the *Jews*, cry'd I, I am neither
' thy Subject nor Inferior : And the Gods, who
' have given me Birth from the noblest Family
' in the World, have not left me to acknowledge
' any superior Power but theirs ; for this Reason
' I have little cause to justify myself to thee, that
' would'st have taken my Life both by Sword and
' Poison, and hast pursued me against all divine
' and human Right, even to the Temple of thy
' God : But the Satisfaction I owe to my Con-
' science, and to the Memory of that Entertain-
' ment wherewith thou hast formerly treated me,
' doth oblige me to declare my Innocence. I
' protest unto thee, *Herod*, both before thy God
' and mine, that I have no way deserved to of-
'   ' fend

'fend thee : In thofe Employments thou gaveft
'me for thy Service, thou haft found it, (and
'poffibly to thy own Advantage) that I neither
'fpared my Blood nor my Life for the Intereft
'of thy State ; and for that which concerns thy
'Perfon, I repeat my Proteftation, that I never
'did thee any Injury.   If that which feems ami-
'able in thy Eye, hath appeared worthy of Ve-
'neration and Refpect, thofe Sentiments, to
'which thou canft only attribute my Crime, can-
'not make thy Complaint againft me legitimate ;
'and I wifh this very Temple, which now ferves
'to fhroud me from thy Malice, may crufh me
'with its own Ruins, if in the moft culpable of
'all my Thoughts, there was any Mixture of
'what might be capable to wrong thee.   Nor
'do I affert this Truth with defign to difarm thy
'Fury, or avoid the Death thou threateneft : I
'cannot fear bafely ; nay, could I now be fhewn
'any occafion to perifh nobly, thou fhouldft
'quickly fee how low I prize my Life ; but I per-
'ceive, that either thy own blind Tranfport, or
'the Rage of mine and thy Enemies, have made
'thee involve, in my impofed Crimes, the pureft
'and the moft entire Innocent that ever yet was inju-
'red. Deftroy him, if thou wilt, whofe Thoughts
'may have difpleafed thee, though they were al-
'ways innocent enough to endure ftripping; but
'do not let fall thy Rage upon her that never un-
'derftood them.   What I have reprefented may
'plant quiet, as well in thy Family as thy Breaft :
'And if thou wilt promife me, at the Foot of thy
'Altars, and before the Minifters of thy God, to
'make me the only Mark of thy Fury, I will
'abandon this Afylum that defends my Head
'from thy Rage, and without further delay ren-
'der it up into thy Hands.

I had

I had further enlarg'd myself, if the enraged *Herod* would have given me a longer hearing, without Interruption. He had endur'd the Beginning of my Discourse with some Patience, or at least had suffered me to speak, because the Excess of Choler that possess'd him, had ty'd up his own Tongue. But when he saw with what Passion I endeavour'd to justify *Mariamne*, and then remember'd that her Goodness had taken the same Care for me, he let himself fall into a cruel Redoublement of his Jealousy; and, not able to dissemble the Rage that Remembrance inspir'd,
' Barbarous Traytor, *cry'd he*, unworthy of the
' Protection I have given thee, against those that
' knew thee better than myself, and would justly
' have cut thee from the World, through the Ex-
' perience of thy disloyal Inclination: Dost thou
' hope to find, that at the Foot of our Altars,
' against my just Resentments, which none but
' my Arm could have given thee, against the
' Pursuits of thy own Brother? Thinkest thou,
' Heaven, that abhors thy Ingratitude, can arm
' itself in thy Defence against a King, that hath
' but too well defended and received thee, not
' only into his Dominions, but with a hospi-
' table Liberality into his House; a Favour thou
' hast unworthily abused? Ah! no, false Man,
' do not hope divine Preservation for such Crimes
' as can neither be excus'd before God or Man;
' nor think thy artificial Words can pacify an
' Anger armed but with too much Justice. Thou
' shalt perish for the Expiation of thy own In-
' gratitude; nor shall thy Counsel direct me
' what Punishment to inflict on the Complices of
' thy Treachery.
He would have said more, and possibly in the end violated all Right of Privilege to get me into

his

his Power, if *Sosius* (followed with a great Guard of *Romans* and *Jews*) had not arrived at the Temple-Gate. This Man was a *Roman* Senator, that some Days since came to *Hierusalem* to treat with *Herod* about certain Affairs concerning the Emperor *Augustus*. And the same *Sosius* that, with a *Roman* Army, had formerly aided him in his War against *Antigonus*, and contributed more than himself to the Defeat and taking of that poor Prince.

Herod highly respected this Man, as well for his personal as his representative Condition, being the Emperor's Ambassador. *Sosius* had formerly known, and fancying something in me worthy of his Amity, gladly consented to be my Friend; and at that time understanding the Danger I was in, he came to find *Herod*, with intent to employ all the Imperial Authority for my Preservation: and so successfully he labour'd it, that *Herod*, as hot as his Rage had made him, was constrained to tame it at the Name of *Augustus*, of whose Power and Greatness he was a timorous Idolater.

Sosius urged, that he ought to permit me to retire to the Emperor, who had oft invited me to *Rome*, and professed an Interest in my Preservation; that his Proceedings were but too violent against a Prince of my Extraction; that it was fit to consider what might follow; his Quarrel being grounded upon nought but weak Suspicion; besides, that he had learnt the Wound of *Alexas* was not dangerous, which I had given him in such a Resistance as was allowed to all Men: Besides these, he represented divers other Considerations, to which, in the end, he join'd the Emperor's Authority, protesting he should render an exact Account of that Action: And to this Menace, *Herod* (that was a Slave to the *Roman* Fortune and

Great-

Greatnefs, and without that Prop, knew it impoffible to fupport his own) rather render'd than
to any other Confideration. At laft, therefore, he
confented I fhould go fafely out of the Temple,
with all that was mine, on condition I fhould
make no ftay in the City, but quit it the fame
Day, and in fix more depart the Limits of his
Realm; pawning his Word to *Sofius*, (who received it in the Emperor's Name) that neither in
the City, nor upon the Way, there fhould be any
Trap laid for me.

This was our Capitulation; and having paid
my Thanks to *Sofius* and the Priefts for their Kindnefs, as well as my Grief to abandon *Mariamne*
would fuffer me, I quitted the Temple, and foon
after the City, under the Conduct of *Sofius* and his
Romans, and they accompany'd me without the
Gates; it was likewife permitted to the reft of my
Train, to repair to the Place of my firft Night's
Lodging, which was at a Town diftant about an
hundred Furlongs from *Hierufalem*. Thus I
efcaped *Herod*'s Fury; but not the Perfecutions of
my unfortunate Love; the Ills I had avoided were
found fcarce worth confidering, when compared
with thofe this cruel Parting procured me; and
though my Refolution was thus imperfect, thus
far I had gone, rather to fuffer a thoufand Deaths,
than renounce *Mariamne* for ever, for fear of one.

We were no fooner arriv'd at the Place where
we were to lodge, but taking *Arfanes* afide, 'My
' dear *Arfanes*, faid I, you fee that I have con-
' defcended to your Reafons, that urg'd my part-
' ing from the Temple, and the City, to avoid
' *Herod*; and poffibly the Confideration of you
' was none of the feebleft Arguments to win my
' confent to preferve a life which I can never love,
' in this condition it is now reduced to; but if
'you

' you believed there was any of those reasons so
' puissant to make me welcome a despair of ever
' seeing *Mariamne* more, disabuse yourself; 'tis
' as impossible to live without her, as without
' respiring: and spare your dissenting reasons, for
' they are all incapable to reverse the resolution I
' have taken to see her this very night, if possible;
' when the Night has spread her shades upon
' Earth, I intend to return disguised to *Hieru-*
' *lem,* and to go to the House of my Friend and
' Confidant *Sohemus*; I have some hopes, that by
' his and *Phylon* the Eunuch's assistance, I may
' gain a sight of the Queen: The design is now
' more easy to effect than ever; for besides the
' service that the Night and my disguise are like
' to do me, in such an infinite number of Stran-
' gers that are now in the City, because of the
' Feast, I shall run no hazard of discovery: be-
' sides, *Herod* will never imagine, that after so
' late an escape from such a peril, I would venture
' afresh to repeat the Precipice. The Queen I will
' see, if Heaven prove so kind that she permits
' me the opportunity, and if her intentions prove
' opposite, I shall receive the Command from her
' own mouth, which her Letter did not clearly
' explain. You will find it in vain to oppose this
' Design, therefore spare the fruitless pains to di-
' vert it; and if my Life be dear to you (as you
' have often protested) remember you ought to
' assist me in all such things are as ordained to
' make it suffer.

Arsanes stood astonisht at my resolution, but
found it impossible to fasten any reason upon it;
and the Night had no sooner made its dark approach, but clad in one of my Servants habits,
with one Attendant I return'd to the City, desiring *Arsanes* to stay with the rest, the better to

hide

hide my departure, and expect the Orders I should
send him as the event advis'd.

I re-entred the City, and found no difficulty to
conceal myself in such a confluence of People,
that fill'd it in all parts, and getting within twenty paces of *Sobemus* his House, I sent my Man
thither, who happily encountred him entring his
own Gate, being newly returned from the Palace. *Sobemus* was amaz'd to see me, not thinking it possible that I should re-attempt the danger
I lately escaped with so much ado. ' Ah! my
' Lord, *said be*, is it possible I see you again in
' a place where to day you ran so great a hazard
' of your life! Be not astonished, dear *Sobemus*,
' *said I*, I have a passion can produce stranger ef-
' fects; they that have courage enough to lift an
' Eye to *Mariamne*, cannot want it to despise
' danger. I am return'd, *Sobemus*, to challenge
' that of your Friendship which you promised,
' and that which I ever expected from you; I
' come to the Queen, by your means, if it be possi-
' ble, and if your assistance can create me so happy,
' that benefit shall compleat your purchase of the
' Heart of a Prince, that you have powerfully
' gained.

Sobemus heard my entreaty, with much desire
to oblige me, but found so little facility in the attempt, as he staid a long time before he could
shape an Answer; at last, when he had thought
enough, ' My Lord, *said be*, you desire Effects of
' my Obedience so difficult and dangerous, as I
' know not in what fashion I shall find it possi-
' ble to serve you; since yesterday the Queen hath
' been more strictly watched than formerly; and
' though the King has not yet discharged the
' thunderbolts, which we fear'd would fall from
' his violent choler, yet he still keeps her in terms
' of

' of diftrufting his fury: neverthelefs, fhe is not
' fo rigoroufly obferved, but (if her confent be
' not wanting) you may fee her; but as I believe
' fhe will not approve your attention, fo I fear
' fhe will not contribute thofe things to the inter-
' view as are in her power to effect; however,
' for your fake, I will run the hazard, and it
' fhall be no fault of mine if you be not fatisfied.

At thefe words I often embraced *Sohemus*, and
weighing the truth of what he had faid, I long
confulted with him upon the order we were to
obferve; all the ways were block'd up with difficulty and peril; at laft we fix'd upon one that
we judged the leaft dangerous; and *Sohemus*, not
willing to ftay me longer in the ftreet, led me
through a private door and up a little pair of
Stairs, not unknown unto me, to the Eunuch
Phylon's Chamber: The Eunuch was then with
the Queen, but his Chamber-door was opened to
Sohemus, by a Servitor that waited there; *Sohemus*
went that way to the Queen's Lodgings, while I
expected his return in the Gallery, without a Light.

My fear to afflict your Patience, makes me forbear the repetition of *Sohemus* and *Phylon*'s Difpute with the Queen to difpofe her to fee me;
the anger fhe expreft againft them and me, and
the pains they took to obtain the grace I demanded, I refer to your apprehenfion; for your reafon cannot be a Stranger to what might be alledged on both fides; and fhall content myfelf
to tell you, that after a long conteftation, at laft
the Queen confented to fee me in *Cleophe*'s Chamber, where by her fhe was only attended; while
Sohemus and *Phylon* were fet Sentinels at both
avenues to prevent a fudden furprifal. You will
poffibly find, *Madam*, fomething worthy of cenfure in this condefcent of *Mariamne*, and judge
with

with rigour, that she ought not to have bow'd to
my Passion with so much indulgence, after she had
given in the whole course of her Life such haughty proofs of a marvellous Virtue; but when you
shall know what she intended, you will doubtless
conclude this action did not spot her whiteness.
Sohemus returned to the place where he left me,
to conduct me to *Cleophe*'s Chamber, where I
entred trembling, and the Queen immediately
after me; I had scarce the assurance to lift my
Eyes to her visage, so weak I grew at the apprehension of an angry look, which my fears
told me I had provoked by importuning a favour
that my merits could no way challenge; indeed
methought I saw some Choler sit upon her brow,
but while I threw myself at her feet, and embraced her knees, without the utterance of a single
word, ‘ Is it possible, *said she*, that you could
‘ have so little consideration of the repose of my
‘ Life and Reputation, to hazard both so visibly;
‘ and after having led my Life, till now, with
‘ such caution, you should force me to see you by
‘ Night in a disguise, without any other necessity
‘ than to sooth your unjust Passion? Have you
‘ done well to exact this from *Mariamne*, when
‘ you had so lately reduced her to the greatest ex-
‘ tremities that ever Princess of her condition and
‘ propension did encounter with? Nay, can your-
‘ self approve that (which in your favour I now
‘ do) against all the Rules of Prudence and Reason?
‘ But do not, *Tyridates, pursu'd she, (sitting her
‘ down, and forcing me to rise)* do not hastily
‘ condemn this Action; see the end, before you
‘ pass a disadvantageous Judgment: If I had not
‘ condescended to see you, as I had many reasons
‘ to disswade it, I had missed the occasion of pre-
‘ venting such attempts for the future; which I
　　　　　　　　　　　　　　　　　　‘ will

' will now do, by putting an Order in force for
' my own repose and yours too, if it be possible.

At these words she stopp'd; and, while her Discourse lasted, having recover'd a little assurance,
I took the advantage of her silence: and lifting
up my Eyes to her face, which till then I had
not dared to behold, but by stolen glances: 'Madam,
' I confess, *said I*, that I am yet more culpable
' than your Words have made me; and though
' my intents have been innocent, the ills you have
' suffer'd through my occasion, do render me the
' most criminal amongst all Men; I am therefore
' come, Madam, to protest at your feet, that all
' my Blood, that a thousand such Lives as mine,
' can never requite the least of your displeasures;
' and to conjure you by all that is capable to per-
' swade, that I may have leave to spend this poor
' Life to purchase the repose of yours; employ
' the courage of *Tyridates* to break the Chains
' of your Calamities. I know I have committed
' a fresh offence in seeking means to petition your
' Goodness for this last Favour, which I never
' have, nor shall ever merit; but it is not just, nor
' can my Passion excuse it, that after having been
' the cause of so many of your Misfortunes, I
' should securely retire from the pursuits of *Herod*,
' and abandoning you to his Cruelties, leave you,
' by shameful flight, in his savage hands, to seek
' a Refuge at *Rome*, while you stay here expos'd
' to his Fury: This only consideration, Madam,
' hath had power to shut my Eyes upon that
' danger, against which you have exposed such a
' Miracle of Goodness: and in fine, I have learned
' to believe, that if any Man may unfetter you
' from your miseries, you ought to hope it from
' none but *Tyridates*, as a glory only due to him.
' I am now no longer retain'd by Hospitality,

' nor aw'd with the Memory of my firſt Obliga-
' tion; *Herod's* Sword and Poyſon have cancell'd
' thoſe; either of which would have infallibly
' deſtroy'd me, had not your adventurous Pity
' prevented the blow. To you only, my Divine
' Queen, this Life, ſuch as it is, is indebted for
' its Being, and you would have me have carried
' it away without offering the Sacrifice where it
' was due; it was yours by Gifts, yours by pre-
' ſervation, and can you think it reaſonable, that
' I ſhould wander with it among the *Romans,*
' inſtead of coming to ſubmit it to my Sovereign?
' Ah! no, *continued I, caſting myſelf at her feet,*
' do not reject that which would reject its own
' being but for you; and that which you cannot
' juſtly diſavow, do not grudge it the hazard of
' *Herod's* Rigour, by dooming my Soul to thoſe
' gloomy Woes, a thouſand times more black
' than the Night, in which he would have clos'd
' my Eyes for ever; or if the preſence of this
' wretch does importune or diſcompoſe your quiet,
' give leave that death may free you of him, from
' which you have but in vain preſerv'd him in *Ju-*
' *dea,* ſince he muſt infallibly receive it elſewhere
' from the rigour of this ſeparation.'

I had ſaid more in the tranſport to which I had
abandon'd myſelf, if the Queen, who ſuffer'd
with repugnance full of deadly fear, had not ſet
bounds to the ſpacious Diſcourſe I meditated;
and after ſhe had interrupted me with a command to riſe: ' Ceaſe, *Tyridates, ſaid ſhe,* to make
' theſe offers which I cannot ſo much as hear
' without offending Virtue, and remember I have
' told you a thouſand times, that the Crime of
' *Herod* cannot authorize mine; If I owe nothing
' to him, as to the quality of a Huſband, yet the
' debt to my God and myſelf, can never be ſatis-
' fied.

' fied.   I will quit the World when it pleases
' Heaven to release me, without the Crimes of
' these Miseries: or if it have decreed them a longer
' date, I must still have patience to endure them;
' 'tis this I oppose, in few Words, to the desires
' you express to wipe away my Displeasure; I
' am neither permitted by Law Divine or Human
' to serve myself of your assistance: For that which
' regards your departure, know, *Tyridates*, it is
' an indispensible necessity that you suddenly re-
' solve it; that I am now half constrain'd to an
' action unbecoming my quality and duty; and
' can no more consent to see you with so much
' danger of life and reputation; and in fine, must
' intreat you never to see me more. Be not asto-
' nished at these Words, you have courage enough
' to be prepared for them, and possibly affection
' enough too for me, to weigh all the reasons
' that oblige me to this Entreaty. I will not speak
' of my Life, which can never be safe while you
' are in *Judea*; for it was never happy to be
' worth the prizing; if my honour be dear to you,
' if you can ballance the prejudice of your own
' repose, and remember the Suspicions of *Herod*,
' the Malice of *Salome*, and the Knowledge my-
' self hath of the fault you have committed, you
' must conclude that the stay of *Tyridates* must be
' incompatible with the Reputation of *Mariamne*.
  She stopped at these Words, while I stood stiff
and motionless to hear the rigorous Sentence of my
Death; and after I had sometime beheld her with
an action that would have let in pity, if too
strong a resolution had not deny'd it entrance:
' Then, Madam, *said I*, you condemn the unfor-
' tunate *Tyridates* to a perpetual Banishment, and
' you believe you are more gentle than *Herod*, in
' commanding him never to see you more: Ah!

‘ if you have that Thought, for the Gods fake
‘ lofe it, and do not believe that any Duty can,
‘ with Reafon, oblige you to that, which you
‘ would not do, but for want of Affection.

‘ The Affection I have borne you, *reply'd the*
‘ *Queen, with an unmov'd Afpect*, is not pro-
‘ bably fuch as you have pretended to, nor could
‘ it juftly oblige me to that I have already done
‘ to pleafe you : Content yourfelf that I have not
‘ been fparing in the Acknowledgment of your
‘ Deferts, nor the Efteem of your Reafon ; that
‘ therein I have pafs'd the precife Limits my
‘ Eftate prefcribed me, and (fince a perpetual Se-
‘ paration permits me to avouch it) I have not
‘ not been fo infenfible, but if Heaven and my
‘ Parent had left me in a Condition to my own
‘ Choice, and *Tyridates* embraced the true Reli-
‘ gion, I had preferred him above the reft of
‘ Mankind.

The Queen ufed fome Violence to bring forth
thefe Words, though they all wore the Badge of
Innocence, when my Soul drew all the Confola-
tion it had then Capacity to hope for : ‘ Ah !
‘ Madam, *faid I*, how glorions is my Deftiny,
‘ and how little Caufe of Complaint hath this De-
‘ claration left me ? But Gods ! yet glorious as I
‘ am, I muft be banifhed for ever : Oh ! hard
‘ Sentence, that alone can ballance the Glory you
‘ have given me ! Rigorous Doom of my Death,
‘ which I cannot, and yet I ought to undergo,
‘ without a Murmur, fince my Queen pronoun-
‘ ced it ! No, Madam, it is not juft you fhould
‘ difturb your Quiet, nor juft I fhould put your
‘ Life in danger, nor juft to fpot your candid Re-
‘ putation ; but it is lefs juft to abandon you to
‘ *Herod*'s Mercy, that I fhould fly to a Haven,
‘ while you ride it out in the Tempeft : Why
‘ fhould

' should I carry this unfortunate and vagabond
' Life among the *Romans*, while you remain sub-
' mitted to the frantick Fits of that savage Man?
' Must I for ever shut my Eyes upon those Lights
' my Soul can only acknowledge glorious, while
' those of *Herod* and his *Jews* are chear'd with
' the divine Beams, to which I must bid an eter-
' nal Farewel? At least set some Limits to my
' Exile, or give me time to prepare for it; and
' while that lasts, let *Sohemus* be once more per-
' mitted to bring me to your Presence: I should
' do what is possible to bow my Soul to an un-
' repining Obedience; but to bid you now adieu,
' now to rend myself from you for ever, is more
' than my Heart can resolve, without leaping a
' most desperate Precipice.

I utter'd some other Expressions full of Tranf-
sport, which the Queen heard with an admirable
Patience, but not with so much Assurance; for,
whether it was the Remembrance of her Condition, (which I had awaken'd) or the Pity she
took of my Misfortunes, her fair Eyes let fall
some Tears: But I saw she was troubled that I
perceiv'd it, and now, desirous to put an end to
this dangerous Discourse, she rose from the Chair
she sat on, and approaching to me with an Action that spoke her resolute, ' *Tyridates, said she*,
' though you appear sensible of the Displeasure
' you take to quit me, I think your Courage ca-
' pable to surmount greater Difficulties. If I
' have any Power upon your Spirit, I desire to
' put it all in my Intreaty, that for my sake you
' will support it patiently; 'tis the last Proof I
' beg of your Affection, but desir'd with so much
' Ardor, as you cannot refuse it, without destroy-
' ing all that you have gained within me: Re-
' lease your Fears for me; though you leave me

' in

'in *Herod*'s Hands, all Succour hath not forsaken
'me, as you imagine; I have still a Defender in
'Heaven, who is not too weak to protect me
'from the Cruelty of a Husband; in him I shall
'ever find my Refuge and my Comfort; and,
'doubtless, so should you too, were you enligh-
'ten'd with his Beams. Adieu, *Tyridates*, take
'my last Adieu; if sometimes you remember me,
'at least forget my Weakness, and the Faults
'you have made me commit.

At these Words, (seeing me fallen at her Feet,
in a Condition that left me no Reason to reply)
she bow'd down, and taking my Head between
her Hands, kiss'd me on the Forehead: And this
was the greatest and most signal Favour I ever received of *Mariamne*; which, so soon as she had
bestowed upon me, she retir'd to her Chamber;
and, shutting the Door after her, disappear'd from
my Eyes for ever.

The Heart of *Tyridates* was so over-charg'd
when he came at this sad Piece of Story, that he
found it impossible to go on, before he had given
passage to some Sighs, that stopp'd the Pursuit of
his Discourse. The fair Queen was so sensibly
touch'd at this Story, as she suffer'd Compassion
to steal some liquid Pearls from her Eyes. But
when he was returned to himself, 'I know not,
'Madam, *said he*, what to say more, for the
'rest of my Life is as unworthy your Attention,
'as my Pains to recount it: You may imagine,
'if you please, the Woes that rent my Heart,
'when I saw myself forced to endure my Life,
'and support my Miseries, by the Command of
'*Mariamne*. I vow by all the Gods, that nei-
'ther Fear nor Cowardice had a hand in the re-
'ligious Observance of my Queen's Injunctions;
'but such an Obedience as must ever be twisted

'in

' in my Thread of Life, difpofed me (by the Af-
' fiftance of *Sobemus*) to depart the Place and
' City ; whence I return'd to my Followers, took
' my way to *Rome*, and prefented myfelf to
' *Auguftus*.

I know, Madam, you will eafily remit the Re-
lations of that tedious Voyage, and the wearifome
Refidence I made with the Emperor, for it con-
tains nothing capable to divert you. And indeed
the Remembrance has fo frefhly fet my Griefs a
bleeding, as I find myfelf unable to be more particular : Be pleafed then only to know, that I
have ever fince lived in Darknefs ; that neither the
Careffes of the Emperor, (who always nobly treated me) the Pomp of *Rome*, nor all the Pleafures
that were daily proffer'd in that great Miftrefs of
the Univerfe, could ever give my Griefs a Moment's Eafe : When after I had there worn out a
Year without an Hour of Repofe, the fear my
Melancholy might render me infupportable to the
Emperor and his Court, made me abandon it,
without defigning any other Retreat or Intention,
but to breathe the Anxieties that denied me Quiet.
When after I had long wander'd upon Earth and
Water, I was caft upon this Coaft, where I have
fince made my miferable Refidence : A Condition,
though mean, yet better fuiting with my Humour
than that I enjoy'd in the Courts of Kings.

It only now remains to tell you, that about a
Month fince I remember'd *Mariamne's* Command
extended no farther than my Banifhment, that
fhe had not forbad me to inform myfelf of her
Condition, which made me fend my faithful
Arfanes into *Judea* to learn.

This Voyage he undertook out of hope to live
there unknown, till poffibly he might find the
Queen in fo relenting a Condition, to repeal my

Exile.

Exile. I attended his return in this folitary Manfion, which, for fome Prefents, I obtain'd of an *Alexandrian* for the Time I fhall ftay upon this Coaft; and I confefs I tafted more Sweetnefs in this Solitude, than I could have hoped from the continual Perplexities of my Soul: Befides, I cannot call it lefs than Comfort to my Grief, that I have had the Happinefs to render fome Service, and to give this poor Retreat to fo great a Princefs.

Thus *Tyridates* clofed his Story, and the Queen, who had lent him a ferious Attention, made both her Action and Difcourfe exprefs how much fhe was interefted in his Fortune.

' Your Relation, *faid fhe, after fome other*
' *Words,* hath fenfibly touch'd me, as the Mif-
' fortune of a great and vertuous Prince, whom
' Heaven hath perfecuted; but if I commend your
' refpectful Affections, I muft not forget to praife
' *Mariamne's* Virtue, that, in fo juft and great
' Occafions to hate her Husband, fo courageoufly
' refifted the Batteries of your Affection, and the
' Motions of that Inclination, which, if I judge
' aright, fhe had toward you: Indeed fhe was
' obliged to the Rules of her Duty; but it is not
' eafy to acquit the Debt that often exacts fuch
' weighty Payments, and defend herfelf from the
' excellent Qualities of fuch a Prince as *Tyridates.*

Tyridates retorted this obliging Difcourfe in very fubmiffive Language; and the Compliment would have lafted longer, if the Queen's Supper had not interrupted it, which made *Tyridates* withdraw, becaufe fhe fupped in her Bed, and (deeming her Wearinefs required what was left unfpent of the Night for repofe) he bad her good Night. But, before he left the Chamber, ' It is ' not juft, *faid fhe,* you fhould longer be igno-
' rant of her Name and Fortune, whofe Life was

C   ' fo

' so lately your Gift; and that since seconded by
' a noble Entertainment.' ' Eteocles (continued
' she, pointing at the Man that was preserved
' with her) shall begin the Relation; and when
' you have learned those Adventures that have
' preceded mine, whereof no Man is better in-
' structed than himself, you shall know the par-
' ticular Accidents of my Life from my own
' Mouth.' Tyridates civilly return'd his Thanks
for this promis'd Favour; and, quitting the Chamber, return'd with Eteocles to his own, whom he
compell'd to sup with him, though, upon Knowledge of his Quality, he would modestly have refused the Honour. After Supper, he caused him
to be conducted to his Chamber, and himself
went to Bed, where he passed that Night in his
ordinary Inquietudes.

So soon as he awaked the next Morn, he saw
Eteocles in his Chamber, that came to give him
good morrow, whom the Prince courteously receiv'd, made him come nearer, and remembring
that from his Mouth he was to expect the beginning of those Adventures he long'd to understand,
invited him to a Seat by his Bed-side; and having
forc'd him to sit down: You see, said he, a very
' inquisitive Man, loath to dispense with the
' Charge the Queen had given you, I can neither
' find Time nor Place more commodiously fa-
' vourable than this, to require Satisfaction; for
' it will not be a civil Hour to visit the Queen,
' till two or three be expir'd.' Sir, said Eteocles,
' I believe what she suffer'd Yesterday will ask
' this Morning's Repose to unweary her; the
' Time I cannot better employ than in rendering
' Proofs of my obedience to both your Commands.
And after a Preparation of a short Silence, he
thus began his Discourse:

F. 5,   The

The Hiftory *of* Julius Cæfar, *and* Queen Cleopatra.

BEfore I can enter the Relation of that great Queen's Adventures, whom I have now the Honour to ferve, I muft of neceffity go back to the Life of another Queen, Illuftrious for Greatnefs, Beauty, and Accidents of her Life, above all others that ever preceded her: You may eafily judge, it is the Queen *Cleopatra* I intend to fpeak of, whofe Name is not only known in this Country, that was under her Dominion, but has ftretched itfelf to the remote Corners of the World, and will doubtlefs be a Task for the Memory of Fame till the laft Age.

Of the Accidents that befel her with *Anthony,* none are ignorant; I fhall only therefore lightly touch them; but becaufe her Enemies have endeavoured to black her Reputation with what happened in her greener Years with the great *Julius Cæfar,* I am oblig'd in Confcience (as he of all Men with whom the Truth is beft acquainted) to defend her Memory from that Calumny, and give you a faithful Account of thofe Paffages compriz'd in as few Words as poffible.

The Queen *Cleopatra* was Daughter (as fure you have heard) to King *Ptolomy,* furnamed *Auletns,* and defcended with King *Ptolomy* her Brother, from that glorious Stock of Kings, that fince the great *Ptolomy,* Friend and Succeffor of *Alexander,* hath continually fway'd the *Egyptian* Scepter. This Princefs was born with all the Graces that the Gods could beftow upon a mortal Perfon; the Beauty of her Body could not be matched upon Earth, nor had that of her Spirit lefs Advantages; and the greatnefs of her Courage, infinitely rais'd itfelf above her Sex: I would fay more,

more, if Renown had not fav'd me a Labour, and those Gifts of Heaven been too fatal to let me dwell delightfully upon the Story.

But the Prince *Ptolomy*, her Brother, was not fo by Inclination; but being naturally prone and propenfe to Vice, he fuffered his Flatterers by pernicious Counfels, to corrupt and deface all that Impreffion of good that his high Birth had left upon his Spirit; which, in fine, tumbled him headlong in his laft Misfortune. He receiv'd the Crown very young, by the Death of the King his Father; and the unbridled Liberty which he found in that abfolute Power, funk him in all his Vices. The *Egyptian* People difcontentedly confidering thefe fad beginnings of his Reign, and fighing to fee themfelves fubjected to a Prince fo unworthy to command, began to turn their Eyes upon the Princefs *Cleopatra*; and perceiving how much fhe differ'd from her Brother, in Spirit, Majefty, and all Things elfe that might render a Perfon worthy of a Scepter, they repin'd that her Sex was an obftacle to their Wifhes; and every meeting would freely confefs to one another, how much more they thought fhe deferv'd their Allegiance than *Ptolomy*, or rather *Pothinus*, *Theodorus*, *Ganymede*, with the reft of the Rabble of vile Flatterers, which he took up from the Duft, to lift them to the higheft Dignities, or rather to give them the fovereign Authority.

This unworthy Crew having once perceiv'd that *Cleopatra*'s Credit was like to extinguifh theirs in every *Egyptian* Breaft, began to render her fufpected to her Brother, and eafily perfwaded that poor Spirit, that it was fit fhe fhould perifh; the ungracious Prince fuddenly refolv'd to give the Blow; but (having Notice of his evil Intention) fhe retir'd from the Court, and fought a Refuge

fuge among thofe *Egyptians* which fhe believed did beft affect her : Nor did they abufe her Confidence ; for a great Part of the Realm arm'd itfelf in the Quarrel, divers Cities declar'd for her, and if her Party was not the moft puiffant, at leaft it was compos'd of the honefter Sort of *Egyptians*, that a long Time kept her fafe behind their Bucklers, againft all the Forces the King could make.

At laft, after Inequality of Number had given *Ptolomy* fome Advantage, he befieged the Princefs his Sifter in the City of *Pelufium*, whither fhe was retir'd.

At that Siege he was bufied, when the infortunate *Pompey* (a dreadful Example of Fortune's Inconftancy) that great Man that had triumphed over three Parts of the World, and by an infinite Number of Victories had juftled for precedency with the Renown of *Alexander* ; flying from the Battle of *Pharfalia*, came to throw himfelf into his Arms, there to feek an Afylum againft the Purfuit of his victorious Enemy. Indeed all forts of Honour and Affiftance were due from *Ptolomy* to the Dignity of that grand Captain ; and doubtlefs any Soul but his would have receiv'd him (that a few Days before was the greateft of all Men) with a fubmifs Refpect to his precedent Condition ; but that difloyal Man (only prizing his prefent Fortune, and not his Virtue) hearkning to the pernicious Counfels of *Pothinus*, *Theodorus*, and *Ganymede*, that reprefented how advantageous an Amity the Death of *Pompey* might gain him with his Enemy, butchered that unfortunate Prince upon the Shore of *Pelufium*, in the fight of his Wife *Cornelia*, who hardly efcaped (by the Succours of her own Men) from the fame Deftiny.

The

The belief I have that Fame has made you acquainted with this pitiful History, the Importance of which spread it over the Earth, makes me contract it in a small Volume. A few Days after, *Ptolomy* understanding that *Cæsar* was come into *Egypt*, and hearing he disapprov'd the cruel War he made against his Sister, rais'd his Siege from *Pelusium*, and bent his Course towards *Alexandria*, where he staid his coming up.

Cleopatra no sooner saw her City ungirt, and herself at Liberty, but by the Counsel of her faithfullest Servants, and especially of my Father *Apollodorus*, who had ever much Credit with her, she resolv'd to throw herself at the Feet of *Cæsar*, and demand his Protection before he arriv'd at *Alexandria*. This Design was presently executed, and she and her Train wafted over with a winged Diligence to the Isle of *Farion*, where *Cæsar* had made some small abode. I was of that Number that attended her, and because of the faithful Service which my Father ever render'd her, none had freer Access nor greater Credit than myself. The great *Cæsar* being advertiz'd of her Arrival, came to meet her with much Civility; and because I was present at that Interview, 'tis fit I should recount some of the Particulars.

Cleopatra, the better to advance her Design, had that Day call'd both Art and Glory to wait upon her natural Beauty, that it might sparkle at the best Advantage; and though in her Habit she had affected a Modesty, conform'd to her Present Estate, and therefore concluded Mourning more becoming than Pomp, in an Action wherein she was to appear a Suppliant; yet both her Mourning and her Modesty were set off with what was more great and pompous than the dazling Luxury of Gold and Jewels could boast. Her Eyes darted

ed

ed. Beams more Glorious than the richest Diamond could sparkle, and the Majesty of her Port and Visage did more loftily express her Quality, than could be done by a magnifick and a numerous Train of Servitors.

If her view put *Cæsar* and his Followers to their Wonder, I confess too the Visage of that brave Man, the greatest not only of his own, but of all the Ages that preceded it, stamp'd a Respect in all our Souls, that made us regard him as if he had been a God. That prodigious Reputation he had gained in a hundred Battles, against the most valiant People of the World, and his last Victory upon the *Romans* themselves, which he came from subduing with a far less Number than theirs, gave us an Astonishment full of Veneration. Indeed, his Face did not belye the Dignity and Grandeur of his Actions: And though there was something missing there that must needs go away with his vigorous Youth; yet there appear'd all the Marks of a perfect Greatness: His Looks so Imperious, and yet so full of Sweetness, that it was not easy to take him for less than the Master of the Universe. *Cæsar* and *Cleopatra*, before they spake, spent some Time in gazing at one another, making their Looks and Silence express their mutual Admiration; but at last *Cleopatra* (considering she was in his Presence that had her Repose and Fortunes in his Hands, or rather was the Master of her Destiny) bowed her haughty Disposition, and forcing a more than ordinary Humility, from the Dexterity of her Spirit, threw herself at the Feet of *Cæsar*, and resisting his earnest and vehement Entreaties to rise, ' You see, ' great Emperor, *said she*, you see at your Feet ' the Daughter of the *Ptolomies*, that is here to ' demand that of you against a cruel Brother,
' which

' which from his Arm she might expect against
' other Enemies.. Oppressed Innocence and Im-
' becillity implore your Assistance, and do proffer
' a brave Employment to your generous Bounty,
' that cannot shew itself in a more becoming
' Garb, then in protecting a Princess, persecuted
' by unnatural Cruelty, in her Fortune, Repose,
' and Life, in the same Estate my Ancestors com-
' manded, Part of which is my legitimate Inhe-
' ritance; I have now no other Retreat but your
' Favour, and if that be denied me, I must ren-
' der up myself to a Brother's Cruelty, in whom,
' neither my Blood, Sex, nor Youth, can ever
' ingender Pity.   Let me not embrace your victo-
' rious Knees in vain, before which, all that is
' Great on Earth, must learn Obedience, and
' confess thee as great and as much *Cæsar* in Ge-
' nerosity, as in that triumphant Bravery, that has
' made thee Master of *Rome*, and with her, of
' all the World beside.

  The fair Princess had doubtless said more, if
Cæsar (no longer able to hear, or suffer her upon
her Knees, though accustom'd to see Kings whole
Days in the same Posture) had not employ'd (after the Tryal of entreaty) the force of Arms to
raise her; and having placed her in an Estate better conform'd to what her Beauty might claim:
' Fear not, *Cleopatra*, *said he*, the *Roman* Arms
' shall defend thee from thy Brother's Threatnings;
' and if he contemns our Prayer, we will not
' leave *Egypt* till we have provided for thy Re-
' pose and Fortune.

  He pronounced these Words with a *Roman* Gravity, and a Majesty that equall'd his Condition;
but a while after, seconding his Parley with the
Princess, his Temper was so softned with the
Charms he there encounter'd, as he lost all his
                                        Gra-

Gravity, and in his following Discourses put a
submissive Behaviour in the Place.

After he had re-assured her Fears by repeating
his Promise not to abandon her, he told her he
would conduct her to *Alexandria*, present her to
her Brother, and put her in possession of her
Partage in the Realm. *Cleopatra*'s Experience of
her Brother's ill Nature, gave her some Difficulty
to resolve it! but at last, she was constrain'd to
obey the absolute Will of *Cesar*, who presently
dispatch'd one of his chief Commanders to let
Ptolomy know, that he could not see him as a
Friend, nor as an Ally to the People of *Rome*, if
he refus'd to receive *Cleopatra*, whom he intended to present him, with all Assurance of Recon-
ciliation. *Ptolomy* entertain'd this imperious Order with a most sensible Despight, and had much
ado to hinder the Escape of some passionate Folly;
but he stood in too much awe of the *Roman* puissance to profess his Indignation, which made him
resolve to dissemble, till Time should offer him an
Occasion to shew it at the best Advantage. He
therefore unwillingly forc'd himself to submit to
the impos'd Command; and in the mean Time
to render *Cesar* more favourable, he sent him by
the wicked *Theodorus* the Head of mighty *Pompey*.
But his Expectation prov'd so erroneous, as that
generous Conqueror, instead of bidding the Present welcome, refus'd to see it, and commanded
the Wretch that brought it, to be chased from his
Presence, after he had express'd how much he detested his Master's Treachery, in Terms full of Contempt and Choler; nevertheless, he enter'd *Alexandria*, where *Ptolomy* receiv'd him with great
Respect, and many feigned Demonstrations of
Good-will. *Cleopatra*, upon this Score, was entertain'd with kind Embraces, *Ptolomy* protesting before.

fore *Cesar*, that he was ready to refign up her Partage, and for the future refolv'd to treat her like a Brother. *Cleopatra* forgot all the Caufe fhe had to complain; and thus accorded, divers Days were confumed in triumphant and magnificent Feftivals.

But the Soul of mighty *Cesar* (wholly invincible as it was) could not defend itfelf from the Charms of *Cleopatra*: That glorious Conqueror, that made the World his Trophy, was now become Captive to a Woman's Eye, and took more Wounds in his Treaties, with her Looks and Difcourfe, than he got in all the Dangers of fo many Combats.

This cannot feem ftrange to thofe that knew this great Queen; for when fhe was pleas'd to fet her Enticements at liberty, it was hard for a Man to try his Strength, and come off untaken: Before he difcover'd his Paffion to the Princefs, he endeavour'd to give Intelligence by his Looks and Geftures; and when he thought he had prepar'd them Audience, he trufted his Tongue to tell her what fhe had made him feel.

Cleopatra was one of the moft ambitious Perfons on Earth; and that Paffion then beginning to gain an Afcendant upon her Spirit, made her regard the Submiffions of that Hero not unwillingly: She had conceived an Opinion of herfelf, high enough to believe that few Hearts were fo well fortified to hold out againft her Batteries; and, obferving *Cesar*'s Behaviour, fhe doubted not but he was ftruck before his Difcourfe affur'd her; the firft Time he ftripp'd his Thoughts to her, was in the Palace-Gallery, where he walked a long Time difcourfing of her Affairs, and the Order his Intention had contriv'd to put them in.

The

The Princess return'd her Acknowledgment for his Courtesies, in Expressions full of Civility, and upon these Terms they were, when finding that no unfit Occasion to unveil his Thoughts, after the Preparative of some amorous Looks that fore-ran the Discovery: ' I should never have believed, *said he*, you would thus have requited ' the Service I render you; were you just, you ' would not ruin my Repose, while I endeavour ' to restore yours; be not amaz'd at this Discourse, ' *pursued he, in a more serious accent;* in procuring your Liberty, I have let my own fall at ' your feet, and humbled myself from the principal Authority in the Empire, that I might give ' it to you in *Egypt*; I had rouz'd the same Courage to defend my self from you, that preserv'd ' me from the Foes that were of Fortune's stirring up, had I not foreseen it would prove too ' weak to withstand your Assault, and found more ' Glory in the Defeat, than disputing the Victory. ' Fair *Cleopatra*, I am your Prisoner, but with ' this satisfaction, that I yield myself to the fairest ' Victor upon Earth, to such a one from whom ' I may implore mercy, without shame or baseness; use your Victory as Virtue shall advise ' you, and remember that you cannot still be generous, and abuse it.

These were *Cæsar's* first Expressions, and to this Declaration the Princess listned without Displeasure: For she could not desire more glorious proofs of her own merit, than in the Conquest of so great a Man; and after she had studied a while for a becoming Answer, she reply'd in these Terms.

' *My Lord*, I never cherished so good an opi-' nion of that little Beauty the Gods have lent me, ' or those other qualities, that may make me a ' pretence to the esteem of common Persons, to

' believe

' believe them able to subdue him who has taught
' the whole World Obedience; 'tis not easie to
' imagine that the Vanquisher of Mankind should
' hook himself upon so weak a Bait, at least too
' feeble to hold such a Soul as his: The Gods
' have formed him of a Nature so approaching
' to theirs, that vain were the Ambition of mor-
' tal Beauties to aim at such a Conquest; nor
' were it just, that (after having ty'd your victo-
' rious Chains upon the Universe) you should lose
' your own Liberty to a Princess, that owes you
' for hers, with all that repose you have so nobly
' restored her. Nevertheless, *my Lord*, I receive
' this Discourse (full of nobleness) with a respect
' due to great *Cæsar*, and my particular Bene-
' factor; and if his Spirit has made choice of
' this kind of divertisement, to unweary it self
' from his grand employments, I am contented
' to afford him matter for it, on condition he takes
' notice, that I suffer all from him as my Protector
' and my Master.

Cleopatra finished these Words, turning her Eyes
upon the face of *Cæsar*, with a smile capable to
perswade him, that her words and thoughts were
not of the same piece; and with an action so
sweet, and yet so majestick, as if the Graces
themselves had compos'd it; her Eyes brandish-
ing such an extraordinary Brightness, as they shot
new flames into Great *Cæsar*'s Soul, who by his
fresh wound, became so transported, as he had
much ado to hinder his amorous fever from
breaking out into the hottest proofs. However,
though with much constraint, he retained it;
and regarding the Princess, with Eyes in which
Passion was not ill represented,

' I should be angry with you, *said he*, if I did
' not know that your tongue wronged your Heart,
' when

' when it mispriz'd those bright powers that con-
' quered me, for they are able to perform greater
' Feats ; the Advantages which my Arms, with
' the aid of Fortune, have given me over Men,
' are all too weak to guard me from you : I will
' give my Life (if you disdain it not) for the con-
' firmation of this truth, and with it submit at
' your feet all the vows and thoughts, not of your
' Protector, and your Master, but of him that
' consecrates the rest of his days to the Divine
' Cleopatra, with an entire Obedience and Sub-
' mission.

'Tis like he had said more, if he had not spy'd
King Ptolomy, whose approach to salute him, hinder'd the pursuit of that discourse. But the next
day he again renew'd it, and as well by Words
as Actions, gave Cleopatra such clear proof of his
Passion, as she found not the least scruple to frame
a doubt of. This knowledge she manag'd with
much Prudence and Reservation, not willing to
give cause of complaint to a Man, from whom
she expected all, and on whom her Fortune and
Tranquillity absolutely depended, yet she govern'd
herself in such sort as he could never take the
least Advantage upon her, nor find cause to blame
her for too much Rigour or Facility. But she
would pleasingly flatter herself with the Glory of
overcoming him, whom the World had not power enough to resist. The knowledge she took of
her own high Birth, and admirable Qualities,
gave her belief she might pretend to all things ;
and she fostered no meaner thoughts than such
as aim'd at the Empire of the Earth.

Beside the Glory that shined in the greatness
of his Actions, Cesar's Person was very capable of
inviting Affection ; and though he was not young
enough to keep all those charms upon his face

undiminished, that are Lovers torches, yet he was
not so short of those Graces, to want much of his
primitive Vigour; for his countenance displayed
such brave and erected looks, as it imprinted respect in every Soul that saw it. *Cleopatra*, who had
Eyes as well as others to regard it, finding herself
deeply oblig'd to his noble offices and affection,
insensibly fell to tye on her own chains, and had already begun to engage herself, when the Affairs
of *Egypt* received that memorable Revolution, of
which you have doubtless heard, and from that
belief, I shall abridge the recital as much as possible.

While *Cæsar* entirely gave himself to his love,
and endeavoured with all the proofs of it to gain
Cleopatra's, the wicked *Ptolomy*, and his perfidious
Counsellors, nursed designs very different.   They
had found in *Cæsar*, as they apprehended, little
Acknowledgment for the Service they had render'd him in the Death of Great *Pompey*; and indeed that high-rais'd Spirit (that could neither approve Villainy, nor esteem those that committed
it) had contemptuously treated all those that had
dipp'd a Hand in that black Treason: Besides,
Ptolomy saw with Despight the Love he bore to
his Sister; and, not without Cause, feared that he
would favour and support her against him, in the
Partage they were to make.   These Considerations, joined with the Counsels which *Pothinus*,
Achilles, *Theodorus*, and the rest of their perfidious Companions were ever fomenting, made him
at last resolve to use *Cæsar* as he had done *Pompey*, and find a way to his Ends by the Death of
him and *Cleopatra*. *Cæsar* had lodg'd none but
his most considerable Persons in *Alexandria*;
and, to satisfy the Citizens, had left the Body of
his Forces at the Isle of *Farion*; which was so

near

near the City, that it might eafily be feen from his Chamber Window. *Ptolomy* believed this Occafion might favour the Execution of his Plot; and fecretly caufing his Army (which was yet undisbanded) to advance, he made it approach to *Alexandria*, and affured himfelf of all thofe in the City, whom he knew at his Devotion. His Defign was ill contriv'd, worfe conducted, and worft of all executed. And it is to to be thought, the Gods that abhor Crimes, forbad Succefs to fo loathed a Treachery, and fo blinded the Contrivers of his mifchievous Intentions.

Cefar was in *Cleopatra*'s Chamber, when one came to advertife him, that the whole City was in Arms; that *Pothinus* and *Achilles*, one of *Pompey*'s Murderers, were marching towards the Palace in the head of a Troop, with a defign to kill him at a Feaft he had made that day. *Cefar* did not defpife this advice, but having rallied fuch of his with an admirable diligence, as had time to range themfelves about him, he quitted the Palace, and marched againft his Confpirators, with an affurance worthy of himfelf. But before he left *Cleopatra*'s Chamber: ' Madam, *faid he*, It is ' not I that feek the ruine of your Brother, but ' Heaven, who, (unwilling fo wicked a Man ' fhould longer reign) does this day prefent you ' the Crown of *Egypt*. I go now to fight for ' you and myfelf, and I promife with the victo- ' ry our common vengeance.

Cleopatra had no time to reply, becaufe he inftantly departed; but her Eyes kept him company as far as poffible; and knowing he went to combat for their common intereft, fhe aided him with vows to Heaven for his fuccefs.

The Traytors perceiving they were difcover'd, refolv'd to fight it out courageoufly; and in effect
dif-

disputed it very hotly; yet the justice of his cause with his own admirable Valour, gave *Cæsar* the Victory; *Pothinus* was killed upon the place with the greatest part of his Forces, and *Achilles* with such as could follow him, fled out of the City to *Ptolomy*, whom the report of that ill success had made retire with his Army.

Cæsar might safely have staid in *Alexandria,* and enforc'd himself by *Cleopatra*'s Faction, which was none of the weakest; but he rather chose to retire with his Troops to give *Ptolomy* Battle; and (hearing the *Alexandrians* of the contrary Part endeavoured to cut off his Retreat, by surprising his Vessels) he ran thither with that Handful of Men that follow'd him, doing such Deeds against them, as in any other but *Cæsar* would have been accounted Miracles. Yet he there ran a greater Danger, than he had done before in all his former Battles; for, no longer able to make head against the great Number of his Enemies, which grew every Moment stronger, by the coming up of fresh Reserves, he threw himself from the Cliff into one of the Boats, to gain the Isle; but being discover'd, he was environ'd by his Enemies, and press'd upon with such desperate Fury, as after he had receiv'd divers Blows and Arrows upon his Arms, he was constrain'd to throw himself into the Water, and swim that Space between him and the Island, not without excessive Pain and Peril. At last he recover'd his Forces, gave order for the Battle, shipped them, and row'd towards *Ptolomy*'s Army; who, conducted by his evil Destiny, advanced with full Sails to meet him. The Battle prov'd very dubious and bloody; but I shall forbear the Particulars, because I believe I have already repeated things, of which no Person can be ignorant. It shall suffice to tell you, that *Cæsar*

was

was always *Cæsar*; that the *Egyptians* were defeated with a mighty Loss; and their King, by a just Chastisement from Heaven, being fallen into the Sea, was drown'd by the Weight of his Arms, and not taken up till the next Day, where he was found armed in a gilded Curass, half buried in the Sand. After this Victory, *Cæsar* advanced toward the City; and at the Gates found the fair *Cleopatra*, with a Part of the Citizens, that begged Pardon for the others, who (through Obedience to their Prince's Authority) had taken up Arms against him. The Princess obtained all her Desires, and he enter'd the City and Palace with her, in a Fashion wholly pompous and triumphant.

Never was there seen so sudden an Execution, nor so many Troubles appeas'd in so short a time. *Ptolomy*'s evil Counsellors were all either perished with him, or had sought their Safety by flight. The rest of the *Egyptians* willingly submitted to *Cæsar*, who told *Cleopatra*, that, for her sake, he was sorry for her Brother's Death; but he knew so well how to represent the small Cause she had to afflict herself for his Loss, as (after she had given some Tears to his Memory, which such an excellent Nature as her's could not refuse him) she accepted the Comforts he proferred. The Funeral Honours she celebrated with much Solemnity; and the following Day, *Cæsar* having conven'd the *Egyptian* Nobility, in their Presence put her in Possession of the Realm, and with an universal Applause, crown'd her with his own Hands. All the *Egyptians*, by whom *Cleopatra*'s Government was much more desir'd than *Ptolomy*'s, receiv'd her for their Queen, with excessive Contentment, and render'd publick Thanks to *Cæsar* for his Magnanimity and Munificence.

One

One Day he was with her by her Bed's Side, when after divers other Discourses, the Length of which would weary your Attention, taking her fair Hands, and joining Lips unto them, ' I die, ' fair Queen, (*said he, with an Action wholly* ' *passionate*.) I die, if your Pity does not draw ' me from my Tomb; and I vow by those fair ' Eyes, which I adore with respective Venerati- ' on, that 'tis impossible my Life should longer ' continue, if your Mercy does not strengthen the ' Thread of it.' ' I should be much afflicted, *said* ' *the Queen*, to see it in any Danger; the Gra- ' titude I owe to great *Cæsar*, and the particular ' Esteem I have of his Person, will never suffer ' me to refuse Means within the Bounds of Possi- ' bility, to comfort him.

' 'Tis in your Power, *replied he*, not only to ' comfort, but create me the Happiest of all Men, ' in making yourself the Reward for what I have ' given you; no other Price can gratifie the Pre- ' sent I have made you, I mean not of a Crown ' (upon which I never set an Esteem) but of a ' Heart and a Soul which can never be but to you, ' and of a Heart and a Soul which I have made ' yours with a Resignation so entire, as I have re- ' serv'd no Power to myself of a further Disposal.

' This glorious Present, *replied the Queen*, ' can never be requited with the Price you demand; ' a thousand such Lives as *Cleopatra*'s can never ' weigh with the Heart and Soul of *Cæsar*: Yet, ' Sir, I would bestow myself upon you, as you ' demand, (*pursued she, letting fall her Eyes* ' *with a kind of Shame*) if Honour could shew ' me the Way to do it; I am born a Princess, ' Daughter to a long Succession of Kings, by your ' Bounty I am now a Queen, and which is yet ' more Glorious, by his proper Confession, I have

VOL. I. G ' triums

' triumphed over the Soul of mighty *Cesar:* Sir,
' these Advantages having plac'd me in one of the
' foremost Ranks of Women, do oblige me to
' preserve myself there in a Reputation pure and
' spotless; and should I render myself unworthy
' of my Birth, my present Dignity, and Affecti-
' on of great *Cesar?* should I yield up myself
' unto him in any other Way, than what his
' Virtue can approve of?

She stopp'd at these Words, supposing she had
said enough to be understood, and that *Cesar*
could well enough construe her Intentions; yet
being by the Maxims of State, and the Ties he
had to the Common-wealth, forbidden to make
a more ample Declaration, he stood, as if surpriz'd at *Cleopatra's* Words; nor was he yet resolv'd to espouse her, fearing that *Rome* would
disapprove the Alliance, and it might prove pre-
judicial to his Design, to make himself Master of
it, as he did in a short time after: But perceiving
himself oblig'd by *Cleopatra's* Words to declare
his Intention, he remain'd silent a while, not knowing in what Manner to evade the Protestations he
had made her; but at last he recover'd his Speech,
and lifting his Eyes from the Earth, where they
had been fix'd, ' You do merit, *said he*, a Con-
' dition yet more Glorious, than what would ren-
' der the Favours I demand, lawful; the World
' cannot afford a Spouse to *Cesar*, more worthy of
' that Quality than the Queen *Cleopatra*, and I do
' vow by Truth itself, that were I free in that
' Election, I should soon make it known, with
' what Passion I desire that Advantage: But I
' am now so ty'd by Interest to the Republick,
' that I cannot apprehend it expedient, to make
' my conjugal Choice without its Approbation:
' Nevertheless, I shall endeavour to express, how

' much

' much I defire to be entirely yours; and paffing
' by thefe Confiderations, in few Days, (If it be
' poffible) make known the Truth of my Affection.

At thefe Words *Cefar* retir'd, without giving
the Queen leave to reply; but after that, fhe liv'd
with him in a Fafhion more referv'd than fhe
had done formerly, and would no longer licenfe
thofe petty Liberties which before fhe had permitted him. He obferved this Change with much
difpleafure; but fo foon as he complained of it
to her, ' My Lord, *faid fhe*, you are too juft to
' defire thofe Things of me which I cannot con-
' fent to, without my own Ruin? And fince I muft
' pretend to a Quality that may authorize them,
' give me rather leave to return the Crown you
' have given me, and refign the Repofe and the
' Life itfelf which I hold of you, than licenfe
' fuch Crimes, as neither your Greatnefs, nor all
' the Obligations I have to it, can ever excufe.
This Difcourfe again ftruck *Cefar* dumb, but after fhe had often repeated her Refolution, it wrought
fuch an Effect upon his Spirit, as made him refolve what he executed a few Days after.

One Day, after he had fent to defire a particular Audience of the Queen, he enter'd her Chamber, only follow'd by *Lucius Metellus*, and *Caius
Albinus*, two of his Friends, in whom he repos'd
the greateft Confidence; he found the Queen prepared to receive him in the Manner he demanded, only accompanied with her two dear Maids,
Charmione and *Iras*, my Father and myfelf:
Cefar that knew us, and in what Manner we
were ty'd to the Queen's Interefts, was well pleas'd
to have no other Witnefs of his intended Action;
and after he had pay'd his ordinary Civilities to
the Queen: ' Madam *faid he*, I have been too
' long reftrain'd by fuch Reafons, as forbad me

‘ to render what was due to my own Love, and
‘ your Virtue; I am now refolv’d to tread upon
‘ thofe inhuman Maxims, that play the Tyrants
‘ with me, and to prefent myfelf to you, in that
‘ honourable and lawful Way, that my ardent
‘ Paffion did ever truly intend. But becaufe this
‘ Marriage which I defire to confummate with
‘ you, cannot be promulg’d, without deftroying
‘ my Defign to fet the Crown of the Univerfe up-
‘ on your Head, let me intreat your confent, that
‘ it may now be known to no other Perfons than
‘ thofe I fee about you, and thefe two Friends,
‘ whom I have brought to witnefs this Action.
‘ In the Gods and their Prefence (if you confent)
‘ I will prefently efpoufe you, and if it may but
‘ remain a Secret amongft us, till I enter *Rome*,
‘ and there eftablifh my Power, as my Defigns
‘ have framed it, it fhall then be publifhed with
‘ all the Pomp and Magnificence your Wifhes can
‘ invent.

To thefe Words *Cefar* added many other affectionate Expreffions, to render the Queen’s Spirit flexible to his Intreaties, and help her over all
the Difficulties fhe found in that Propofition. She
took a long Time to ballance the Refolution fhe
was to take, and in fine, betook herfelf to the
Counfel of her Maids, my Father, (and if I may
dare to fay fo) myfelf; but above all other Per-
fwafions, the Belief prevailed fhe had of *Cefar*,
as a Man that could not confent to violate his Promife given to a Princefs of her Condition, in the
Prefence of fix Witneffes, enough to convince
him of Infidelity before Men and Gods, which
he folemnly invok’d in that Action. At laft, whether vanquifh’d with Reafon, or undermin’d by
her own Weaknefs, fhe yielded herfelf: When
Cefar putting his Hand in hers, after he had called

led all the Gods to the Myftery, he protefted that he receiv'd her as his Spoufe, and folemnly fwore, that he would never own nor acknowledge any other. Thefe Proteftations he feal'd with a Kifs in our Prefence, and to contract the Relation, the Company judging their Prefence no longer neceffary, retir'd, and left *Cæfar* alone with the Queen, to take Poffeffion of thofe admirable Beauties (envied of all the Princes of *Afia*) which were then with an unbridled Liberty abandoned to his Defires.

'Oh Gods! *cryed* Tyridates, *with a profound* '*Sigh,* Gods, Sovereign Arbiters of our Defti- 'nies, and what has the unfortunate *Tyridates* ' done to you, that you fhould force him thus to '*trail* on his Life, without either Happinefs or ' Hope, when you difpenfed fo much Felicity to ' the reft of Mankind?' Thefe few Words he paf- fionately utter'd, with his Eyes lifted up to Heaven, when *Eteocles* thus purfued her Story.

Hymen's

Hymen's Præludia :

OR,

Love's Master-Piece.

PART III. BOOK I.

ARGUMENT.

The Rebellion of King Pharnaces *calls* Cæfar *out
of* Ægypt, *and invites him to an eafy Victory.
He leaves* Cleopatra *with Child. The Birth of*
Cæfario. *The early dawning of his rare Qualities, both of Mind and Body.* Cæfar's *Victory
in* Syria *againft* Cato, Scipio, &c. *He wins
the Battle of* Munda *againft* Pompey's Sons,
which compleats his Conquefts. Comes to Rome,
*and is made perpetual Dictator. His Ingrati-
tude to* Cleopatra. *He adopts* Octavius, *and is
kill'd in the Senate-Houfe. The Triumvirs revenge his Murther, by the Death of all the
Confpirators.* Cleopatra's *Care in* Cæfario's
Education. Anthony, *in his Parthian Expedition, fummons her to appear before him. He
is taken in the Snare of her Beauty : Repudiates*

Octa-

Octavia, *and marries her.* This rais'd a Quarrel betwixt him and *Augustus,* which is decided in the Battle of *Actium.* Anthony *is overthrown, and flies with* Cleopatra *into* Ægypt. *The Conqueror pursues, and besieges them in* Alexandria. Cæsario *is sent for safety to* Hydaspes, *King of* Æthiopia. *Is betray'd in the way by* Rhodon, *and preserved by the loyal Policy of* Eteocles. Hydaspes *receives and treats him as his own Son.* Cæsario *falls in love with* Candace, *the King's Daughter.* Anthony, *through a Mistake, kills himself.* Cleopatra *dies by the Bite of an* Aspick. *The Character of* Britomarus, *and his haughty Pretences. The gallant Combat between him and* Cæsario. *They are parted.* Cæsario *protects him : Moderates the King's Anger to a Banishment. The brave Speech of* Britomarus *to* Cæsario *at their parting.*

SINCE that fatal Day, which I know not whether I may call happy, or unfortunate, the great *Cæsar* and the Queen *Cleopatra* entirely dedicated themselves to their unreſtrained Delights: And tho' the Marriage continued ſtill a Secret among us, and while the Day laſted, they obſerved the ſame Ceremonies before Company they had formerly uſed ; yet the Nights, by the Means of *Iras,* *Charmione,* and my Father, (in whom the Queen repoſed a clear Confidence) ſtill reviv'd their Contentments. Never did Love appear more amiable than in theſe two Perſons. *Cleopatra* liv'd not but in *Cæsar* ; *Cæsar* was *Cleopatra's* Idolater ; and they forgot nothing that might prove their Paſſion the ſtrongeſt ; and yet the moſt ſincere

that

that ever invaded Lovers. The whole Court, nay, all *Egypt*, took part in their Contentments, tho' they knew them not: And, I think, *Rome* herself scarce ever shew'd so much Pomp, as then our *Alexandria* was daily dress'd in.

The whole World knows *Cleopatra* was the most magnificent Queen that ever lived, not only in the Pride of Entertainment, in the Splendor of her Festivals, and the Gifts she bestow'd on *Anthony*, but in the whole Course of her Life kept up her royal Grandeur at that lofty Pitch of Glory, where she should still have flown: And then perceiving herself the Sovereign of his Will, that was like to be the Sovereign of all Men, she forgot nothing that might help her to hold those Advantages: And *Cæsar*, not less satisfied with his Fortune, judging her most worthy of his Affection, was never weary of admiring the rare Qualities of her Body and Mind, which daily served to make his Love flame higher.

But at last Fortune interrupted the Course of their mutual Felicities; and *Cæsar* (that was not born to waste his Life upon a Woman's Lip, for whom all great Actions were reserv'd, and to whom the World's Empire was destin'd) was constrain'd to quit *Egypt*, and with his Army to pass into *Syria*, where he had learn'd that *Pharnaces*, King of *Pontus*, Son of *Mythridates*, and Inheritor of the Hatred which he bore to the *Roman* Name, though not of his Virtues, was up in Arms, and had spoiled a Part of *Armenia*. I shall forbear to repeat the Adieus of these two Lovers, for I do but touch upon their Life as I pass by it, and only take it in my way to another Story, to which it serves me for a Conduct. Should I enlarge myself upon the Loves of *Cæsar* and *Cleopatra*, Truth would engage me to defend the Memory
mory

mory of that great Queen, who, doubtlefs, hath
been foully blotted by the Ignorance of thofe that
knew not of her Marriage ; but in that which
befel her fince with the deplorable *Anthony*, I
fhall make but a fhort ftay, their unfortunate Loves
and lamentable End being known to all Perfons in
the World, that are capable of underftanding.

Cleopatra's Tears were too weak to retain
Cæfar in *Alexandria* ; but he comforted her with
the folemn Repetition of his Promife before us, to
call her to *Rome*, fo foon as he fhould be eftablifhed in the Dignity (which his Ambition aim'd at)
of perpetual Dictator, and then to declare their
Marriage to all the World. At that time the Princefs began to perceive herfelf with Child, and
gladly believed that the Affurance fhe gave to
Cæfar of it before his Departure, would yet more
deeply engage him to remember his Vows, and
the dear Pawn he left behind him.

Thus *Cæfar* marched into *Syria*, leaving *Cleopatra* in *Alexandria*, where fhe govern'd her People with fuch Moderation and Prudence, as fhe
taught all Men to admire thofe politick and mo-
ral Virtues in her Sex, that were rarely found even
in Men of uncommon Parts : She fupported the
Abfence of her dear *Cæfar* with much Anguifh ;
but fhe receiv'd frequent Comforts with the news
of his continued Victories. Not long after his
Departure, fhe learned that *Pharnaces* was defeated
by him in a fignal Battle ; and the War, which,
in all appearance, was like to laft many Years,
thus terminated in half a Day. A little after, fhe
received Intelligence, that in *Africa* he had vanquifh'd *Cato*, *Scipio*, and the King of *Juba*, with
a Prodigy of Fortune and Diligence ; and having
gained that Victory with the Slaughter of 50,000
of his Enemies, and the Lofs of but fifty of his

own Soldiers, he was return'd to *Rome*, where he had made three triumphal Entries. The Fame of these great Deeds pleasingly flatter'd the Soul of *Cleopatra*, and she dismissed all her Anxieties, with a Confidence that such a Man could not be capable of Infidelity.

In the mean time, no longer able to hide the swelling Fruit of her Womb, and unwilling to contract the ill Opinion of her Subjects, she was constrain'd openly to declare the Truth of her Marriage; and instead of the shame and confusion her Fear suspected from that Discovery, she found her *Egyptians* possess'd with new Joy, in the Expectation of such a King from her Loins, as might prove a perfect Copy of *Cæsar* and *Cleopatra*.

The Queen was brought to bed in *Alexandria*, (almost at the same time that *Cæsar* made his Entry into *Rome*) of a Son, not only worthy of his Father and Mother, but of all that the most fruitful Hope should conceive; never did the Light salute a thing so beautiful; the Astrologers never knew a Birth so advantageous; for this Royal Infant immediately became the Admiration and Delight of all that saw it: But because his Childhood was but the Spring to that Lustre, which hath since appeared in him with riper Advantages, I will not stay upon the Beginnings of his Life, because they are of less Importance. By a general Consent, he was called *Cæsario*; and we all hoped, that, though there was little Difference between his and his Father's Name, there would be yet less in their Qualities, and the Greatness of their Actions. The Queen took a marvellous Care of his Education, and made the whole World to be searched for the most expert and knowing Persons in all Sciences and Exercises, wherein he was to be inſtructed, when his Age permitted him, and (though I did but weakly merit that Honour, and a better Choice might have been made among the *Egyptians*) ſhe was pleaſed to make me his Governor; for my Father was too old for that Employment, and only deſir'd it for myſelf.

In the mean time, the Queen, whatever Conſolation ſhe taſted in the Enjoyment of her Son, was galled with bitter Grief, ſeeing there appeared no Proof of *Ceſar*'s Promiſe. Not long after, ſhe underſtood he had given the laſt Blow to that War, by the Defeat of *Pompey*'s Sons; that in *Rome* he had uſurped the Sovereign-Authority, and forced a Maſter upon that proud City, the imperious Miſtreſs of ſo many Kings, and ſo large a Part of the Univerſe.

Then her Hopes began to ſwell with the Expectation of his Promiſe; and *Ceſar*, by frequent Letters, endeavour'd to confirm them, excuſing his Abſence from her Delights with very ſpecious Reaſons, which for a time appeaſed her; but when ſhe ſaw a whole Year waſted, and yet no Haſte made to accompliſh his Vow, ſhe began to loſe her Patience, and complain of his Infidelity. Yet, before ſhe thought fit to make her Reſentments ſpeak louder, ſhe ſent my Father *Apollodorus* to *Ceſar*, as well becauſe he was the faithfulleſt of her Servants, as that in his Preſence *Ceſar* eſpouſed her, and might therefore better than any other reproach the Violation of his Word. This Voyage of my Father's proved ineffectual; yet, when *Ceſar* ſaw him, he hugg'd him in his Arms, entertain'd him nobly, gave him rich Preſents, and often mention'd the Queen with dear Reſentments of Affection; but could afford him no other Reaſons for his Delay, than what he had written to *Cleopatra*. He proteſted, that ſo ſoon

as

as he had felt himself fit sure upon his Imperial Throne, he would accomplish his Promise; but in that Condition, while his Monarchy was yet infant, feeble, and staggering, he found it not safe to enterprize any thing against the Consent of the People and Senate, whom he had already exasperated with imposing his Yoke.

Cleopatra was contented for a time to flatter herself with the Likelihood of these Excuses; but, in fine, after her Patience had learned another Lesson, as tedious as the first, she broke into Reproaches against him, gave herself up to the Sway of a just Passion, and probably was hatching Thoughts to make it known in some deadly Blow, when News came, that Heaven had revenged her, and that her faithless *Cesar* was murder'd in the Senate-House, with twenty-three Wounds, by those that he thought his dearest Friends.

This Report fell like a Clap of Thunder upon her Spirit, and all her Choler could not dissuade her from receiving it at first, as the greatest Blow that Heaven and Fortune could contribute to her Overthrow. She solemniz'd this Loss with a Deluge of Tears, and such Actions as could best express most Passion; and would possibly have abandon'd herself to Grief, if the last Marks of *Cesar*'s Ingratitude had not brought her Comfort; for she learned, that, a little before his Death, he had adopted his Nephew *Octavius* (who is now the Great *Augustus Cesar*) for his Son, declared him his Heir, and obliged him to take his Name and Dignity, without making the last mention of his Son *Cesario* or *Cleopatra*. This last assurance the Queen received of her Husband's ingrateful disesteem, kindled a despite that dry'd up all her tears, and shewed her cause to rejoyce in the same death she so lately bewailed; however, she

she ceased to bemoan his loss in publick, though she rendered to *Cesar's* Memory the Funeral Honours, which she believed due as to her lawful Husband; but her resentments against the Father descended not to the Son; for she nourished the little *Cesario* with as dear Indulgence, as if his Father had been still Faithful; and remembring that (perjur'd as he was) he had been the greatest of all Men, in his face she beheld the Image of his mighty Sire, as another dawning of her comfort. To him her resolutions intended the Crown of *Egypt*; and (though the *Egyptians* perceiving the *Ptolomean* Race was almost extinct) did oft petition her to make choice of another Husband, she always denied their entreaties, and at least so won upon them by her mild and prudent Government, as they were content to approve her design of passing the rest of her Life in Widowhood.

Alas! how happy had the poor Queen been, had she held her resolution; she had avoided those famous Misfortunes that made so much noise in the World; and her miseries, with the lamentable Catastrophe of her Life, had not forced tears from her rudest Enemies.

Sir, I suppose you know that a few years after *Julius Cesar's* death, the unfortunate *Anthony* having shar'd the Empire of the World with young *Cesar*, since called *Augustus*, and with him revenged the Murder of their Predecessor, by the defeat of the Conspirators, and by that bloody *Triumvirat* which produc'd such fatal effects in *Rome*; passing through *Cilicia* to make war upon the *Parthians*, he summon'd *Cleopatra* to appear before him; and because the Queen was too weak to resist the puissance of that great Master of half the World, by the advice of her Council

she

she went to find him in that stately Galley, whereof the Stern was all of pure Gold, the Sails of Purple, the Oars of Silver, and all the rest drest in that proud Equipage, that has since found the World so much Discourse. You have heard of her meeting with *Anthony*, and the Feasts they made so full of Pomp and Profusions : but as *Anthony* was first vanquished with *Cleopatra*'s magnificence, so he gaz'd not long before he was subdu'd with her beauty, to which he became a slave, not with a servitude parallel to his Predecessor, but such an one as only expired with his Life ; and would have endured a thousand Ages had the Gods lengthned their days to so remote a period.

    Anthony was something inferior to *Cæsar*, and therefore *Cleopatra* in bestowing herself upon him, might seem to descend a little from the height of her pretences : But since she was resolved to give *Cæsar* a Successor, she could not chuse a greater than *Anthony* amongst Men, whose Glory was not yet blasted by the Fortune of *Augustus* ; his Birth was of the most Illustrious, his Person recommended by a number of fair Qualities, and brave Actions, and his Rank no less considerable than the chief upon Earth. *Cleopatra* rendred herself to these considerations, and to the Loyal Affection of *Anthony*, who for her sake deserting the Amity of young *Cæsar*, and his Sister *Octavia*, whom he had married at *Rome*, gave up all his interest in the Common-wealth, and his own Fortunes that were fastned to it, to give himself intirely to her, and confining his Ambition within her Embraces, espoused her in *Alexandria*.

    I know the *Romans*, irreconcileable Enemies to *Cleopatra*'s Memory, have endeavour'd to disprove

that Marriage, as they did the former, and perfecuted that deplorable Queen in her reputation,
after they had sent her to her Tomb by their cruelty: But my Eyes were witnesses of what might
serve to upbraid their inhumanity, and justify
her Memory against those cruel ones that would
still disturb her repose in her very Sepulchre.

Anthony ty'd the Conjugal knot in publick, but
with an inauspicious augury, which their misfortunes did since prove too prophetick. They
are so well kown, that I believe you are not ignorant of the least particular; I shall therefore
inclose them in a few Words, and swiftly follow
the thread of my discourse, till I arrive at what
chiefly engages this Relation. Within the first
year of their Marriage, the Queen disclosed a
double Birth, a Son and a Daughter; the Son
was called *Alexander*, the Daughter *Cleopatra*, and
if I had not named *Cesario*, I would have said
that human Eye never saw any thing so fair as
these Twins: Indeed I think their Beauty was
fatal to their House, and a cause of calling down
the Divine Vengeance upon *Anthony*, for so oft
provoking the Gods, by shewing these Children
at publick spectacles, with the usurped names of
Apollo and *Diana*, causing them to be dressed in
the same fashion those Deities were usually represented in, and commanding the same honours
should be rendred them as were ordinarily paid
to those Divinities.

I saw them not since they were eight or nine
years of age; but at that time they were the
wonder of all that beheld them, and it was
thought the Beauty of young *Cleopatra* would not
only equal the Queen her Mother, but out-shine
all that ever were accounted fair.

‘ Those

' Those that conceived such hopes of the Prin-
' cess *Cleopatra*, (*said* Tyridates *interrupting*
' Eteocles) had much reason on their side; my-
' self saw her at *Rome*, while I made my Resi-
' dence in the Emperour's Court, and agreed with
' the general opinion, that nature never shap'd a
' face so triumphantly beautiful: She now lives at
' Court with the Empress *Livia*, who tenders her
' with as dear an esteem, as if she were her proper
' Daughter; the fame of her perfections have al-
' ready nois'd them in a large part of the World;
' and were I not loath to interrupt your Narrati-
' on, I would speak more amply of them. Young
' *Ptolomy* her Brother was then at *Rome*, in an
' high esteem for handsomeness; but the Elder,
' *Alexander*, whom you mentioned, was a while
' since lost at Sea, without any news of his escape.

' Sir, *said Eteocles*, your Relation doth sensi-
' bly touch me, for while I have life I must own
' so passionate an interest in all that pertains,
' either in blood or alliance to our dead Queen, as
' I cannot hear them spoken of without extraor-
' dinary motion; may the Gods frame them a
' fortune different from their Parents, and do me
' the grace to let me see those dear Reliques of
' that Illustrious Family recover their splendour.'
But to continue my Story, a year after *Alexander*
and *Cleopatra*, was born that *Ptolomy* you saw
at *Rome*, little inferiour to the other two, carrying
in his visage the fair marks of a glorious Birth.
Never was there seen a Court so pompous as *Anthony*'s and *Cleopatra*'s; most of the Kings upon
Earth came thither to pay their Homage, and many
of them sent their Children, that they might have
the honour to be educated with our young Princes. Indeed they were brought up with such care,
as was due to them only; and though *Cesario*

was not Son to *Anthony*, yet his respect to him was proportion'd to that great veneration he preserv'd for his Father's memory; he caus'd the Marriage of *Julius Cesar* with *Cleopatra* to be publickly proclaim'd in all his Dominions, declared *Cesario* the Legitimate Son, and indubitable Heir to his Father, rendred him honours suitable to that dignity; and whether it were to endear his Mother, or to appear kind to *Cesar*'s memory, he caus'd him to be styled the King of Kings, as he had already *Cleopatra* the Queen of Queens; and, disdaining she should bear a barren Title, he gave her the Realms of *Egypt, Cyprus, Soria*, and the lower *Syria*. To young *Alexander, Armenia*, all *Media* and *Parthia*, when it shall be Conquer'd. To young *Cleopatra, Lybia* and *Cilicia*; and to little *Ptolomy, Syria* and *Phœnicia*. Of these several presents he sent the Decree to be confirmed at *Rome*, which nevertheless was suppress'd by the Consuls *Domitius* and *Sosius*, the very same you mentioned in your discourse.

In the mean time you know what Wars were waged while they lived together both in your own Country, and in *Syria* against *Antiochus*; the good success he had against *Parthia* by his Lieutenants, and the ill luck that befel him when he carried the War thither in person; his resentments against *Artabasus* King of *Armenia*, whom with his Children he led Captive to *Alexandria*, where a while after he lost his Head by *Cleopatra*'s Command, as your recital exprest it. You are not ignorant of the many Voyages he made to *Rome*, where he always resisted the Senate that would oblige him to forsake *Cleopatra*, and at last fell foul with *Augustus* by that scornful repudiation that he made of his Sister *Octavia*.

In

In fine, the War being openly declared between these two Masters of the World, their grand Factions almost intirely divided it, according to the sway of several affections; two greater powers than these never met in opposition, and the World never regarded an event with so much interest as that, which was to decide its Empire.

My Lord, you have understood the beginnings of this War; with the divers Encounters, wherein Fortune sometimes lifted herself in one, sometimes in the other party, till the Battel of *Actium*, where, after she had long ballanced her good will, she declar'd for *Cesar*. The miserable *Anthony* was betray'd both by Love and Fortune, and whatever Courage the Queen disclosed in the spring-tide of her Life, was all resign'd to the horrour of that one Battel, where she assisted in person; whence flying with sixty Sails in her company, she drew along the amorous *Anthony*, who rather chose to abandon with the Victory, the Empire of the World, than to lose his *Cleopatra*. You must needs have heard how after that signal defeat they were forsaken by all their Troops; and sure Fame has told you of the pitiful effects that errour produced among them; how upon a false report of *Cleopatra*'s death, spread by herself with a design to cure *Anthony* of an unjust suspicion he had conceived of her; that desperate Prince flew himself with his own hand, and breathed his last between the Arms of his dear *Cleopatra* in the Tomb wherein she had shut up herself. You have heard it related how *Cesar* (having render'd himself Master of *Alexandria*) came to visit her, brought her Comfort, and entreated her to hope for all the civil Usage his Power could afford: All which, the great-hearted Princess courageously disdained; and not enduring to survive her dear

An-

Anthony, nor to see herself in danger to be led to *Rome* in triumph, she called Death to her Rescue, which she gave herself by an Aspick's Tooth, for want of other Weapons : And how *Cæsar*, after he had pacify'd *Egypt*, and left *Cornelius Gallus* Governor at *Alexandria*, returned to *Rome*, whither he led *Alexander*, *Ptolomy*, and *Cleopatra*, the Children of *Anthony* and our Queen. Thus, compriz'd in a few Words, I have given you the lamentable Destiny of this unfortunate Prince : But you are yet to understand that of *Cesario*; and I assure myself you believed, with the greatest Part of the World, that *Augustus* had caus'd him to be put to death, as Fame did openly divulge it.

‘ 'Tis true, *said Tyridates*, and I had my Be-
‘ lief from the general Confidence at *Rome* that
‘ it was so, where I have often heard, that *Cesar*
‘ having taken *Alexandria*, and advising with his
‘ Friends what he should do with *Cesario*, the
‘ Philosopher *Arrius*, who was in great Credit
‘ with him, whisper'd some Words in his Ear,
‘ that, alluding to a Verse in *Homer*, might thus
‘ be interpreted :

Plurality of Cæsars *is not safe.*

‘ And from that Hint *Augustus* (fearing that he
‘ might one Day dispute the Succession of his Fa-
‘ ther's Empire) put him to to death.’ ‘ Such,
‘ *reply'd Eteocles*, was the general Opinion, and
‘ we are happy that it got so much Credit among
‘ the Prince's Enemies ; who possibly, without
‘ that Prevention, would have made their Pur-
‘ suit and Persecution reach to the Place that pro-
‘ tected him. But to you I shall unmask the
‘ Truth, whatever Danger the Discovery may
‘ threaten, knowing well I do not hazard my
‘ Prince in declaring the Truth of his Life to an-
‘ other

' other Prince, that equals his Virtues ; and it
' was but to come the right way to his Adven-
' tures, that with a few Words I touch'd a Part
' of the Queen his Mother.

The History of Cæsario *and the Queen* Candace.

AFTER the Loss of the Battle of *Actium,*
and the disloyal falling away of the greatest
Part of the Forces, the unfortunate *Anthony* and
his Queen shut themselves up in *Alexandria,* and
there attended the Approaches of their victorious
Foe, with the rest of their Forces, resolving to
defend it to the last Man, and the latest Moment
of their Lives : Their Courage was not revolted
with their Fortune ; for they might yet have protected their Fate, and again debated the World's
Command, if the Prevention of that disastrous
Mistake had not contrived their Ruin. Nevertheless, the Queen, not able to refute her just
Fears of a sudden Wreck, began to cast an Eye
upon her deplorable Family, that in so short a time
were tumbled from the sublimest Pitch of Fortune,
to the Foot of Calamity. Oh Gods ! what Words
(that were fittest to shew the Marks of a signal
Grief) did she not give to those sad Considerations ? There was much Reason in her Fears that
the Victor would make his Hatred reach to the
Children of his Enemy, and so choak all the
Seeds of War, that might grow up to give another
Shock to the Tranquillity of his Dominion, by
rooting out the whole *Antonian* Race. And these
Suspicions made her oft sollicit that the Children
might be put in some Place of Safety ; and either
sent to the King of *Æthiopia,* a great and puissant
Prince, their Friend and Ally, who had neither
felt nor fear'd the *Roman* Arms ; or to *Herod,* a
faith-

faithful Friend to *Anthony*; or at leaſt to ſome others, whom the Change of Fortune had not perſuaded to diſavow their Amity.

But *Anthony*, who tenderly indulged his Children, could not reſolve to ſee them ſo pluck'd from him, or ſend them to ſeek their Safety from the Hands of a Stranger: He repreſented to the Queen, that the Gods that were yet able to ſend them Succours, (contrary to the Opinion of Men) might miraculouſly repair the Ruins they had made; and, ſhould ſuch a Change arrive in their Favour, they ſhould repent the expoſing them to a Flight, whoſe Succeſs was uncertain: That if Heaven had reſolved to compleat their Deſtruction, they might expect a better Fate for their Infants from the Clemency of their Enemy, than the Loyalty of any barbarous Prince, whoſe Friendſhip, the Child of their Fortune, no doubt would follow it to the Conqueror's Party.

Cleopatra perceiving his Reſolution not to be mov'd, and herſelf not able to wreſt the Diſpoſal of the Children from him, fell to conſider of his Preſervation, whom he had no Part in; and judging with much prudence, that though *Auguſtus* might pardon the Progeny of *Anthony*, yet he would not do ſo to the Son of *Julius Ceſar*, who (profeſſing himſelf the Off-ſpring of a lawful Marriage) while he lived, would at leaſt be armed with Juſtice, to bid fair for his Father's Succeſſion, which the other poſſeſſed by no other Right than that of Adoption; the lawful Power of his diſpoſal ſolely remaining in herſelf, (for *Anthony* pretended not to it) ſhe concluded that it was not ſafe to truſt him to the Mercy of that Enemy, and could find no other Way but ſuch a Flight to ſecure him.

Ceſario

Cæsario was five or six Years elder than the rest, and then newly arriv'd at the fifteenth Year, but at that Age was become the most accomplish-ed of Princes; his Beauty never found an equal among those of his own Sex: In the Vivacity of his Eyes, and all the Features of his Visage, was seen an Air so Majestick as could belong to none but *Cæsar* and *Cleopatra*: His Stature was extra-ordinary for his Age, his Force prodigious, his Agility and Nimbleness in all his Exercises attract-ed the Admiration of all Beholders; his sprightly dexterous Wit express'd such an enchanting sweet-ness, and his Inclinations were always so levell'd at great Actions, that in his tenderest Years, I ne-ver knew him nurse a Thought that was not wing'd for an uncommon Flight. He was enfla-med with an Emulation at his Father's Glory, and it kindled the same desires in him, that it had done in the Soul of young *Alexander*: But in the Relation of his Life, which was made him, and which I oft represented to his Eyes, as a Model for his Imitation, he never set a lower Esteem upon his Clemency, Liberality, and Moderation, than his Valour, and prudent Conduct; and all the Glosses he made upon it, were so many de-lightful Demonstrations to me of his ardent Love to Virtue. In an Age so tender and feeble to sup-port a Cuirass, a hunder'd Times has he offered to precipitate himself into military Dangers; and had not an absolute Authority retain'd him, he would have followed *Anthony* to his Battles, with an Ardour which he found very difficult to moderate. Such a one, or rather a thousand Times better than what my Expression had made him, was *Cæsario*, when the Queen his Mother (preferring his secu-rity to her own delight in enjoying his lovely Presence) resolved to lose it for ever, and being

con-

confirmed in that purpose, and prepared to execute it, I was commanded to attend him from his
Chamber to her Presence.

She could not behold him with a Design never
to see him more, (at least if the Gods restor'd not
their Fortunes) without resigning that Constancy,
wherewith she temper'd all her Actions, to abundance of tender Tears; which so softned the
young Prince's Soul and mine, as it set our Eyes
for a while to the same Task.

At last she made an Assault upon her Grief;
and struggling to recover an assured Look, after
she had wiped away her Tears, 'My Son, *said
'* she*, though your Years be few, your Apprehen-
' sions do much o'er-top those of an equal Age;
' and I know you are already capable to make
' Reflection upon our present and past Fortunes:
' You are derived from a Father that was the
' greatest of Men, and a Mother that may boast
' to have held some Rank among Women, and
' will leave a Report of her Life behind her, that
' is not ordinary in her Sex. I see nothing in
' you (the Gods be thanked) that belies your
' Birth, or forbids me to hope that you will not
' make the Soul of mighty *Cæsar*, (now placed
' among the Gods) to blush at your begetting:
' If Fortune frowns upon your budding Age, and
' bereaves you (with those from whom you had
' your Being) of the Advantages, which in part
' you should hold of her, learn in time to slight
' her, and strain your Virtue to captive her Smiles,
' and force her back again. You wear a Sword,
' after your Father's Example, that may one Day
' recover the Crowns you have lost; and if the
' Gods decree, (as there is much appearance) that
' we fall in this War, and period our Empire
' with our Days, you shall stay behind us to win

' that

' that back again by the Glory of your Actions,
' which we loft by the laft of ours, revive the
' Memory of *Cæfar* and *Cleopatra*, and perhaps
' revenge the Fate of *Anthony* and *Cleopatra*, up-
' on thofe Enemies that deftroy'd us. Thefe are
' the Hopes, my Son, that move me to ftudy
' thy Safety, when I neglect my own : My Affec-
' tion to thee makes me commit a cruel Violence
' upon my tendereft Inclination ; 'tis fit we part,
' young *Cæfar*, that thou may'ft go beyond the
' Reach of thy Enemy's Arms, and go in the
' Queft of a better Deftiny, than that thou muft
' expect at the Knees of a pitilefs Conqueror ; and
' indeed it is unfit that the Legitimate Son of
' great *Cæfar* fhould tamely beg a Life of his
' Adoptive, which he cannot take of him with-
' out a Blufh, and which he muft never look to
' obtain from him, who, in bearing the Name
' and Power of *Cæfar*, does neither inherit his
' Clemency, nor any one of his other Virtues.
' To preferve thee, I defpoil my Heart of its
' deareft Sentiments, but (whatever Violence I
' fuffer) I fhall always think it a more gentle Ca-
' lamity, to part with thee for ever, than to fee
' thee cold in thy Urn before I enter mine ; to be-
' hold thee a Suppliant at the Feet of our cruel
' Enemy, or dragged in triumph behind his Cha-
' riot, to that City, which thy Father firft ranged
' under his Obedience.

The Queen ftopp'd at thefe Words, to dry fome
difobedient Tears, which rebell'd againft her Refolution ; and, removing her Eyes from the Face
of her Son, to faften them upon mine, ' *Eteocles*,
' *faid fhe*, this is the laft time that I remit into
' your Hands the things which I count moft pre-
' cious : I trufted you with his Education, as I
' do now with the Confervation of his Life, and
' with

' with it all my own Hopes; let the Fidelity I ex-
' prefs you, by the Proofs I ask, to be the wor-
' thy Son of *Apollodorus*, who died as he liv'd
' in my Service, after he had got the Repute of
' the moft loyal Servant that ever breathed. Take
' the Prince, my Son, and your Pupil, whom I
' releafe to your Care and Conduct, and with
' your moft winged Diligence conduct him out of
' *Alexandria*, and the unfortunate *Egypt*, into
' *Æthiopia*. The King of that puiffant Realm
' is our Friend and Ally, and the only Neigh-
' bour we have, that dares think himfelf ftrong
' enough to defend his own againft their Inva-
' fions, and therefore ftands not in awe of the
' *Roman* Arms: Of him, in my Name, demand
' a Refuge for this young Prince, whom I not
' only truft with him, but beftow upon him:
' Tell him our Alliance does not only oblige him,
' nor the Laws of Generofity, that preach the
' Protection of the Miferable and Oppreffed, but
' the Intereft that is common to all that weild
' Scepters, to oppofe himfelf againft the Violence
' of the *Romans*, thofe cruel Enemies of Man-
' kind, that would ftretch their Tyranny over all
' the Kings on Earth. I know he will receive
' you, and allow my Son all the Shelter you can
' ask. This Night you fhall fet forwards; for I
' defire your Voyage may be fecretly carry'd, left
' your Enemies take notice of it, and fo endea-
' vour to ftrike at the Life of this poor Prince:
' You fhall have *Rodon* and *Alexander* for Com-
' panions in your Flight, with a few Officers,
' moft neceffary for fo fmall a Number, left a
' greater Train might difcover the Defign, and
' betray my Son to fuch Dangers, as my timorous
' Apprehenfion is apt to frame. I fhall furnifh
' you with Money and Jewels enough to keep

VOL. I.   H   ' off

' off Neceffity, while you ftay from us in fo re-
' mote a Refidence. If we make Peace with
' Octavius, or by the Favour of divine Aid re-
' cover Strength to rear our drooping Fortunes, I
' will call you back again, and with all the Hafte
' that Affection can make, draw you from an
' Exile, which I cannot fupport without a bleed-
' ing Grief.

The Queen exprefs'd herfelf in thefe Terms,
when the young Prince, throwing himfelf at her
Feet, protefted he would rather die than abandon
her ; that inftead of leaving her expofed to the
Menaces of fo much Peril, he had Courage enough
to run her Fortune and Anthony's.

The Queen, drawing new Arguments from the
Difcourfe and Action of this brave Spirit, and excellent Nature, felt a painful Increafe of her Affection ; and turning her Eyes from his Face, where
they did but gather frefh Caufes of Grief, ' Great
' Cæfar, faid fhe, if thou be'ft rank'd among the
' Gods, fince he carries fo many Marks of thy
' Life, protect the Son that thou haft left me.
And then turning to her Son, at firft fhe gently
ftruggled with his Refolution ; but perceiving that
would not do, fhe fternly employ'd all her Authority : And after fhe had abfolutely forbid his further Oppofition of her Will, fhe commanded me
to carry him away by Force, if he refufed to follow.

Young Cæfario bearing fuch a Refpect to the
Queen, as he knew not how to difpenfe with Obedience, fubmitted to this laft Command, and
only in Tears exprefs'd his Grief to forfake her.
I fhall not further enlarge upon the Queen's and
our Regrets, to which, and to our Preparations
for departure, we dedicated the reft of that Day.
The Queen fent by Iras and Charmione (her two
faithful Maids that died with her, with fuch conftant

stant Fidelity, as will be the Wonder of all Ages)
a Cabinet full of Gold, with some rich Jewels,
which she trusted to my Hands; and so soon as
the Night approach'd, after she had utter'd her
last Adieu to us, bath'd in a River of Tears, she
bruis'd the Prince in her Arms: And when she
had left her last Kiss upon his Cheek, ' Go, *said*
' *she*, young Prince, where thy Destiny calls thee,
' the Gods will undertake thy Protection; in the
' mean time, forget not thy Father's Greatness,
' and let none of Fortune's rude Blows over-tame
' thee to Actions unworthy of thy Birth.

After these Words, the last I heard from her,
untying herself from her Son's Embraces, she
caused us to mount on Horse-back in her Presence, and, without further Delay, to quit the
melancholly *Alexandria*.

My Lord, the Beginning of *Cesario's* Adventures carrying much Resemblance to yours, like
yourself, he was forced to fly his Country, in an
Age little differing from that wherein you quitted
Parthia. He went out of *Alexandria* with not
above a dozen Horses in his Train; and he that
a while before, with so much Pomp, had been
proclaimed the King of Kings in divers Nations,
was forced to abandon his native Country, and
in that petty Equipage to seek a Covert for his
Life in a foreign Land.

This sudden and strange Revolution of Fortune,
may serve for a memorable Example to those that
trust to her Favours, and suffer themselves to be
blinded with treacherous Prosperity. The Magnificence of *Anthony* and *Cleopatra* had been ex-
cusable, if they had not stain'd that Grandeur
that placed them in the chiefest Rank of Mankind, with Actions that pull'd the divine Anger
upon their Heads; and those that a little before
saw

faw fo many Kings at their Feet, bereaving one of his Crown, another of his Head, (as the unfortunate *Antigonus*, King of *Judæa*, and the wretched *Artabafus* of *Armenia*) beheld themfelves reduced to attend his Deftiny in the laft City that was left them ; and, a few Days after, conftrained to take the Succours of Death from their own Hands, which *Cleopatra* (to compleat her Calamities) had much ado to obtain, and did at laft by an Artifice.

We parted from *Alexandria* almoft at the fame time that *Octavius Cæfar* encamped on the other Side, in view of the Walls; and had we longer delay'd the Voyage, we had found no Paffage free. Young *Cæfario* had fo long practis'd Horfemanfhip, under thofe Mafters that taught him his Exercife, as it render'd him the lefs unfit to undertake the Toil of fuch a Journey : Befides, he had inured himfelf to travel, by his Cuftom to follow the Chafe, which he would do with much Eagernefs, being of a Conftitution ftrong beyond his Age ; and this proved very ferviceable to our Defign. The firft Night we ftrived to reach fo far, as any Perfon, lefs hardy than himfelf, would have been weaken'd with Wearinefs ; and about the Break of Day, we ftaid at a Village three or four hundred Furlongs from *Alexandria*, where we found it fit to let the young Prince repofe himfelf, while we refrefhed our Horfes. In that Place we ftaid three or four Hours ; which expired, we again got to Horfe ; but had not marched many Furlongs, before I efpy'd the Prince's Horfe, with my own, *Rodon's*, and three or four others in the Company, to halt ; and not fo much as dreaming of the Treachery was intended us, I only imputed it to the Wearinefs they had contracted with hard Riding and extraordinaay Hafte.

We

We might have taken thofe that continued found, but loath to part with fo many neceffary Officers, and befides, ignorant of the Mifchief that purfued us, we were conftrained to march fo foftly, that we had much ado, in that whole Day, to reach another Town, that was not diftant above one hundred and fifty Furlongs from that where we refted in the Morning; and there arrived, (our Horfes fcarce able to fuftain themfelves) we were compell'd to ftay that Night; but fending for fome Smiths that lived there, to fearch them, we found that they were all pricked, and the Nails that hurt them no fooner drawn out, but they were much mended, yet not fo recover'd as to endure that Night's Travel. I then began to entertain fome Sufpicion, and to believe this an intended Treachery to retard our Voyage; but yet I knew not whom to diftruft. Our little Troop was compofed of no Perfons, but fuch from whom indeed we had reafon to hope an untainted Fidelity; myfelf excepted, *Rodon* and *Neander* were the Principal: *Rodon* was made the Prince's SubGovernor in his tendereft Years, and had not a Iefs Part in his Education than myfelf; befides, he had a Son there of the fame Age with the Prince, that was brought up with him, and then follow'd him in that Voyage: *Neander* was a Man of approved Fidelity, and the reft all eminent Officers of *Cleopatra*'s Houfe, as fhe had culled from fuch as fhe thought moft true; yet, even among thofe, we found Monfters capable of the blackeft Treafon, and the moft prodigious Villainy that ever was hatched by human Invention.

After I had almoft wafted that Night converfing with Cares, too reftlefs to admit Sleep, I threw myfelf from my Bed; in which I was laid in my Clothes; and paffing into a little Gallery

H 3 adjoin-

adjoining to our Chamber, I open'd a Window, to see if I could spy the approach of Day. Under this Window was a Garden, in which I overheard some Persons discoursing ; and though I had little room for Curiosity, unless such as regarded my Prince's Safety, yet then, and peculiarly then, I think the Gods inspir'd me with it : The first Words had no sooner deliver'd themselves at my Ear, but I knew the Voice was *Rodon's* ; and presently after discover'd him that talk'd with him to be a Kinsman of his, and one that he deeply trusted, call'd *Arcetes*, for whom he had formerly procur'd a beneficial Grant from the Queen. The Time and Place made them exchange their Thoughts with a Confidence fearless of Overhearers ; but Heaven was awake in my Prince's Behalf, and by that miraculous Occasion becken'd me to his Preservation.

Rodon and *Arcetes* did but enter the Garden when I open'd the Window, and therefore I believe I heard all their Parley. ' Thou hast made ' great Haste, *said Rodon*, but is it possible thou ' couldst dispatch so many things in so short a ' time, coming out of *Alexandria* but with us !' ' Content yourself, *reply'd Arcetes*, that the Affair ' is driven to the Mark of your Desires, that I ' spake with *Cæsar* himself, who well remem- ' ber'd your Name, and mention'd the Sollicita- ' tions he had formerly made, to obtain that ' which now you have offer'd him. There I staid, ' by his Command, a full Hour, while he con- ' sulted with his Friends upon the most requisite ' Resolution : At last he called me to his Presence, ' commanded me to return unto you, and assure ' you, that he would not only bestow those Jewels ' on you, which the Queen had committed to ' *Eteocles's* Custody, but bids you hope for more

' im-

' important Favours ; and this Day to expect
' News from him upon the Way, which your
' Letter told him you were to take. Myself over-
' heard the Command he gave to a Centurion to
' be ready, and I believe they will overtake us be-
' fore we reach the Forest of *Agria*, thro' which
' we are to pass.'   ' They will have time enough
' to do that, *reply'd the disloyal* Rodon, for our
' March has been so slow since I nail'd our Horses,
' while *Eteocles* and the rest were at their Repose,
' that the *Romans* will need but a little Diligence
' to reach us : But now let us talk no more of it,
' for we cannot carry too much Caution and Dis-
' trust in an Affair of this Nature.'   And thus,
whether they fear'd to be lessen'd or surpriz'd by
the Day's Arrival, which then began to appear,
they left the Garden, and me still at the Window,
in such a Confusion, as is impossible to represent.

Gods ! what a strange Agony of Thoughts was
I then distracted with ?   To what Extremes of
Grief, Astonishment, and Anger, did the Know-
ledge of that loathed Treason hurry me !   I had
much ado to credit my own Ears, in a thing so
unlikely ; it had almost surpriz'd the Use of my
Reason and Judgment.   The first thing I did was
to detest *Rodon*'s Infidelity ; then, upon my Knees,
I gave thanks to the Gods for the Miracle of this
Discovery, and petition'd the Continuance of their
Aid for the Prince's Safety :   Yet I was much to
seek for the Continuance of my Endeavours, for
I saw myself, on all sides, menaced with so much
Difficulty, that I almost wanted Power to con-
ceive a hope of Success.

And now the Day had withdrawn all the Curtains of Darkness, before I could fasten upon
any other Resolution than to kill *Rodon*, and at
least revenge my Prince, if it were not permitted

ted me to preserve him; nevertheless, having no time to lose, I return'd into my Chamber full of mortal Inquietudes; and after I had given order for the Horses to be ready, I waken'd the Prince, and caused him to rise with a hasty Diligence. While he was apparelling himself, I drew *Neander* aside, (having learned by *Rodon*'s Discourse, he was not of the Conspiracy with that Traytor) in a few Words let him know our Destiny, which shook him with as great a Fit of Confusion as my self: While we were talking of it, the unfaithful *Rodon* came to us, the sight of whom had almost put my Power into the Hands of Passion; and I was even ready to fly upon him and strangle him, yet, with much ado, bridled it; and advising *Neander* to the same Reservation, we got the Prince on Horse-back, concealing the Truth from him, lest his tender Years, being too weak to disguise his Apprehension, should betray it in troubled Looks, and so deprive us of the Means to endeavour his Preservation.

Thus leaving the Town, we took the same way was first resolved, for fear *Rodon* should scent the Discovery of his Treason; and we had scarce marched a quarter of an Hour, when the Gods sent me a Thought, which I resolved to act without further Deliberation.

I confess, at first I felt some Repugnance, for the Danger to which I was to expose an innocent Person; but the Safeguard of my Prince outweighed the rest of my Considerations, and helped me in a Moment to level all the Obstacles that opposed my Intention: For that Reason, making a Sign to *Neander* to keep up with the Prince and the rest of the Troop, I marched softly after with *Rodon*, whom I had engaged in Discourse; but when the rest had left us a little behind, (feign-

ing that fomething was broke about my Saddle)
I alighted, making fhew to amend it, and oblig'd
Rodon to ftay for me, telling him that a little
galloping would foon recover our Company: Befides that, I had fome Authority over him, the
Eftate whereto his Confcience had reduced him,
left him not Confidence enough to gainfay me;
nor was he unwilling to accept of any Occafion to
retard our Voyage, becaufe he knew it might advantage his Defign.

Thus, when our little Troop had gained more
Ground of us, and, by the help of a little Hill
betwixt us, I had loft fight of them, I remounted my Horfe; and approaching *Rodon*, with a
Look that reprefented part of the Paffion that
fwayed within me, 'Traytor, (*faid I*) thy
'Death is at hand; and if thy Prince muft die
'by thy Difloyalty, thou fhalt yet want the Sa-
'tisfaction to fee him perifh, or reap the Profit
'of thy horrid Treachery.

I had no fooner utter'd thefe Words, but my
Sword was in my Hand; and the faithlefs *Rodon*
(more combated with his Confcience, than the
fear of my Valour) receiving my Menace with a
pale difmay'd Look, had much ado to put himfelf
in any Pofture of Refiftance; neverthelefs, with a
trembling Hand he drew his Sword, but defended
himfelf fo ill with it, that, with a Facility which
took away all the Glory of that Action, I paffed
mine twice through his Body, and tumbled him
upon the Sand, where he vomited out his perfidious Soul with his Blood.

After this Execution, fheathing my Sword
again, I hafted after the Prince with all the fpeed
I could make; but cafting my Eyes back from
the top of the Hill, I perceiv'd the Squadron of
Horfe that *Cefar* had fent after us, marching out

H 5 of

of the Town where we lodged, which I prefently
judg'd to be the fame that the falfe *Rodon* expected: This fight made me fpur up to my Company,
and when I had overtaken them, approaching to
Neander's Ear, 'Neander , *faid I*, Rodon is dead,
' but our Enemies appear ; take the Prince with
' you and two of our Men, gallop on afore to the
' Foreft of *Agria*, thruft yourfelves into the thick-
' eft Part of it, and there expect my coming up,
' with good News : The reft of the Day, I will try
' to abufe our Enemies ; and, if Heaven favour my
' Intentions, hinder their further Purfuit of us ;
' if you fee me not come back to you fome time
' to Day, at Night purfue your Voyage, under
' the Conduct of the Gods, who will not aban-
' don you.

I faid no more ; and without giving him time
to anfwer, made him fpeed away with the Prince
and the two that were to follow them, one of
which (becaufe of known Fidelity) carried the
Jewels and Gold the Queen had given us. *Cefario*,
who had a moft docile Ingenuity, abfolutely
obeyed my Will, and made no fcruple to follow
Neander, becaufe I counfell'd it : I could not fee
him part fo fuddenly without letting fall fome
Tears, as a Tribute to my fearful Incertainty of
ever feeing him again : And in the mean Time,
turning to thofe that ftaid with me, 'My Friends,
' *faid I*, we are betrayed ; our Enemies are with-
' in a hundred Paces of us : *Rodon* ftays behind
' to make difcovery of them : And behold the
' Traytor, *fhewing them Arcetes*, fee, the Vil-
' lain that hath fold us, has the Confidence to
' ftay among us.' At thefe Words, I flew at him
with my Sword in my Hand, but was prevented
by two of my Companions that ftepp'd before him,

as he was preparing to fly, and with two Blows threw him dead at our Horses Feet.

Rodon's Son, whom I caused to stay with us, though he would gladly have followed the Prince, who, as I told you, was of an equal Age and Stature to him, and had much in his Looks that over-topp'd his Condition, beheld the Death of *Arcetes* with Astonishment, when approaching to him, and taking him by the Arms, I shewed him the *Romans*, that were advancing to us a good swift Trot: ' We are all dead Men, *said I*, ' if we do not deceive our Enemies, by making ' you pass for the Prince *Cesario*; the persona- ' ting this Dignity will save your Life; for if the ' *Romans* take you for the Son of *Cæsar*, they ' will only content themselves to lead you Priso- ' ner to their Emperor; if you tender your own ' and our Lives, favour this just Deceit.

The fear of Death had so seiz'd the Youth, as it disposed him to follow my fatal Counsel, which I had scarce ended when the *Romans* were upon us, and spreading themselves upon the Plain, began to inviron us, and shut up the Passage to our flight.

I then perceiv'd the Danger at hand I had exposed myself to, and had well fore-seen it, before the Attempt: But the Gods can witness, that I felt no regret to hazard my Life for my Prince's Safety, and that there came no other Care to my Thoughts but for him and his Conservation. At a Sign I made to my Companions, we all threw ourselves from our Horses, and putting our Knees to the Ground, we encompassed the Son of *Rodon*, whom I had only caused to keep his Saddle. The *Romans*, who ran upon us with an impetuous haste, perceiving us in that suppliant Posture, were staid by the Command of their Captain, attend-

attending his Orders, without offering a Blow:
But so soon as my Voice could be heard; ' Ah!
' whatever you be, *cryed I*, if we have merited
' your Anger, turn your Weapons upon us only,
' and spare great *Cæsar*'s Son; Sacrifice us to your
' Rage, if we have offended, but give our Prince
' his Life.

These Words, with our submissive Action, turned the *Roman* Swords (fatal to the innocent Son
of *Rodon*) from our Throats; for the Captain approaching to him with his drawn Sword; ' For
' you, *said he*, we give you your Lives; but 'tis
' this same Son of *Cæsar* we only seek to take.'
At these Words, making his Way through us,
he ran the Youth through the Body with his
Sword, just as he was about to speak, and probably to tell him, he was not *Cæsar*'s Son. I cannot remember that poor young Man's unripe Fall
without the Sense of some Remorse for my own
Treachery: But my Lord, it was otherwise impossible to save our Prince; and since one must
perish, it was but just that the Son of that Traytor should be sacrific'd to his Father's Treachery:
Besides, I had indeed conceiv'd a Hope (if Hope
could shape itself in so short a time) that the *Romans* would forbear the Cruelty of his Murder,
and only content themselves to lead him to their
Emperor; in the mean time, I cast myself upon
his Body, and (the better to abuse our Enemies)
I made my complaints swell to as high a Tide,
as I should have let fall upon the Corpse of our
own true Prince. The *Roman* Commander being
a Man of Quality (as good Fortune would have
it) was touch'd at my Piety, and protested to me,
that he had executed *Cæsar*'s Command with regret: He oppos'd himself against many of his Men,
that would have cut off the Youth's Head, to pre-

sent it to the Emperor; and told them they might assure him of the Truth without exercising that Inhumanity upon the Son of *Julius Cæsar*; nevertheless, at their Sollicitation, he demanded the Jewels which *Cleopatra* had given us; but I reply'd, they were in the Hands of one of our Companions, called *Rodon*, whom we had not seen all that Day, and that I believed that it was he that had betray'd us. At this the Soldiers fell to threaten, and began to search us, but they found little about us; and their Captain remembring his Name was *Rodon*, who in effect betray'd us; and knowing the Emperor had design'd him the Jewels; as a Price of his Treason, easily believed that he was gone away with them; and desiring he should rather possess them by that Title, than as the Gift of *Cæsar*, commanded them to unhand us, restore us our Horses, and set us at Liberty to retire where we pleased. And thus his Men marching after him, they left us about the unfortunate Son of *Rodon*, upon whom I continued still my Laments.

When our Enemies were marched out of sight, (after we had covered the Body of that innocent Youth with a little Earth, and indeed contributed some true Tears to his Destiny) we remounted our Horses, exalted with our happy Success beyond Expression, and followed the Track of our true Prince.

See, my Lord, what has passed about *Cæsario's* supposed Death; they were abus'd that believed he was ever in the Hands of *Octavius*, for I dare assure you he never saw him; and that if he did consult upon what was to be done with him, and resolved to put him to Death, as you related, by Advice of *Arrius* the Philosopher, it must either be while *Rodon's* Messenger was with him, or before,

before, while the War was hot between him and *Anthony*; during which, 'tis true, he had oft follicited us to deliver the young Prince into his Hands, or put him to Death.

Two Hours after we had thus escaped our Enemies, we arriv'd at the Forest of *Agria*, and at the End of it found the Man that *Neander* had set Centinel near the High-way, to conduct me to the Place where the Prince was hid; without this Precaution, our Task would have been difficult to have found him, because the Forest was vast and full of Thickets. But Gods! what a Joy exalted me when I recovered the Sight of my dear Prince! what Words did I not utter! what Tears shed, when it was permitted me to embrace him, for whom some Hours before, I had been shook with such just Apprehensions? But then what a pleasing Satisfaction was given me! when (after I had receiv'd my Prince's Caresses overflowing with Affection) I learned of *Neander* the Inquietude he had suffered for my absence; and his Resolution (after he knew the Truth from *Neander's* Mouth, who could not refuse it to his pressing Importunity) to return back and run our Fortune, without permitting us alone to expose our Lives for his Safety: A Design so Noble (from which *Neander* only withheld him by Force) in so young a Soul, pleasingly confirmed me in those Hopes I had already conceived of the height of his Courage, and after I had express'd my Resentments of his Nobleness, and he rewarded us with Tears of Acknowledgment for what we had done for his Preservation; and, as Proofs of an excellent Disposition, paid some to the Memory of that innocent Son of *Rodon*, I caused him to mount on horseback, and so we got out of the Forest, and continued our Voyage.

My

My Lord, the particular Paſſages by the Way deſerve nothing but Silence, and to give way to Things of more Importance, which I muſt inform you of.   Within a few Days we left *Egypt* at our Backs, and having traverſed Part of the Deſarts of *Nubia*, which are contiguous to the two Realms, we enter'd *Ethiopia*, and took our Way toward the great City of *Meroe*, where that mighty King then made his Reſidence.   Our young Prince ſuffered the Incommodities of the Voyage with an admirable Courage and Patience; he was ever the firſt that urged our departure from thoſe Towns in our Way, where I had obliged him to ſtay and take ſome Repoſe.   We called him not by his right Name, left the News of his Safety coming to his Enemies Ears, ſhould make them try to find Traytors in *Ethiopia*, as they had done in *Egypt;* and for that Cauſe we accuſtomed to call him *Cleomedon*, with deſign that none there ſhould know him by any other Name, except the King, and ſuch other Perſons as muſt neceſſarily be truſted with the Truth.   But why ſhould I detain you longer ? We arriv'd at *Meroe*, whether we had ſent *Neander* ſome Days before, to advertiſe the King of our Prince's coming, and excuſe the entrance of his Dominions without Permiſſion, with the preſſing Neceſſity of his Flight.

The King of *Ethiopia*, (one of the beſt and juſteſt Princes upon Earth, who hated the *Roman* Tyranny, and ever honour'd *Cleopatra*) expreſs'd much Joy at the confidence that great Queen repos'd in him, and diſpos'd himſelf to treat the Prince her Son as his own; he would have given him a magnificent Reception, if *Neander* had not diſſwaded it, inſtructed by the Fear that we had to divulge that, which former Conſiderations taught us fit to be concealed.   The King, to favour

vour our Defign, was content to receive him in his Cabinet, where he gave us a particular Audience, without admitting any to be prefent, but fuch as he knew would guard the Secret.

The Magnificence and Furniture of his Palace had doubtlefs aftonifh'd any Perfons but fuch as had dwelt in the Court of *Cleopatra*, where there glifter'd more fumptuous Pomp and Glory, than all the World befide could boaft of; yet we there faw fuch an abundance of Riches, as cuftom to behold fuch Sights could not keep us from furprizal: For (as I believe you know) in *Ethiopia* Gold is fo common, that it is employed by Perfons of the loweft Rank, upon the moft vile Offices: But to contract my Difcourfe upon this Subject, I fhall only tell you, That as the Majefty of the King challeng'd our Veneration, fo the Countenance of my Prince wrought an Effect upon his Spirit, that foon made him confider'd as the Son of *Cæfar* and *Cleopatra*; for he accofted him with a Garb that juftified his Birth, and faluted him with a ftately Modefty, that had nothing in it but what was great and graceful, which rather ftirr'd up Admiration and Refpect than Pity: I had prepoffeffed him with fome few Inftructions, which he made ufe of with a moft becoming Grace; and after he had render'd his due Salutes to the King,

' Great Prince, *faid he*, my Parents, whom
' Fortune hath abandoned, have bequeathed me
' to you, with a belief that you will not refufe
' me your Protection; and with them I demand
' it of you, as the fole Prince of the World, from
' whom I am willing to receive it.

He faid no more than thefe few Words, which he utter'd in a Kingly fafhion; and at the fame time I prefented the King with the Queen *Cleopatra*'s Letter, who prefently acknowledg'd the Seal to be hers, and in it found thefe Words.

The

The Queen Cleopatra *to the Great* Hidaspes,
King of Ethiopia.

'THE knowledge I have of your Vertues bids
' me hope that your Affections will not
' change with our Fortune; and that having been
' our Friend and Ally in prosperity, one Calamity
' can neither make you forget our Amity or Al-
' liance: Upon this confidence, I give you mine,
' and the Son of mighty *Cæsar*, whom the Arms
' of his Enemies have chased from his Native
' Country, and reduced to ask a Refuge, which,
' but from you, I would not beg of any. If the
' Gods consent to guard us from the *Roman* Yoke
' and Oppression, I shall dearly preserve the me-
' mory of this obligation: But, if (for expiation
' of our faults) they have resolved our ruine, at
' least I shall perish with this comfort, That I
' trusted not the dearest thing I had in the World,
' but to him, who of all Princes is most worthy
' of the Confidence and Amity of *Cleopatra*.

King *Hidaspes* having read these Words, and
heard the Prince's, with a visage moistned with
some tears, that *Cleopatra*'s Misfortunes drew from
his Eyes, he turned to him, and taking him in
his Arms: ' Son of *Cæsar* and *Cleopatra*, *said he*,
' welcome, I see and receive you with an unfeign-
' ed joy; the Memory of your Father, and the
' Person of the Queen your Mother, in me shall
' ever challenge a sacred Reverence: Promise your-
' self, not only the same Offices from us, you
' might expect from your own, but be confident
' of our Protection so long as I have a Man that
' can hold a Sword.

And thus my Prince was received by the
Ethiopian King, who presently caused him to be
lodged

lodged in the Palace, gave command for the pro-
visions of his House, and made his intention
known to us, that he would have him Treated
as his proper Son.   His orders were so punctually executed, as in a few days we beheld ourselves
in as high a condition in *Meroe*, as we had formerly appeared in *Alexandria*; the Prince had a
great number of Officers, a large proud Equipage,
and indeed wanted no respect that was fit for the
Son of a mighty King in his Father's Court.

His proper Name and true Birth were only
known to such as the King honour'd with most
confidence :   Among the rest he pass'd under the
Name of *Cleomedon*, for a Prince only a-kin to
Cleopatra, and something allied to King *Hidaspes*.
Tyridates at that passage interrupted *Eteocles*:
' Though I have been ignorant of *Cesario*'s de-
' stiny, *said he*, I have heard of *Cleomedon*, and
' the distance that divided us, could not hinder
' renown from bringing his Name amongus, and
' with it the report of his grand Actions that car-
' ried it.   Under that name, replied *Eteocles*, my
' Prince did things considerable ; and such as
' doubtless their reputation reach you ; but I shall
' relate them in their order.

You know the *Ethiopians* are black, but the
Kings having been oblig'd by reason of State, to
make Alliance with their Neighbour Princes, and
so espouse White Women, have partly lost that
scorched Complexion of their Family.   This
King, who was born of a White Woman, was
only a little swarthy, and the Queen his Wife,
who died a year before we arrived in *Ethiopia*,
being purely white, and a most beautiful Princess, brought forth a Daughter that not only Heired her Mother's complexion, but became Mistress
of so fair a Beauty, as made her the wonder of
her

her own, and the better part of the World befide. This was the fair Princefs *Candace,* and the fame bright Queen now in your Houfe, which you delivered from the greedy Waves, where fhe had perifhed without your fuccour. To come to the relation of her Life, with my Princefs, I have begun you a Narration, which though fomething remote from them, will not altogether appear unneceffary; and now I fhall conduct your knowledge through all thofe accidents that compofed the prefent Fortunes of thofe two Great Perfonages.

The Princefs *Candace* exceeded not eleven years of age when we entred *Ethiopia*; and we had not refided there above a year, before my Prince render'd his Arms to her triumphant Beauty, and delivered up unto it a precious liberty which he could no longer hold against the rare perfections of that Princefs. This paffion that entirely feiz'd his Soul, came feafonably to banifh a dangerous grief, and arrefted him fhortly after our arrival, with the news of *Cleopatra's* deplorable end, and the lamentable fall of that unfortunate Family.

This ftruck my Prince fo deep, that all the comfort we could urge, had much ado to keep him from his Tomb; nor had we fo foon appeafed his forrow, if *Candace's* Beauty had not ftrugled more fuccefsfully with it than our arguments: indeed it was half impoffible for a Prince fo born, and newly entred an age capable of the fweet impreffions of love, to refift fuch uncommon puiffance. And though at firft *Cæfario* ftrove hard to preferve his liberty, yet all his luctation fainted at laft, to the confeffion of his weaknefs, and buckled to the yoke of a Tyrant, that handled him more rudely becaufe he refifted.

I 3

I did not difapprove the birth of this Paffion, for (finding nothing in it fit to cenfure) I no fooner knew it from my Prince, but indulg'd him in it, inftead of diffuading. He ever dearly loved and refpected me, and not only confidered me as his Governor, that had over-feen the growth of his greeneft years, but as him that had faved his Life, with the dangerous hazard of his own, and to embrace his interefts, had cafhier'd all other thoughts that had Eyes for his own: This knit him to me with the tender ties of fuch a confidence, as indeed was only due to the Queen his Mother. He open'd his heart unto me, fo foon as he felt the wounds that Love had given it; and having demanded my counfel and affiftance, and found me wholly difpofed to contribute all to his defires: ' Father, *faid* ' *he*, at Love's fiift Alarm, I feel a delightful pain; ' but becaufe 'tis cruel enough to rob me of my ' Reft, methinks it refembles that Fire, whereof ' I have oft heard the Queen my Mother and ' yourfelf difcourfe; and I fear it will ufurp as ' much power in my Soul, as it did in the un- ' fortunate *Anthony*. ' Gods! *faid he*, a while ' after, what a bright wonder is this Princefs *Candace*! how impoffible is it to fee and not turn ' flave to her Beauty?' Thefe Words were accompanied with divers fighs, which I had neither will nor power to condemn. In the mean time his flame grew daily higher, and in a fhort time, made him a moft ardent Paffionift.

I fhall forbear to importune you with the larget difcourfes he made at the firft fentiments of his Love, and only infift upon fome particulars that fell out in the blooming years of this young Couple; and though I am willing to ftep haftily over thofe, that I may bring them to an Age

more

more rational, yet I cannot filence thofe paffages, which methinks deferved better than to be fwallowed in oblivion.

The fair *Ethiopian* Princefs was born to all thofe excellent Advantages, that the confpiring bounty of Heaven and Nature can beftow; but the Beauties of her Afpect, which I prefume you have noted, are dim to thofe that fhine within her Soul; they began with her earlieft youth to break out with fuch beams, as were not to be feen but in herfelf: Her extraordinary vivacity was always accompanied with a marvellous folidity; a Judgment elevated above her Sex, and Courage great enough to challenge a rank among Perfons the moft generous: Of this fhe hath given fuch clear proofs, as will foon claim your Credit: But before I pafs to their recital, 'tis fit I ftay upon fomething that preceded.

The Divine Qualities of this Princefs twifted fuch a refpect with my Prince's Affection, that he long fmother'd his fighs, before he durft declare his Paffion; and though the fublimity of his Birth, and the merit of his Perfon might have arm'd him with a boldnefs capable to attempt any thing; and the tender age of the Princefs, younger by four or five years than himfelf, might well have help'd to difcard part of his fears; yet he always beheld her with fo much refpect, as he wanted the affurance to ferve himfelf with any of thefe Advantages; he daily faw her with more freedom than any of the other Princes that were educated in the *Ethiopian* Court; and the King, who dearly lov'd him, gave him a more free and familiar accefs to his Daughter than any of the reft. She gladly admitted him a Companion to her Sport: And though he had already a folidity that over-topp'd his years, yet his affection had
found

found the way to fweeten the moft ferious and important employments; he paffed all his Evenings with her, and in the day-time upon her Walks; but ftill kept himfelf about her with fo profound a reverence, that he took no other advantage from the Princefs's civility, to licenfe the declaration of what he felt, but by his fighs, his paffionate looks, and his actions full of extraordinary complacency.

The Princefs (young as fhe was) was not yet fo innocent, but fhe had already begun to difcern a difference between Actions of Civility, and fuch as parted from another motive; and (as her knowledge furmounted her age) fhe obferved part of that in my Prince, which his own mouth durft not bewray.

Cefario, by his excellent parts, was already become the darling of the *Ethiopian* Court. He was grown fo accomplifh'd in all thofe fervices and exercifes, to which he had given marvellous beginnings in *Egypt*, that he was look'd upon as a Perfon of moft refined qualities; neverthelefs, I am bound to confefs, that there was a Youth of his age at *Meroe*, which my Judgment tells me was no way inferiour, but in Birth; and indeed fince fome remarkable events will have him mingled with my Prince in his Hiftory, he doth merit a particular mention, and cannot without injuftice be deprived of that which is due, even from his Enemies.

Among a great number of Servitors, of which the Princefs's houfhold was compos'd, there were divers young Men particularly dedicated to her fervice, that always kept near her Perfon, but at fuch times when Women only had accefs; thefe were always ready to receive her Commands, took care of her Divertifements, and for that

they

they were particularly employ'd; for the most part they were of Noble Extraction, chosen by the King from the best Families of the Realm, and from some strangers that came thither to inhabit.

Among these the young *Britomarus* appear'd with wondrous Advantage, and though he was the Son of a Stranger, who for many years had made his residence in *Ethiopia*, and it was something difficult to prove his Nobility; yet the qualities of his Person prevail'd with the King to pass by that consideration: Indeed, I never beheld a person better shaped, neither for Body nor Mind; he had a most comely proportion; in his Face there was that rare mixture of sweetness and gravity; his Eyes full of a sparkling liveliness; but in his Air, Port, and Actions, he bore it out with a garb so fierce and haughty, that he seemed to be sensible of nothing less than his own base and obscure Birth: And though his knowledge taught him submission to such as he believed had right to a legitimate Obedience, he could never bow to those who had no other pretence to command over him, but such as their Birth or Fortune gave them. He lived with his Companions, as if he had been their Master; and though there were some among them of the most considerable Houses of *Ethiopia*, yet he never regarded any but for their Vertue; only to the Princess he was most flexibly officious, and when any particular service was requisite, he never could suffer, but with much regret, that any of his fellows should be employ'd.

This Youth was near about the age of *Cæsario*; but he quickly cherished an aversion against him, a part of which I believe (considering the qualities that got him the esteem of others) his

Nature

Nature contributed; but there were ftronger reafons to exafperate him againft my Prince, that in the end tranfported him to things that merit the re-cital, and fuch as have obliged me to give fome-thing too curious a defcription of a perfon of his condition.

My Prince one day entred the Palace-Garden, to go look for the Princefs, and in croffing an Al-ley, he met young *Britomarus*, who had gotten a Nofegay in his hand, with intent to prefent it to the Princefs; *Cefario* perceiving it to be a fair one, defir'd to make this prefent himfelf, and for that reafon ftaying *Britomarus*, ' I pray thee, *faid he*, ' beftow that Nofegay upon me, that I may give ' it to the Princefs.

' My Lord, *anfwered* Britomarus, it was for ' that defign I made it, and do intend to prefent ' myfelf, if you pleafe to permit it. For that, ' *replied the Prince*, you may get another, but ' muft needs confent that I may give her this, and ' I affure you fhe fhall know it came from you.

Britomarus could not well refufe my Prince's demand, well knowing how high his credit ftood with the King; but he obeyed him with an acti-on that plainly told him with what repugnance he did it. *Cefario*, inftead of being offended at his behaviour, efteem'd his courage, and, to appeafe his difpleafure, would have reftor'd him his Nofe-gay, if he had not fuddenly left him, and fhortly after quitted the Garden : He would have call'd him back, forry to do him fuch a petty injury, if I had not diffuaded it, telling him, that *Britoma-rus* was not a perfon confiderable enough for him to value his difpleafure ; but this was not the only encounter wherewith my Prince gave him caufe of complaint. As *Britomarus* was the for-wardeft undertaker among all his Companions,

fo

so he still carried away the chief employment for the Princess's Service; wherewith, while he was often busied, *Cesario* entring the Chamber, and envying the honour was done him, would oft take the Work out of his hands, and so constrain him to leave the place; but he always did it with such a reluctance, as made the print of itself upon his visage. This behaviour did not provoke young *Cesar* against him, though the Eye of his affection often looked upon the other's officious forwardness about *Candace*, not without some Jealousy: but besides that, he was of a most sweet disposition, and far from doing the least injury; the obscure condition of *Britomarus* hindred him from heeding any occasions that might kindle displeasure; for he was remote from any imagination that his resentments sprang from the true motive, that caused them; and suspected not the young Man of any other ambition than to raise his Fortunes.

In the mean time my Prince's fire burnt inward, without daring to give his passion vent, though his face and actions plainly told what he suffer'd. At last, after a long contestation, he gave fire to the Train; the first time he attempted it, was in the Temple of the Sun, where the Princess being at her Devotion, *Cesario* approached to the place where she kneeled, and standing a long time behind her, let her go on in her Prayers, without interruption; but at last turning her head she spy'd him, and sweetly reproving the faintness of his zeal, invited him to bear her company in her Devotion. The Prince presently obey'd her, and prostrating himself behind her, *I bend* ' my knees, *said he*, as you command; but the ' Gods must pardon me, if I say it is you, as ' the chief Divinity, I must ever adore.

At these Words he let fall his Eyes, and the Princess signified by a blush, that she was not such a novice as not easily to apprehend the meaning: And being already confirm'd in the truth by *Cæsario's* gesture, she would fain have dissembled, as if she had not understood him: But her blushes betray'd her, and the confusion that seized her would not suffer a reply; her silence made the Prince a little more hardy, and desirous to put a progress to this beginning, he recover'd his discourse, and without removing his Eyes from the Earth, ' If you refuse my Ado-
' rations, *said he*, you do not imitate the Gods,
' whom you commanded me to pray to; in their
' Presence I protest, that the resentments I have
' for you cannot strike sail to the respect I owe
' to them: *Madam*, let me then be suffer'd to
' avow this in their Temple; I confess it is a
' presumption, and the thoughts that ripen'd it
' too soaring to hope for pardon from a less
' goodness than yours; but I have kept them
' cover'd with a whole year's silence, and should
' not now have adventur'd to let them go, had it
' been longer possible to hide them; if you find
' ought in it to be condemn'd, to you I will not
' dare to excuse it, nor alledge any other justifi-
' cation than the violence yourself has done me;
' against which, greater forces than mine are not
' capable of resistance.

Doubtless he had said more, if the Princess had not interrupted him. This language could not justly offend, coming from a Prince, that by the greatness of his Birth, and the qualities of his Person, might dispute priority with all the Princes on Earth: Besides, his tongue said nothing that she had not read before in his actions; neverthe-less, this unmasking did a little surprize her; and

not

not willing to suffer him to go on, ' I am sorry
' *said she*, you should interrupt my Prayers with
' language I cannot like, and henceforth you shall
' do well to find other subjects for discourse. If
' I have displeas'd you, *reply'd the Prince*, I will
' not repine to endure the punishment you shall
' ordain, and if I have been so unfortunate to
' kindle your anger, by discovering thoughts full
' of veneration and respect, I shall think nothing
' too unjust or rigorous, to expiate the offence I
' have committed.

' 'Tis not for me, *answer'd* Candace, to ap-
' point punishments for Princes of your extracti-
' on; I have only right to complain of the dis-
' pleasure you have done me, in holding a dis-
' course which I neither understand nor approve.

She pronounced these Words with such a serious coldness, as the Prince durst venture no more
replies; and receiving the Anguish, which Can-
dace's displeasure had given him, at the Centre of
his Heart, he retir'd with a Countenance so sad
and troubled, as almost put his Face out of knowledge: and I think this grief had gone further,
if at the recital which he made of his Adventure,
my counsel had not stopp'd it, by representing, that
he had no cause to afflict himself; but that in all
likelihood he could not hope a more favourable
answer from the Princess, who before had never
heard any Language of that nature. *Cesario* drew
comfort from my Words, and resolved this first
repulse should not disarm his courage.

In the mean time he liv'd with her after the
same manner he had done formerly, and inter-
mitted not the payment of his observances full
of respect and discretion; but she appeared to
him more reserv'd than usual, call'd him not so
freely to her Recreations, and her Walks; and
I 2   though

though she still continued to him her first Civilities; yet she kept him off from occasions to renew the discourse that had displeas'd her: But if his tongue was mute, his Eyes and Actions became Orators so eloquent, that though her tender years had contributed less understanding than she had, she would have needed no other interpretation of the respect that ty'd his Tongue, and might easily perceive that my Prince his passion, instead of abating, daily took a greater inflammation from her coldness: And in this condition he was with her, when there arriv'd a memorable accident that merits your attention.

At a solemn Feast that was celebrated at *Meroe*, upon the Princess's Birth-day without the City, there were made most magnificent Courses on Horse-back, at which the King, with the most eminent Nobility assisted; the young Courtiers were engag'd for this exercise, where they appear'd in all the bravery they could make; they ran arm'd at all points, and in the Course launc'd their Javelins against a mark; and made divers other active trials of their force and dexterity: *Cesario* was enter'd his seventeenth year; and being already strong enough to make a stout performance in all manly exercises, presented himself into the Lists, clad in gallant Armour which the King had given him; his Casque was shaded with white and black Feathers, he was mounted upon a Horse white as Snow, which he manag'd with an admirable grace and agility. This was the first time I saw him in Armour, and methought he became it so gracefully, as my Eyes could not be satisfied with a spectacle so agreeable. The King, Princess, with the whole Court, fastened their regards upon him with marvellous hopes; and possibly the whole Assembly yielded

but

but one Person, whose affection he had not attracted. Before the Courses began, all the young
Gallants presented themselves before the Ladies
they lov'd, and publickly demanded their Favours, and upon such an occasion they were
hardly permitted to refuse them: There was
scarce any that did not obtain of their Mistresses,
either Knots, Scarfs, Bracelets, or other Presents
of that nature; only *Britomarus* made no address, but stood almost alone at the foot of the
Scaffold, where the King, the Princess, with the chief
of the Ladies were seated, without expressing the
least desire of what the other so eagerly entreated: he
had purchased so high an estimation at Court, that
divers persons became interessed in his coldness;
and the King himself having caused him to be call'd,
demanded the reason why he sought not to gain some
Favour, as well as his Companions, to shew his
activity in honour of her whom he best affected.

The bold youth lifted up his head at the King's
demand, and beholding him with a bravely assured look, ' Sir, *said he*, I have lived till now
' among all the Ladies of your Court, without par-
' ting with my Liberty; and though I have ho-
' noured them all as I thought, I have made no
' single present of my Heart to any, nor indeed
' am I willing to bestow it: I am entirely vow-
' ed to the Princess's service, to whom your Ma-
' jesty has done me the honour to give me, and
' though I ought to look upon her as a Subject
' and domestick Servitor, I hope she will pardon
' me if I take the Liberty to protest before her,
' that I will not ask a Favour from any but her-
' self: I never had other aim but at her service,
' since I was made happy in my dedication to it;
' and, if I may not enter the Lists under her
' Cognizance, I am resolved to beg no other's,

I 3   While

While young *Britomarus* spake in this manner; the boldness of this Action became the wonder of all that stood near him: This raised a cry among them, which re-doubled his assurance, and, swelling with the flatteries of those Acclamations, he advanced to the Princess's Seat, and throwing himself at her Feet, 'If your Highness, *said* 'he, will vouchsafe to honour the meanest of 'your Servitors with some badge of your Beauty, 'I dare promise that there is not a person in this 'company able to dispute the Prize of this day, 'nor to carry away the Victory in any kind of 'Combat I shall undertake for your Service.

The words and behaviour of *Britomarus* were diversly receiv'd by the company; many of the assistants consuted them as inconsiderate and over-bold; and some excused his Youth, and imputed it to that true height of Courage, that had shewn itself in all his other Actions. Of this number was the King himself, who, instead of checking the young Man's confidence, witnessed, that he approved it, and commanded the Princess to bestow something on him: *Candace* was ready to obey, when my Prince, who regarded *Britomarus* his Action, with thoughts very different from the rest, and felt himself stung with Jealousy at the young Man's hardy demand, could not suffer the honour was intended him; and conceiving the Princess's favour due to none but himself, was loath that a person so much below him, should carry away advantages, which he durst not petition for; and, in the heat of this thought, approaching the Princess, and bending his Knee before her; 'I was not bold enough, Madam, *said* 'he, to aspire to the grace *Britomarus* has demanded, deeming myself unworthy of it, as 'doubtless he is: But if you must stoop to bestow

'it

'it on one of us, I hope I may believe that my hopes
'have the fairer Title, and will not come behind
'him in defending that glory in all our Combats.

The Prince had no sooner spoke, but his desire
was granted, and the King not permitting the
Princess to reply, 'Give the Prince *Cleomedon*
'a Favour, *said he*; *Britomarus* must not dis-
'pute his pretences; and to satisfy him, command
'some of your Maids to give him a Present.

If these Words seem'd cruel to *Britomarus*, they
were as pleasing to the Prince, who receiving a
Bracelet of Jewels from *Candace*'s hands, after he
had kiss'd it with abundance of respect, mounted
on Horse-back with a transport of contentment,
and presently put himself in the head of those
that were to begin the Courses.

Britomarus was call'd to receive a Gift offer'd
him by *Artimis*, one of the Princess's Maids; but he
would not vouchsafe to look upon her; but leaping on his Horse in a furious discontent, convey'd
himself out of the company, without so much as
entring the List.

The Courses began, of which I shall pass
particular Descriptions, and be content to tell
you, that my Prince behav'd himself with so
much active strength and bravery, as he asto-
nish'd the whole Assembly, eclips'd the repute of
all the rest, and confirm'd the King and Court
in the pregnant hopes they had entertain'd of
him; after a great part of these Exercises were
finished, my Prince, desirous to breathe a while,
and withdrawing about one hundred paces from
the Prease, to the fresh Air, he spied *Britomarus* leaning against a Tree, and looking upon
the manly sport his Companions made, in the posture of a Man much afflicted. Though his carriage had displeased the Prince, yet the rejection

I 4   he

he had procur'd him, and the esteem of his good
qualities, with the grief his looks confest at the affront was done him, exchang'd his Jealousy for Pity: In fine, his excellent nature could not give
him leave to see his affliction, and himself the
Author of it, without endeavouring to give him
the redress of some comfort. With this resolution
he softly gallops up to him, spies his Face covered with Tears, and him in a condition sad enough
to require a just compassion. 'What *Britomarus,*
' *said he,* in Tears? Is it possible so great a Spi-
' rit (the marks of which we have acknowledged)
' can descend to weep for so trivial a cause of dis-
' pleasure? Yes, my Lord, *answered Britomarus,*
' I do weep, and I should weep Tears of Blood,
' for the injustice of my Fortune, that exposes
' me to miseries my Courage cannot brook. And
' have you no greater subjects of sorrow *reply'd*
' *the Prince,* than those we know of? No, my
' Lord *said Britomarus,* yet those are strong enough
' to drag me to my Grave, since Heaven, in giving
' me Courage, has not given me a Birth that
' will permit me to make use of it. I am born,
' my Lord, with an Heart as big as yours, and
' possibly thoughts about it that look as high,
' only Fortune has put a difference betwixt us,
' which it may be Virtue intended not: From
' this blind chance you daily take commissions to
' wrong me, and my condition ordains me to
' suffer it; you have oft provoked me with shame
' and displeasure, which though respect hath taught
' me to pocket without complaint, my Spirit
' could not learn to support it without sinking
' under sadness. Had I taken these injuries from
' a person with whom I might have measured
' my Sword, (wherewith I one day expect to
' reap some glory) you should soon see this dis-
' content

' content difpell'd that clouds my brow ; but
' fince I am abus'd by a Prince, from whom I
' cannot hope that fatisfaction, I will turn my
' Sword againft my own Breaft, and punifh the
' ambition there, for lifting its head fo high above
' my extraction.

While *Britomarus* fpoke in this manner, the
young Prince heard him with admiration, and
thought he found fomething in his Words that
tafted of an unweighed irregular ambition, yet
he took notice of a Spirit fo bravely daring, as
he could not difapprove it : But withal, clearly
difcovering his intentions, and (not willing to
fmother his own) he anfwered him with a ferious coldnefs : ' I did believe, *Britomarus*, that our
' diftance in quality did forbid all competition
' betwixt us ; that you need not have afflicted your-
' felf for fome Advantages I have feiz'd, which
' to my thinking, you ought not to difpute ; and
' this perchance has made me pafs by that cir-
' cumfpection which I would preferve with my
' Life, not to injure perfons of Courage : I am
' forry I have offended you, and really to wit-
' nefs that I am fo, I will not feek excufe in my
' condition, to refufe that fatisfaction that may
' content you ; I will grant that to your Courage,
' which your Birth could not fuffer you to hope,
' and poffibly may make you know, that Fortune
' has not put all the difference betwixt us.

' Ah ! my Lord, *cry'd the young* Britomarus,
' *ravifh'd with joy,* now you prove yourfelf a
' perfect Prince ! Poor *Britomarus* is a debtor to
' your Noblenefs, for the honour you proffer : My
' Lord, I accept it with more gladnefs than I
' would do the gift of a Crown, and will no
' otherwife ufe the favour, than to let you fee, that
' he that durft not demand it, was not wholly
' un-

I 5

' unworthy of it: And since you have offered it
' with so much generosity, I cannot slight an oc-
' casion that proposes so glorious a remedy, for
' the displeasures you have made me resent. Let
' us go then, *reply'd the Prince, beginning to be*
' *angry*, and if you desire this consolation, let us
' fly the sight of such persons that may hinder it.
' Our Arms are equal, for I would be loath to
' use any advantage which you want.' At these
Words, he spurred away from the company, and
Britomarus hastily following with a fierce joy,
they soon lost the sight of the Assembly. Yea,
they were loath to stay near it; and the Prince,
unwilling to be interrupted in the first essay of his
Manhood, ran on about fifty or sixty Furlongs
further, till they came into a Valley where none
could discover them.

There *Cesario* stopp'd, finding the place commodious, and turning again towards *Britomarus*,
' We will go no further, *said he*, let us give our
' Horses a little breath, and then end our difference.
' *Britomarus* his courage was so high flown, as it
would not permit him to make an answer; and
suffering his Horse to breath a-while, he beheld
the Prince with Eyes that spoke nought but defiance. The age of both was equal, their stature
little different, and this the first time that either
had worn Arms: They had both Javelins in their
right hands, and Swords at their left; their Horses
were both good, both chosen for the solemn Exercise of that day; scarce had they patience to give
them leisure to breathe, when after a loud defiance, they lanced their Javelins at one another,
with a force so impetuous, as scarce was ever
more fury shown by any of the rudest hands that
ever were inur'd to the Trade of War, which
they then but began to practise: Their Javelins
were

were both shivered upon their Shields into a thousand pieces; and the young Combatants passed by one another, without the least staggering in their seats; but they soon return'd with their drawn Swords, as yet unused to this imployment, and advancing them in the Air, with an action bravely menacing, turning their Horses heads, they flew the second time at one another, more eagerly than before: The first blows drew Blood, and the second made two deep wounds: *Britomarus* was run through the left Arm, and *Cesario* in the Thigh. Never did two young Lions see their own blood drop from the Hunter's Spear, with a rage more violent than that of my Prince, and the ambitious *Britomarus*. They equally breathed Vengeance and Victory, and rushed together with so lavish a fury, that if the Gods (like them) had forsook the care of their lives, their practice in Arms had there begun and ended together. They had each received another slight wound, when my Prince coming close up, laid hold on *Britomarus* his Arm, and he not refusing to close with a like intention, streightly ingaged him in his; and thus locking one another in friendless embrace, and putting spurs to their Horses, they fell both to the Earth, where they began to rowl o'er each other with a most dreadful fury; sometimes one was uppermost, and then the other, yet neither could keep the mastery: But in this struggling they lost so much blood, that at last both rising by a joint consent, they were scarce able to hold their Swords; however, in that staggering condition they fell to fresh blows, and doubtless would have ended their Combat, and possibly both their Lives; for as yet there appear'd no advantage on either side, when we happily arriv'd to stop the mischief.

Their

Their sudden departure had given us some outrage: We were far from suspecting *Britomarus* his rashness: But, as faithful care would seldom suffer me to keep my Eye from my Prince, I had no sooner learn'd in what manner he departed, but without stay, mounting my Horse, I ran after him with all the company I could engage, and we came, as I told you, in a happy time to part these young Combatants, whom we found in an estate that spake our arrival very necessary.

So soon as *Cæsario* saw me, he even sobb'd with grief to see himself interrupted, and suspecting (not without likelihood) that we would do *Britomarus* some outrage, he put himself before him in a posture of defence, and crying out to me as I first came in; ' Father, *said he*, as you tender ' my Life, do not hurt *Britomarus*; it was I ' that first assail'd him, I compell'd him to de- ' fend himself, and I will rather suffer death, ' than him to be injur'd. I will defend myself ' as well as I can, *said the fierce young Man*, for ' it is not fit I should hold it of you, having ' done my utmost to take away yours.' These generous and gallant Words on both sides gave us new wonder; in the mean time having taken care, according to my Prince his desire, that *Brito-marus* should not suffer, we hastily lighted from our Horses, and ran to the two Combatants, just as they were ready to fall to the ground with weakness: I snatch'd my Prince in my Arms, and wetted his Face with my Tears; but whilst I was helping him on Horse-back, and getting up myself behind him, he desired the same office might be done to *Britomarus*: And not only content to take that care of him, he made *Neander* get up in my place, and sent me before to the King to beg the young Man's Pardon, and to protest,

teft, that he would never come in his Prefence till he had granted it. I obey'd his command, but found it not fo eafy a task to reverfe the King's refolution, who had abfolutely defigned *Britomarus* for punifhment; but at laft he granted mercy, upon condition, that fo foon as his wounds were healed, he fhould leave the Court, and never more return, upon forfeit of his Life.

In the mean time, my Prince was conducted to his Lodgings, prefently put to Bed, and fearched by Surgeons; his wounds were found not dangerous, only the lofs of Blood had done him the greateft Mifchief: And after the Application of fome neceffary Remedies, they enjoined him a filent Repofe, without any Difturbance, till the next Day.

In the mean time, the Fruit of his generous Gallantry fpread itfelf in a Moment; and the Relation of *Britomarus* himfelf to his Friends, of the Bravery and Noblenefs of his Behaviour, fill'd the whole Court with Admiration. Oh how gladly I drank up his Praifes from every Mouth! how fweetly was my Fear and Difpleafure vanquifhed that his Wounds had given me! the Gentlenefs and Grandeur of that firft Action made me gladly conclude him worthy to be what he was; and though I blamed the Prince for that Paffage, to prevent future Hazards by the like, yet I did it in fuch Terms, as gave him a clear Difcovery that I could not difapprove it.

So foon as the Surgeons would permit him to be feen, the King came to vifit him; and after he had exprefs'd the Intereft he took in his Recovery, with Words full of Affection, he fell a commending that Action, as indeed it merited, and yet in fome fort gently blam'd him, by the Confequence of an Intreaty, no more; with fo carelefs

a

a Valour, to hazard the Son of *Cæsar* and *Cleopa-*
tra, against a Man of *Britomarus*'s Condition.

The King was scarce parted from him, when,
by his own Orders, the Princess his Daughter came
to visit him; but at that Sight his Joy was so excessive, as his Wounds had like to have broke
loose; and by the change of his Countenance,
had they but mark'd it, they might easily know
what his Heart meant by it. The fair Princess,
having taken a Seat by his Bed's Side, accepted his
Thanks for her Visit with a majestick Modesty,
her Answer expressing, in very obliging Terms, the
Grief she took of his Hurts. This conducted
Cæsario's Passion into the Scene; for, perceiving
the Princess's Attendants keep themselves at a distance, through Respect, 'Madam, *said he*, it
' was but just that I should buy your Favours
' with the Blood they have cost me; but had I
' added all that is left in my Veins, to what is
' already gone, it would not have paid for the
' meanest Part of them.' 'I am sorry, *said*
' *Candace*, the King should command me to give
' you so dangerous a Present, which at best has
' cost you some Blood, too precious to spill for
' so mean a Toy.' 'You undervalue that, *said*
' *Cæsar's Son*, that the most ambitious Princes
' would prefer to Empires: But might I dispute
' this Subject against any other but yourself, the
' World has not a Person from whom I would
' not force a Confession, that all Things else, tho'
' of the highest Value, become worthless and con-
' temptible, when compar'd with the Princess
' *Candace*'s Favours; and indeed it should teach
' me a higher Pride, if your own free Choice,
' without the King's Command, had bestow'd it,
' and it had not only been the Child of Obedi-
' ence. Madam, I know this Desire has too
' much

' much Ambition, but I am grown too weak to
' repulse it ; and if it has kindled your Displeasure,
' Madam, behold me in an Estate to quench it
' with the rest of my Blood that is left, and so
' make my Life the Expiation.

' I demand no such Reparation, *said the Prin-*
' *cess,* as you offer for the Offence ; your Life is
' not priz'd so low, but we can rather chuse to
' suffer something from you, than put that in
' hazard ; but I should take it well at your Hands,
' would you turn the Tide of your Discourse up-
' on another Subject, and not oblige me to hear
' that which must make my Visits less frequent.

These Words came so seriously from her, that
the Prince began to fear indeed he had displeased ;
and from that Thought, ' If either my Discourse
' or Action, *said he,* have made me so wretched
' to urge your Displeasure, I do here vow to pu-
' nish myself with a Rigour that shall satisfy
' your Anger ; the Gods raised *Britomarus* to
' call to an account my unjust Ambition, for
' teaching my Eyes such aspiring Looks : But if
' his Arm was not strong enough to do it alone,
' I will enforce the Justice of his Quarrel by the
' Assistance of my own : And since it is a Rash-
' ness worthy of your Anger, to speak of a Pas-
' sion you cannot brook, I am resolv'd to doom
' my Tongue to an eternal Silence.

The Prince put such a passionate Action to these
Words, as it soften'd *Candace* to some Pity ; and
not willing, with a harsh Reply, to exasperate his
Afflictions, ' I have already told you, *said she,*
' that I desire no such cruel Reparations of you,
' and do tell you again, that it behoves you to
' mind your Recovery, in a Place where none can
' with you ill.

She

She had gone further, if the Arrival of divers Perfons, who then entered the Chamber, had not interrupted the Difcourfe; among whom was *Tyribafus*, the King's Favourite, or rather the fecond King of *Ethiopia*, whom, though I have not yet mention'd, muft make up a principal Part in the Progrefs of this Hiftory.

This Man was of illuftrious Extraction among the *Ethiopians*, of a great Courage, and a greater Ambition; comely of Perfon, dexterous in every thing he undertook, and indeed worthy to fit where Fortune had placed him; his Credit with the King, was not greater than with the Soldiery, in whofe Hearts he had got the Power (by commanding them in feveral warlike Expeditions) of an abfolute Difpofal. In fine, he was the chief Man of *Ethiopia*; and though others were born nearer to the Crown, their Authority not only fell fhort of his, but was entirely ftrangled by it; and, as then there being no Diffention between my Prince and he, knowing that the King defir'd it, he appear'd his Friend, and at that time gave him a very civil Vifit; where, after he had ftaid with him till the Princefs withdrew; he attended her back to her Lodgings: After this, my Prince often faw her, while his Wounds confined him to his Bed, without gaining the leaft Intelligence by her Difcourfe how to faften any Judgment upon his Fortune, or know what was hid within her Breaft.

And now he had left his Bed, and was refolv'd the next Day to quit the Chamber; when one came to tell him, that *Britomarus* (whofe Recovery had been as forward as his) was at the Door, and defir'd Permiffion to fee him. We much diffuaded this Interview, fufpecting that *Britomarus* whofe defperate Rage had fo lately made the

Danger

Danger of it known) had carried some Design against the Prince's Life; but he knew his Heart better than we, and not having Power to distrust him, commanded us to conduct him in,

Britomarus enter'd the Chamber with a Visage something pale, and his Arm in a Scarf; but with a Countenance so noble, and so bravely assur'd, that, in spight of Prejudice, it even wrested both Esteem and Affection from us: *Cæsario* rose up to meet him, whom *Britomarus* having respectfully accosted, tho' with a very sad Look, 'My 'Lord, *said he*, I could not carry away myself 'from this Court, without leaving my Thanks 'behind me for the Favours you have made me 'receive; you have permitted me (a poor Soldier 'as I am) to draw my Sword against a Prince, 'defended me from the Fury of your Servants, 'and employ'd your Credit with the King to save 'my Life. These Obligations, great as they are, 'cannot make me your Friend; the Dishonour 'you have done me, and the Displeasure I resent 'to abandon a Place for your sake, where I had 'so strong a Tye, have forced my Disposition to 'oppose and resist it. Nor is it only to discharge 'my Heart of these Words, that has brought me 'to take my Leave of you; but to assure you, 'though I must be your Enemy, I shall diligent-'ly seek Occasion to be quit with your Genero-'sity. I am now going in quest of Glory, and 'possibly may find a Fortune in some other Coun-'try, that will be less ungrateful than this. I 'hope the Sword, which I had the honour to 'draw against you, will reap me Advantages that 'may permit me to see you again upon the same 'Occasion. My Heart tells me my Birth is not 'inferior to your's, and if it deceives me, I will 'punish the Falshood, by making it dig for that,

'in

‘ in a Mine of Danger, which my Extraction
‘ hath refused me : I have appear'd worthy to be
‘ scorn'd by the King of *Etbiopia*, the Princess
‘ his Daugher, and yourself; but I must presume
‘ to tell you, that none of you yet have known
‘ me, and I dare hope, one day, to appear in a
‘ Condition that may challenge a better Notice.

When he had ended these Words, and given a
respective Reverence to the Prince, without staying for an Answer, he departed the Chamber,
though the Prince call'd him back, and follow'd
to speak with him ; and, immediately mounting
his Horse, he quitted *Meroe*, with the *Ethiopian*
Court; and was never seen there since.

Tyridates stay'd *Eteocles* at this Passage : ‘ I
‘ am deeply deceived, *said he*, if I be not able to
‘ learn you News of this *Britomarus* you speak
‘ of ; and they are such, and so great, as I won-
‘ der they should miss the way to your Ear: But
‘ this merits a particular Discourse, and I will
‘ not interrupt your's.' *Eteocles* was going on
with his Story, when one told him the Queen
was awake, and had call'd for him, which made
him take leave of *Tyridates* for some Moments.
In the mean time, the Prince called for his Clothes,
and quitted his Bed, where *Eteocles*'s Story had
detained him longer than ordinary.

Hymen's

Hymen's Præludia :

OR,

Love's Master-Piece.

PART IV. BOOK I.

ARGUMENT.

The Sight of Alexandria *renews* Candace's *Complaints for her* Cæsar's *loss.* Tyridates *invites her to take the fresh Air, with the promise of a pleasant Walk ; where, preparing to go on with her Story, she is interrupted by the Arrival of a strange Knight, who is known by* Tyridates *to be* Coriolanus, *Prince of* Mauritania. *He ignorantly rescues* Zenodorus *from* Britomarus, *as he was ready to kill him : While the Knights fight, the* Pyrate *escapes.* Tyridates *interposes his Persuasions in vain. The Arrival of* Cæsario *disorders the Combat, and for a while makes it tripartite. His Cask is struck off by* Britomarus, *and* Candace *knows him. They are parted.* Zenodorus *returns with*

with twenty Horsemen, who assail the Knights while he carries away Candace. Britomarus *saves* Cæsario's *Life, who spurs away in pursuit of* Zenododrus. *The Pyrate's Men are all slain but three, by the prodigious Valour of the Combatants.* Candace *is miss'd by* Tyridates, *who engages the rest to join with him in pursuit of the Ravisher. Their Search proves vain, and they all return to* Tyridates's *House.*

F the fair Queen walk'd late that Day, it was not so much to be imputed to the Weariness of the former, as to her cruel Cares, that refused to be charmed by Sleep till Day was ready to break; the Consideration and Complaint of her Disasters had almost swallow'd the whole Night; and that Courage that had shewn itself great in all the Accidents of her Life, could not sometimes deny Homage to a Grief too just to be condemned. The Troubles of a Kingdom (either lost or very staggering) could not feed her Griefs so high, but the continual Fears for the loss of that which her Soul indulg'd, batter'd it with more Violence.

These just and cruel Apprehensions, not only drew Sighs from her Breast, but Laments from her Mouth, with a Brook of Tears from her fair Eyes, which they let fall in such abundance, as her Pillow was wholly steep'd in the Stream.

' Good Gods! *said she,* What are the Offen-
' ces have provoked your impetuous Rage against
' me? And what could a poor Maid commit
' worthy of so many Marks of your protracted
' Anger? Was it so great a Crime for *Candace*
' to love the Son of *Cæsar,* that the Loss of one
' of the fairest Crowns in the World, such unpa-
' rallel'd

' rallel'd Perfecutions of my Sex and Condition,
' with fo many dangerous Hazards that I have
' run both of my Life and Honour, could not
' expiate it; but I muft ftill be tortur'd with the
' remembrance of Perils, to which you have ex-
' pofed that which is more dear to me than my-
' felf? Alas! *continued fhe*, 'tis too probable my
' dear *Cæfar* lives not; for, if Heaven did not
' fend him particular Affiftance, he could not but
' be crufhed with fo many Dangers (joined with
' his Sorrow for my Lofs) that my malicious
' Fortune has thrown upon him: Ah! if it be
' fo, juft Heaven do not fuffer the wretched *Can-*
' *dace* to furvive him one Moment; fnatch her
' no more out of the Jaws of *Neptune*, nor the
' Hands of her Enemies, by a Refcue a thoufand
' Times more cruel than that Death from which
' you have guarded her.

The fair Queen had inlarged her Complaints,
if the Maid that lay with her, who had much Influence upon her, had not turn'd their Current by
the fweeteft Comforts fhe was able to apply. *Can-*
dace would hear her, both becaufe fhe dearly loved her, and befides, delighted to have her Mif-
fortunes flatter'd, and to ftay herfelf upon the
Hopes fhe gave her of the Recovery of her Empire,
and the Safety of *Cæfario*. And thus they wafted
the greateft Part of the Night, till, a little before
the birth of Day, Sleep came to becalm her Cares,
and drew the Curtains of her bright Eyes, which
fhe kept fhut about four or five Hours: At the
End of which, being awaked, and feeling no In-
difpofition that could perfwade her to lie ftill, fhe
caus'd *Clitie* to rife (that was the Name of her
Maid) and give her her Cloaths; a Part of which
when fhe had put on, fhe quitted her Bed, and
in that Eftate took fome turns in the Chamber;
at

at laft fhe opened a Window, whence the Eye
might freely fpread its View over the adjoyning
Sea, and the ftately City of *Alexandria*.

The Sight of that City (heretofore the Abode
and legitimate Inheritance of her dear *Cefario*)
awakened her Complaints, and after the Prologue
of two or three Sighs, tying her Eyes to thofe
proud Walls that *Alexander* built,

' Defolate *Alexandria*, *faid fhe*, fince thou
' haft loft thy faireft Ornaments; fince thy *An-*
' *thonies*, *Cleopatra's* and *Ptolomies*, dwell no
' longer with thee, but in thy Duft: Pompous
' and Triumphant as thou wert; thou doft now
' languifh under tyrannick Yoke. Oh! that I
' could at leaft repair Part of thy Loffes, in re-
' ftoring that to thee which thou gaveft to me:
' Within thy Bofom my young *Cæfar* firft faw
' the Light; to thee I owe the Education of his
' tendereft Years; and of thee I received him,
' with all thofe lovely Graces that he brought
' among us: And now I am come without him
' to thy forfaken Walls, to expofe myfelf to the
' Reproaches thou may'ft throw upon me, for ha-
' ving unjuftly detained him from thee. But par-
' don me, my beloved's native Soil, if I cannot
' reftore what myfelf hath loft: He is pull'd from
' me by the Cruelty of my Deftiny; and I bring
' thee as much of him as is poffible, by offering
' thee a Heart, where he ha▪ as lively and per-
' fect being as in that Place he now inhabits.
' Ah! my Eyes, *faid fhe*, (*wiping away fome*
' *Tears that had newly forced their Paffage*)
' muft every Object give a frefh warning to your
' Tears? Can you prefent nothing to my Imagi-
' nation, but what renews my Difquiets? Since
' you firft became Fountains, you have been fo
' lavifh of your Streams, as your Spring might
' well

" well be exhaust ; but you still over-flow as much
" as when my Miseries first alarm'd you: Ah !
" could my dear *Cesar* yet come and dry you up,
" I should delightfully remember with what Fide-
" lity you have kept me company in my Disgra-
" ces, and then how zealously should I bless the
" most dangerous and sad Occasions I have had,
" to witness of the Height of Affection? But alas !
" how uncertain are those Hopes! How cruel the
" Arms of our barbarous Enemies! And then how
" dangerous are you inconstant Billows that rowl
" before mine Eyes !

She had enlarged her Plaint ▓▓▓▓▓ these
sad Considerations to waste ▓▓▓▓▓▓▓ the
Day, had not *Clitie* interrupt▓▓▓▓▓▓ her
it was time to dress her, recei▓▓▓▓ *Tiri-*
dates, who could not fail to ▓▓▓▓▓ so
soon as she could be in a Condi▓▓▓ permit his
Visit. *Candace* came to herself at *Clitie's* Sollicitation, as one newly waked from a deep Sleep :
and regarding her with a languishing Eye : " I had
" abandoned myself, *said she*, to some melan-
" choly Thoughts, which the View of *Alexan-*
" *dria* had rouz'd within my Soul; and I assure
" myself, thou canst not (without some tenderness)
" cast thy Eye upon these Places where my belo-
" ved *Cesario* took his Birth. See, *said she*,
" (*opening the Window again*) look upon this
" same City, where the lamented *Cleopatra* deli-
" vered him to the World, where she nourished
" and brought him up to bestow upon me: And
" ah ! how gladly did I receive the rich Present
" of a Person so Illustrious? How tenderly and
" dearly would I have preserved him, whose ab-
" sence (and it may be utter Loss) I now regret
" with such violent Resentments.

The

The Queen would never have given over, still
finding fresh Subjects to entertain her Sorrows, if
Eteocles, advertiz'd by *Clitie*, had not enter'd the
Chamber; yet she would needs draw him to the
Window, to shew her (as well as the Distance
would permit him) all that might be discovered
of the Palace where the Prince was born and nourished: With such other Places as he and the rest
of his Royal Play-fellows (often mention'd to her
by *Eteocles*, in the Story of his Master's Youth)
had chiefly frequented in his greenest Years. After the Queen had allowed some Time to this
pleasing Employment, she made an end of dressing h....... when *Tyridates* understood, he
come .... good Morrow, and was met and
receiv......... with an Air full of Sweetness and
Majesty...........

' *Tyridates*, who was now grown acquainted
' with her Name and Condition, accosted her
' with all the Respect due to her Person and Dig-
' nity. You see, said the Queen, a Person very
' slothful, yet not altogether inexcusable, for ha-
' ving wearied out so many cruel Nights and Days
' without Repose: I assure myself you will not
' take it ill, that I have now tasted it from your
' Bounty.' ' Madam, would it please the Gods,
' said *Tyridates*, that I had Power to perform
' more than what this miserable Retreat can con-
' tribute, and you should soon know, that the
' most difficult and dangerous Occasions to serve
' you, would always be delightful to such as For-
' tune shall honour with the Employment.

' Indeed I ought not to expect less Generosity,
' replied the Queen, from a Prince of the *Arsa-*
' *cidæ*; for, 'tis so natural, that you cannot want
' it, without belying your Blood.' ' 'Tis true,
' said *Tyridates*, the House of *Arsaces* had a fair
' Stock

' Stock of vertuous Reputation, before the inhu-
' man *Phraates* diſhonoured it with his Cruel-
' ties; but it is now the infamous Shame of all
' Royal Families; nor do I believe that any can
' paſs a more gentle Thought upon it, without
' ſharing in the Guilt that is faſtened to it.' ' The
' Crime of *Phraates*, *ſaid the Queen*, cannot
' reach to you, the Spots of his Cruelty are ſolely
' limited in himſelf, and cannot ſo much as dim
' the Luſtre of your Virtue.

That fair Queen had gone on, if the Modeſty
of *Tyridates* would have ſuffered it; but interrupting her Diſcourſe, to change the Subject, he
demanded how ſhe had paſſed the Night. ' Could
' my Mind, *ſaid Candace*, have ſhared in the
' Repoſe you have given my Body, I ſhould ſay,
' by your means I have reſted well. But as the
' Troubles of my Soul have received no Comfort,
' but from your Aſſiſtance, I think I may ſay,
' I have number'd the tedious Hours of the Night
' with more unquiet than yourſelf.' ' The Gods
' preſerve you, *ſaid Tyridates*, from ſuch rack-
' ing Pains as drag my Days through eternal
' Death; for could your Apprehenſion but reach
' them, you would doubtleſs give them another
' Character.' ' I ſee well, *ſaid the Queen*, that
' *Eteocles* has not yet told you my Story, or has
' but related a few of the firſt Events.' ' 'Tis
' true, *ſaid Tyridates*, that I am yet but acquain-
' ted with the beginnings of it; for *Eteocles* has
' gone no farther than the generous Combat that
' the Prince *Cæſario* had with young *Britoma-*
' *rus*.' Then you have yet heard nothing of my
' Life, *ſaid the Queen*; but when you ſhall once
' know it, you will confeſs that I have Miſeries
' enough to match yours, and ſome to ſpare, ſuch
' as your Patience never traverſed. I am baniſh-

VOL. I.   K   ' ed

' ed as well as you from my native Country,
' possibly despoiled of a most flourishing Empire,
' separated, like you, from the Person I love,
' whom I left exposed to Dangers far greater than
' such as threaten *Mariamne*'s Life, such as Hea-
' ven itself cannot rescue him from, without a
' Wonder.

' These Calamities, *replied the afflicted Tyri-*
' *dates*, are very considerable, especially in the
' Person of so great a Queen as yourself. But
' your Majesty may permit me to tell you, that
' I have some too cruel to be pattern'd among the
' worst of yours. You are bereaved of that hap-
' py Person whom you have judged worthy of
' your Affection; but the Subjects of our Losses
' are very remote in Nature; I assure myself, that
' the Prince you love, does support the separation
' at least, with as much Impatience as you; and
' the Loss of you makes him outsigh you for his
' absence: Besides, your displeasures have not
' struck you in the most sensible Part, since the
' Blows you receiv'd came only from the rude
' Hand of Fortune, and not the Will of him you
' love: But Gods! how different is my Destiny?
' the only Will of *Mariamne* creates all my Mi-
' series; it was that banished me her Presence;
' and (which wounds me deepest) while I die for
' her, she does not so much as dream of me.
' Would Heaven that every raving Wave were my
' professed Enemy! that all the Arms of the Em-
' pire bent their Points at my Happiness! Nay,
' that every thing in Nature defiled me, on Con-
' dition *Mariamne* were for me, I would encoun-
' ter all their Traverses with Contempt, and either
' not feel them, or at least with an invincible Pa-
' tience sustain them: For as my Joys and Griefs
' are entirely dependent on her, so 'tis she alone

' can

' can make me Happy or Miferable: And from
' thofe that fpring from any other Source, in me
' they will find but little Senfibility.' ' I fee your
' Affection, *faid the Queen*, is truly worthy of
' yourfelf, and the Object it aims at: But if I
' miftake not, your Evils are not fo great as you
' have figured them, if they only depend on *Ma-*
' *riamne's* Will; my Thoughts tell me fhe yet
' loves you, and had not the Care of her Reputa-
' tion, with the fevere Rules of her Duty, lain
' too heavy in the other Balance, fhe would never
' have banifhed you her Prefence, but rather be-
' ftowed fome Proofs of her Acknowledgment up-
' on you, which fure fhe could not bridle with-
' out much conftraint: That laft Condefcenfion
' fhe granted in your Favour, when fhe fuffered
' you to fee her in the midft of fo many Dangers
' that menaced her, could not come from fuch a
' Perfon as *Mariamne* (who was never accufed of
' Levity or Imprudence) without the confent of
' Affection, which was all the Excufe fhe had
' for it: Nor do I believe her wholly exempt
' from that which your being divided makes you
' fuffer for her fake; and am confident fhe paffes
' not a Day wherein fhe calls you not into her
' Memory.' ' Ah! Madam, *cry'd the amorous*
' *Tyridates*, how agreeably you flatter me, and
' how neceffary is the Authority of fuch a Perfon
' as yourfelf, to perfuade that which Appearance
' could never manifeft; I am unworthy of the
' affection and remembrance of *Mariamne*, and
' the Gods can witnefs, I never cherifhed a Thought
' fo arrogant to believe I deferved them. Yet I
' cannot liften to your Difcourfe without fome
' Comfort, reprefenting to myfelf, that a Perfon
' fo Divine as you, cannot (like our common
' Spirits) be capable of Error.

This

This Difcourfe had been enlarged, had it not been interrupted by thofe that brought up the Queen's Dinner; *Tyridates* din'd with her, and fo did *Eteocles* and *Clitie*, becaufe they would have it fo; not being then either in Place or Condition to obferve the regular Method of all Ceremonies.

After Dinner, *Tyridates* told the Queen, that though the Place was defart and favage, it afford-ed fome unfrequented Walks not unpleafant, which gave her a defire to take the Air; when, after her Eyes had fpent fome time in turning over feveral Objects at the Window, fhe went out of the Houfe, propp'd by the Arm of *Tyridates*, and only follow'd by *Eteocles* and *Clitie*: They walk-ed a while upon the Downs, where their Eyes had liberty to converfe with the fucceffive Waves, and thofe wondrous Flows and Ebbs that had fo puz-led the Science of all Philofophers. But the Queen beginning to be wearied by the Sand, *Tyridates* led her down a very pleafant Valley, femi-circled on the one Side with divers Points of a Rock, cover'd with Mofs, and on the other Side with a little Wood; which joining crefcent-wife with the Extremes of the Rock, left a green Meadow in the Middle, beautify'd with divers Chryftal Fountains.

This Place agreed with the Queen's Inclination to Solitude; and fuiting her Intention to be pri-vate, fhe accepted that Invitation to difcourfe the reft of her Adventures to *Tyridates*; and fpying a Space between two Rocks, cover'd with Mofs, and framed by Nature into a Seat, fo fecretly con-triv'd, as it concealed them from the fight of any in the Meadow, though they might eafily difcern what pafs'd in any part of it, fhe fettled there, inviting *Tyridates* to fit by her, while *Clitie* and

Eteo-

Eteocles made choice of a Place to lie down in, some five or six Paces from their Miftrefs.

After the fair Queen had been a while filent, fhe look'd upon *Tyridates* with a little Blufh, that with a glad Ambition was newly climb'd into her Cheeks; 'If I give you the Relation of my Life, ' *faid fhe,* I muft be obliged to uncover fome ' Follies, which the precife Rules of Modefty ' would keep conceal'd; but as it is not juft, that ' I fhould either ferve myfelf of your Affiftance, ' or demand your Counfel in Affairs whereof you ' are ignorant, I fhall freely give you the naked ' Account of my Life, with that Adventure that ' conducted me into this Country; and, in fine, ' crave your Advice about the fitteft Order to be ' obferved for the Compofure of my Affairs, and ' Security of my Perfon.' 'I fhall always be ' more able to ferve you in Perfon than Counfel, ' *reply'd Tyridates,* being very incapable of di- ' recting a Perfon of fo much Prudence as your- ' felf; however, I fhall employ (fince you ordain ' it fo) all the Judgment is left me, without ex- ' pecting the Trouble of this Relation from your ' Majefty, which I may as well learn from the ' Mouth of *Eteocles,* and fo efcape a Solecifm in ' Civility.

Candace was about to reply, and had difpofed herfelf to take up the Story where *Eteocles* let it fall; when they were interrupted by a Noife of Horfes, which trod very near, and gave warning to their Eyes to look about them; which they had no fooner done, but they efpy'd two Men on Horfe-back coming out of the Wood into the Meadow; the chief of the two that appeared the Mafter, quickly drew the Regard both of the Queen and *Tyridates,* as well upon the Beauty of his Arms, as his graceful Deportment on his

Horfe : The Ground of his Armour was black,
but very richly gilt, fet round with Rubies of great
Value, and in all the other Places moft remarkable ; the Plates of Steel that were below his
Taffes, reached to his Knee; and thofe upon his
Arms, to his Elbow, which were of the fame Materials and Workmanfhip.   His Horfe was black,
with fome white Spots upon him; but then all
white with his own Froth, which his Pride and
Courage had newly drefs'd him in.   His 'Squire
carried the Shield, of the fame Materials with the
reft of his Arms, on which he bore a Crocodile,
with a Motto under it of the *Roman* Tongue.

In this Equipage, leaping a little Hay, he enter'd the Meadow, with intent to let his Horfes
feed there, while himfelf took fome Repofe; and
alighting from his Horfe, his Approach gave *Ty-*
ridates and the Queen a more perfect Defcription of the Beauty of his Shape, which appeared
with an admirable Proportion; all his Geftures,
and every Action fo becoming, as it faften'd their
Eyes upon him with a more ferious Regard; but
their Satisfaction was much improv'd, when (the
better to refrefh himfelf) he took off his Cafque
and gave it to his 'Squire, lending them a fight
of his unarmed Head and difcovered Face, which
made them confefs they had never feen one better
fhaped among all the Perfons of his Sex; all the
Lines of it fo evenly regular, as it was too hard
for the skilfulleft Defire to mend any thing about
it ; his Complexion was fomething brown, his
Eyes black, but full of fuch a fparkling Vivacity,
as it required a fteady Eye to behold them, without fhrinking at the Luftre ; his Hair of the fame
Colour, being very long, and curling naturally,
fell in large Annulets upon his Shoulders : In fine,
his whole Compofure carry'd fo compleat a Sym-
metry,

metry, as it would have pofed Envy's felf to have found fault.

This Stranger, (fuch, and much better than my Words have copied him) after he had fet his Horfe at liberty, fought a Place to lie down on, and difcharge fome Wearinefs he had lately contracted in a long Voyage; and, to favour their Curiofity, Fortune led him to the choice of a Place very near the Corner of their Rock, which, though it hid him from their Eyes, yet it could not hinder their over-hearing the Difcourfe betwixt him and his 'Squire; who, after he had taken care of the Horfes, laying his Shield, Cafque, and two Javelins in readinefs, came and laid down at his Feet, and defir'd him, if it were poffible, to releafe his Griefs to an Hour of Reft: 'For, 'Sir, *faid he*, I think no Force, no Health but 'your's, could have ftood the rude Shock of fuch 'violent Pains as you have fuffer'd; nor can you 'long refift it, if you perfevere in this cruel man- 'ner of tormenting yourfelf.

The Mafter, fetching two or three deep Sighs (as a Prologue to his Anfwer) 'Ceafe, dear *Emi- 'lius, faid he*, to trouble thyfelf for a Life which 'is not worth the Pains thou takeft about it, and 'which I cannot regard but as my deadlieft Ene- 'my. I lov'd it once, when it was near to *Cleo- 'patra*; but now fhe has refus'd an Intereft in 'it, I abandon it to Defpair as well as fhe.' 'But, 'my Lord, *reply'd the faithful 'Squire*, to what 'then ferves that undaunted Courage, which (fur- 'mounting the Growth of your unripe Years) 'hath carried you to fuch a Height of Reputa- 'tion? To what your Study in Philofophy, 'which you beftowed fome of your budding Age 'upon, with fuch a rare Succefs?' 'My Cou- 'rage and Philofophy, *faid he*, indeed have help-

K 4   'ed

' ed me to support that with some Moderation,
' which, possibly, without their Succour, would
' have forced the Effects of Fury and Transport,
' as well as those of Folly ; that, in all likelihood,
' Report was carried to the Limits of the *Roman*
' Empire : But they cannot cure a Disease of this
' nature, without stripping my Soul of that sen-
' sitive Faculty, of which herself is in part com-
' posed : The Advantages I have gain'd above
' others that wanted my Education, to dissuade
' me from repining against the Gods, from de-
' spairing of their Goodness, and holds my Hands
' from falling foul upon Subjects of Innocence,
' upon which the Tempests of my Grief (without
' their Assistance) might possibly throw me ; but
' they cannot hinder me from sighing, lamenting,
' and proving myself a Man, by afflicting myself
' with Causes of Affliction, as I was formerly
' abused into an Opinion of Happiness by an Im-
' posture of Prosperity ; and, wouldst thou call to
' mind, in what manner I resisted Affronts con-
' siderable enough, when they sprang from other
' Causes than the Will of my ungrateful Princess,
' thou wilt remember, that neither Courage nor
' Moderation fail'd me.　What I suffer'd by the
' cunning Malice of *Tiberius*, the tyrannick Au-
' thority of *Augustus*, with many other cross
' Blows that thou knowest of, I felt myself able
' to sustain, and possibly I should not have shrunk
' under any Weight, that had only power to bow
' an ordinary Spirit ; but after Explication of the
' ingrateful and artiless Intentions of *Cleopatra*,
' 'tis not enough to complain ; 'tis fit to die, *Emi-*
' *lius* ; nor can either Courage or Philosophy urge
' a just Diversion from such a purpose.

He utter'd these Words with a Tone so passionately heighten'd, as it drew Pity from his con-

cealed

cealed Auditors; and Prince *Tyridates* was about
to tell the Queen a Conjecture of his, when they
over-heard him go on in his Complaint : ' For-
' get, inhuman Princefs! *faid he*; were fo many
' Services, fo many Proofs of Affection no more
' than to be infenfibly driven from your Memo-
' ry? Have I deferved to be thus ufed for an in-
' violable Fidelity? and think you this does not
' ftain the Blood of *Anthony* and *Cleopatra*, to
' facrifice an innocent Life to Defpair, which,
' without the leaft Refervation, was efpoufed to
' your Service? Juft Gods! Gods whom I have
' fo often invoked, and of whom I have received
' fo many favourable Affiftances, if your Anger
' be ftill decreed to perfecute the miferable Re-
' liques of our Houfe, which you have fuffer'd to
' fall under the *Roman* Arms, turn all the Points
' of it againft me only; but do not punifh me,
' becaufe I love, with fuch Pains as fhould only
' be referv'd for the Guilty. If *Cleopatra* pro-
' vokes your Indignation by her Ingratitude to
' me, confider fhe is the Mafter-Piece of your
' Hands; and that however my Confcience avows
' me innocent, yet fure I am not fo; her Spirit
' is incapable of Error, and I, by the Weaknefs
' of fome Action, have furely plotted my own
' Difgrace. If it be fo, as I owe that Belief to
' her Judgment, my Life, my Actions, my
' Thoughts, I difavow you all, if you have any
' other Aims than the Love, Service, and Glory of
' *Cleopatra*. The Gods all know I never owed
' any fuch; and if you flily crept into my Breaft,
' it was in fuch Difguife, as I difcerned you not
' from thofe fhe might fafely approve.
   The Stranger would have ftretched his Complaints further, if his 'Squire, who began to be
weary of that kind of Life, had not thus ftopp'd

K 5   him :

him: ' My Lord, *said he*, I befeech you be not
' fo lavifh to your Griefs, as to give away the
' Power of reflecting both on what you are, and
' what you ought to be; 'tis true, your Misfor-
' tune is great, but yet not defperate: And, as I
' believe, this Change in the Princefs proceeds
' from fome Impreffion has been given from you;
' fo I hope (the Truth once difcovered) to fee you
' reftor'd to the fame Eftate in her Favour. I am
' more than confident this Mifchief was plot-
' ted by the Artifice of *Tiberius*; for that peevifh
' Man will omit no Occafion to deprive you of
' what he pretends to fo unworthily. But the
' Princefs *Cleopatra*'s Spirit cannot be poffefs'd,
' but Time will open her Eyes upon your Inno-
' cence: Befides, the Friendfhip of *Agrippa* and
' *Marcellus* will be active in your Behalf; and
' methinks Fortune begins to intend you fome
' Kindnefs, by conducting *Cleopatra* hither, who
' you know is fhortly expected at *Alexandria*,
' with the Emperor and Emprefs *Livia*, whom
' fhe always attends: All things confpire more
' Affiftance to your Defigns here, than at *Rome*;
' efpecially, the Place of your Refidence being un-
' known, and probably 'tis doubted in the Em-
' peror's Court, whether you be ftill living. They
' have reafon to doubt it, *faid the Mafter*; and
' had I liften'd to the rational Motions of my
' Grief, thy Fidelity had mifs'd this daily Trouble
' of urging fruitlefs Confolations. Indeed, I am
' glad at the coming of *Auguftus* to *Alexandria*;
' but 'tis lefs out of hope to fee *Cleopatra*, before I
' fhall dare to appear in her Prefence, than for the
' Revenge I intend upon *Tiberius*. I know that
' difloyal Man thinks his Subtleties have deftroy'd
' me; but he fhall find I am ftill living, to give
' him death in the very Arms of the Emperor
                                    ' and

' and Empress his Mother, that support him so
' unjustly against me. This is rather the Design
' of my stay upon this Coast, than to justify my-
' self before my Judge that sovereignly condemns
' me ; and possibly this sole Intent preserv'd my
' deplorable Life, that else should have been sacri-
' ficed to my just Resentments.

The Stranger, thus ending his Discourse, gave
Occasion to his Over-hearers to communicate their
Thoughts. *Candace* had oft heard the Name of
Cleopatra pronounced with such Interest, whom
she could take for no other than the Sister of
her dear *Cæsario*. But *Eteocles*, who ever kept the
Blood of his dead Mistress in sacred Veneration,
could not hear the Name of that Royal Maid without appearing transported. *Tyridates* read both
their troubles in their looks ; and not ignorant of
the cause, ' I do not wonder, *said he*, to see you
' amaz'd at this encounter, for my own surprisal
' is little less than yours ; but I think I am able
' to give you some light in this mist : for, if I
' be not deceiv'd, this Stranger, whom we have
' all so justly admir'd, is the valiant Prince of *Mau-*
' *ritania*, Son to the Great King *Juba*, who with
' *Cato* and *Scipio* was vanquished in *Africa* by
' *Julius Cæsar:* His Love to the Princess *Cleo-*
' *patra* made itself known to all *Rome* by the
' marvellous effects it produc'd ; and there was
' scarce a person that was ignorant of his Quarrel
' with *Tiberius*, link'd with divers other events
' that deserv'd remembrance. During my stay at
' *Rome*, he was absent ; but if the general opini-
' on might be credited, she could not boast a
' braver Man, nor one whose Valour was more
' advantageously accompanied, with such other
' qualities as render an accomplish'd Prince : I
' must not let him go, *said Eteocles*, before I
' see

'see and know him better, and demand some
'news of that Princess whom I have carried a
'thousand times in my Arms, whose Birth, Person,
'and Name are so sacred unto me. And indeed,
'*said Candace*, though my concealment be re-
'quisite, I cannot but wish to see him that loves
'my *Cæsar*'s Sister so passionately; the praises
'you have given him, with what I have dis-
'cern'd in his looks, have gain'd him much of
'my esteem, and made me already interest my-
'self in his Fortune. Madam, *said Tyridates*,
'I am glad to hear you say so; if you think fit,
'we will shew ourselves to him; and with your
'permission, I will offer him that poor retreat
'you did not scorn to accept; there we shall have
'leisure to know him, and learn, whether I guess'd
'right at his Name and Quality.

To this the Queen gave an easy consent, and
they were rising to salute him, when a great noise
of clashing of Arms, and loud voices, that sent itself to their ears, from a neighbouring Valley prevented them. This retir'd the Stranger from his
profound thoughts; and unwilling to hazard a
surprizal in that estate, he suddenly snatcht up
his Casque, and commanded the Squire to bridle
his Horse; which done, he was no sooner leap'd
into the Saddle, when he saw two Men on horse-
back coming towards him in their full speed from
the Valley, in a different estate and posture. The
first (having no other Arms but his Sword) fled
before the other arm'd at all points, who with his
Sword in his hand pursu'd him with loud threatnings, and wanted but little of overtaking. The
Arms of the hindermost were of a brown complexion, and (as if Art had studied disorder) confusedly filleted with Gold and Silver; his Coat
of Mail was suitable to his Cuirass; upon his

Casque

Cafque he bore a Lion, with a long Horfe-tail in his paw, that fell backward from his head upon his fhoulders. The fame Beaft was pourtray'd on his Shield, with a Motto under him, that could not be read at that diftance.

The Garb of this Warriour was not fo proud and fierce, but the other was as poor and timorous; the fear of Death, that hung out its pale badge upon his Vifage, would let him exprefs no anger, but to his Horfe, which he fpurr'd moft furioufly; and as he turn'd his Eyes round, as if he hunted for hope of fuccour, he fpy'd *Cleopatra's* Lover, whom he faw in a condition to defend him from his Enemy's rage; and fpurring up to him with his hands ftretched out in a fuppliant pofture: ' O fave me, Sir, *cry'd he*, from this cruel Man ' that has taken this Advantage to murder me!' He had no time to enlarge his entreaties, nor was it neceffary to a Man in whom the fentiments of Vertue had too deep an impreffion, to fly any opportunity that might fet his Courage a-work to relieve the oppreffed. He returned him no other anfwer than a preparation to give what he demanded: And to that end, putting himfelf between him and his purfuer, and firft defirous gently to try the force of perfwafion, he cry'd out to him afar off, to moderate the violence of his paffion, and pray'd him to confider the glory he was like to purchafe, for a Man arm'd as he was, to fet upon a perfon that had fo little to defend himfelf.

The Stranger, whom a moft violent choler and animofity againft the fugitive, had wound up to a haughty fiercenefs, could not fee the way to his revenge block'd up, without converting his fury upon him that deny'd it paffage, and inftead of a reply, he advanc'd his Sword in the air, and flew upon him like a Lion: ' Thy life *faid he*, fhall
' pay

' pay the forfeit of this Traytor's, which thou
' rob'st my just indignation of.' With these Words
came so weighty a blow, as his Enemy having
scarce time to ward it with his Shield, was half
astonished; but he, desirous to make use of that
disorder, (Revenge over-powering Glory) would
have quitted the Combat to continue the pursuit:
But *Cleopatra*'s Servant suddenly recovering himself, catched hold on the rein of his bridle as he
was passing by, and gave so rude a tug to the
tender-mouth'd horse, as made him rise so high
before, that he wanted but little to overthrow himself backward upon his Master; but he slacking
his hand, with a sharp remembrance of the Spur,
prick'd him forward; yet not so soon but his
fugitive was already got out of sight, and (that
he might leave no certain tract to his follower)
had betook himself to the Covert of an adjacent
Wood. But when he saw his hopes of overtaking him were fled with him, he turn'd his anger
afresh upon his new Enemy; and beholding him
with Eyes that darted flames of rage: ' Thou canst
' not, *said he*, but be base and perfidious, since
' thou favourest those that are so; but thy death
' shall repair the displeasure thou hast done me.
' Take heed, *said the other*, and defend thy own
' life carefully; for, believe it, thou wilt have
' more need of all thy force against me, than
' him whom thou wouldst have kill'd at such
' an advantage.

The two brave Combatants, valiant as any
that ever got a name in Arms, follow'd these
Words with such weighty blows, as he that first
enter'd the Lists, with an unwilling complement,
was forc'd to bow his head to the Saddle's Pommel,
and the other to touch the Croupe of his Horse.
But recovering fresh force and fury, each finding

ing the valour of his Enemy, and expecting by
the firſt blows what was like to follow, quitted
the thoughts of an eaſie Victory, and wak'd all
the dexterous force that Nature and Exerciſe
had given them, to find advantages. The Prince
of *Mauritania* (for *Tyridates* was not miſtaken)
at firſt was leſs angry than his Enemy; but when
he ſaw his Arms died in his own Blood, he ruſh-
ed upon his Foe with ſuch an unbridled, yet skilful
fury, as would quickly have given him the Victory,
had he not diſputed with a courage ſo invincible,
as the World could not boaſt a braver.

The proofs they had given of their mutual
Valour were ſoon become the wonder of their
Spectators. And while *Candace* was wrapt in a
deep amazement at the ſight, *Tyridates* and *Eteocles* quitted their places, and advanced into the
Meadow, with an intent (if it were poſſible) to
part them; an undertaking ſomething difficult,
they being both on foot, and only armed with
Swords : *Tyridates* therefore judging the gentler
way the beſt, and approaching ſomething near
them; ' Gallant Men, *cried he*, will you kill one
' another without a ſubject for a quarrel? Might
' you not better reſerve your Valour to employ
' againſt your Enemies whom you have cauſe to
' hate?' The Knights were ſo deaf to diſſuaſion,
as all the anſwer they return'd was a hot continuance of the Combat, each ſo vehemently ſpur-
ring up his Horſe to gain the Croupcr of his Enemy's; that *Tyridates*, fearing to be trodden under
foot, was conſtrain'd to retire a little, and become
a quiet Spectator, ſince he could not be an Arbiter;
attending the event of that furious Combat, not
without much fear it would prove too bloody.

It was yet fought on both ſides with ſuch an
evenneſs of Fortune and Courage, as no judgment
could

could allow either the least advantage; when the appearance of a third that came galloping up to the Combatants, gave *Tyridates* some hopes of assistance in his design to part them. The Arms of this last comer were very richly embroidered with Gold, and artificially engraven with the *Roman* Eagles; upon his Shield was painted that Royal Bird turning her undazl'd Eyes upon a Sun in its Glory; and upon his Casque she erected her two Heads, and expanded her Wings, as she is represented in the Arms of the Empire.

The arrival of this new Cavalier, not more considerable for the gallantry of his Armour, than the bravery of his Garb and Posture, made *Candace* and *Tyridates* (wholly fixed as they were upon the former spectacle) to take off their regards, and bestowed them upon him: But he allow'd them but little time to observe; for he no sooner cast his Eyes upon him of the two that bore the Lion in his Casque and Shield, but he clapp'd down the Visor of his Beaver, then half up, and approaching the Prince of *Mauritania*: ‘ Valiant Sir, *said he*, I conjure you, by the re- ‘ membrance of what you love dearest, to quit ‘ your place unto me, and permit me to continue ‘ a Combat with your Enemy, which I began ‘ before yours, and is possibly of greater importance.

The Prince turning his Eye upon him that entreated so strange a courtesy, lik'd him so well at the first sight, as he should not have stayed his consent, had he not been exceedingly provok'd by a resistance, which he was not accustomed to find among other Enemies; nevertheless, he was about to reply, when he was prevented by the other, who having heard the request of the last comer, at the first glance knew and received him with a joyful clamour; ‘ Come, come, *said*
‘ *he*

' *be aloud*, and join your forces together; I do
' not fear to fight you both, nor doubt the Victo-
' ry, though your number were greater.' This
said, he flew from his first Antagonist, and rush-
ing in with his Horse upon the other, gave him
a rude shock with a blow upon the head that made
him reel in the Stirrups; but the other Stranger
was not long in his debt, for having his Sword
ready in his hand, he discharged it with such a
puissance upon him, that the blow carried away
part of his Shield, and so benummed the hand
that held it, as it forced him to let fall his reins,
and his Horse feeling himself at liberty, started
away, and so saved his Master from the second
blow : But he quickly recovered his Bridle, and
being much ashamed of the accident, he bravely
turned head to both his Enemies, that approach'd
him with equal fury : A while he doubted upon
which to bestow his first blows; but having little
time to consider, he addrest himself to the Moorish Prince, and witnessing with his hand, that
he had something to say : ' I do not doubt, *cried he*,
' but I have courage and force enough to dispute
' the Victory against both : But if thou dost value
' the request of an Enemy, stand by a while, and
' give thyself the pleasure of seeing us decide a
' quarrel of greater importance than what is be-
' twixt us two, and I promise that immediately
' after my Victory, we will end our difference.

' I fear, *said he*, he will not leave thee in a
' condition to give me such resistance as my Ho-
' nour can accept; for methinks his forces are so
' little inferiour to thine, as I cannot hope the
' success of this Combat will tend to thy advan-
' tage. Finish first then what thou hast begun
' with me, and if Fortune decrees that thou 'scapest
' my hands, thou shalt have leisure enough to de-
                                          ' bate-

' bate they first quarrel.' These last Words of the
Prince were not so much as heard by the Enemy,
who staying for no answer, had eagerly renewed his
Combat with the Knight of the Wings, and was received by him with as much bravery as he brought.
The valiant Moor angry to be so slighted, ran up
to him with his Sword in a posture to express
it; but seeing him engaged with the other, and
ashamed to assail him at such an advantage, he
held his Sword advanced in the Air, as yet uncertain how to dispose of it; very unwilling he
was to give over the Combat, and as loath to
wound his Credit by striking one that was so hotly match'd by another as valiant as himself: But during his Irresolution, the two Chevaliers charged
one another still with such mighty Blows, as
made their Lives indebted to the Goodness of their
Armour; nor could that longer hinder their Swords
from cutting Passages for the Blood in divers Parts
of their Bodies, the sight of which rather animated then enfeebled them, urging each to crave his
Revenge upon the other, with such height of Fury, as there was never seen a Combat between two
Men so terrible. Their Blood had in divers Places dyed the Earth in its own Complexion, when
after many cruel Blows that came too thick to be
counted, at last there fell two together with so
huge a Force, as they wanted both but little of
kissing the Dust, but they reeled a long time upon their Saddles, before they could recover their
Stirrops; the Knight of the Lions broke his Sword
upon the Casque of his Enemy, but with the Blow
cutting the Laces (that fasten'd it) asunder, it threw
the Roman Eagles to the Ground, and left the Head
of his Master naked and disarm'd; which discovered to the Lookers on, one of the handsomest
and most majestick Faces that ever credited Nature's

ture's Workmanſhip: at the firſt Glance *Candace*
and *Eteocles* knew it, and advancing towards him
with a tranſport of Joy, ' Ah! my Prince, *cried*
' *they at once*: Ah! *Cleomedon*, *Ceſar's* Son;
and indeed it was *Ceſario*, whom the heat of the
Fight had deafen'd to their Cries; for covering
his head with his Shield, with his Sword ready
to cut out Work for the Surgeon, he re-advanced
towards his Oppoſite that attended him with an
equal Reſolution: But the Prince of *Mauritania*,
who had lent Attention to the Words, and Regard to the Viſage of *Candace*, was willing to
do Homage to the Empire of Beauty, in a deſire
to oblige her: And ſeeing the Combatants in a
very deſperate Condition, threw himſelf between
to part them, believing *Ceſario*, with whom he
had no Quarrel, would not ſtrike him, and the
other's Truncheon he did not fear.

Tyridates and *Eteocles* joining with him, at
the ſame time laid hold of their Bridles, and by
that Means hinder'd the Progreſs of the Combat,
which they fretted at with exceſſive Choler: *Ceſario's* appear'd in Flaſhes at his Eyes, and bluſhes
in his Face, but at laſt lending an Ear to the Words,
and an Eye to the Faces of *Eteocles* (who held
his Bridle) and *Candace* that ſtood by ſtill crying
out, *Cleomedon*, *Cleomedon*, immediately he knew
them both, and with a Joy that broke out into
loud Accents, ſeeing his Enemy held by the *Mauritanian* and *Parthian* Princes, he forgot all
Thoughts of Enmity, and was flying into the
Arms of his Princeſs, when they all took a freſh
Alarm, from fifteen or twenty Horſemen, that
with their Swords in their Hands, came up towards them upon the Spur, conducted by the
ſame Man that fled from the Knight of the Lions,
and at him only they all ſeemed to bend their
un-

unmanly out-rage: But the two others (then quitting, or at least suspending all Animosity) of Enemies were quickly become Parties; which known, without ballancing the baseness of the Act, they pour'd themselves upon them all; but the first that aborded them, carried away incurable Marks of their Treachery: For they coap'd with such Enemies as were incapable of being dismayed at such a Number. The Prince of *Mauritania*, who was the freshest of the three, sent the first he met without a Head to the Ground, and cut off the Arm of the second, just as it was advanc'd in the Air to strike him. These two first Blows gave *Cesario* time to put on his Casque, which *Eteocles* had given him, and the Knight of the Lions leisure to recover a Sword instead of his own that was broken: Which done, they both bravely joined with the valiant *Moor*, and help'd him to distribute Death among their Enemies: The first that fell under the Sword of *Cæsar*'s Son, had his Head cloven in two Pieces; and he that died on the other Hand, was run through the Body, his Point finding a Way through the Weakness of his Cuirass, to tumble his Soul from the principal Seat of Life. These were no sooner fallen, but *Tyridates*, covering his Head with one of their Casques, and snatching up a Shield, leaped upon a Horse, which a new Blow from the gallant *Moor* had made Masterless, and came and joined his Assistance, like a considerable reserve ... est.

... les, ... th the Prince of *Mauritania*'s ... wed his Example, only the Queen and ... d remained Spectators of the Combat: ... ed it was almost a Prodigy to see Men so ... and wounded in a former Fight, with ... eyond human Puissance, in so few Moments

ments to reduce such a Number of their Enemies to despair of Victory.   *Tyridates*, though but half arm'd, quickly tumbl'd two at his Feet, and *Eteocles* courageously cut his Passage through the Press, and joined himself with the Prince his Master.   But while these four gallant Warriors, stung with brave Emulation, like so many new *Mars's* display'd their invincible Valour; the Captain of their Enemies, whom fear of Death had rang'd in the Rear, contenting himself to animate with Words, but not daring to give the Encouragement of a personal Example, chanced to cast his Eyes upon the Queen of *Ethiopia*, who was seeing Heaven with her Silver Tears to rescue her *Cæsar* from the Perils that menac'd him: he no sooner saw, but knew her, and breaking into an out-cry, ' Oh ye Gods ! *said he*, and do ' you then restore me my Fugitive, that was wre- ' sted from my Hands with so great a Danger of ' my Life ?' When presently commanding one of his Men that was nearest to follow him, he ran to her, just as she was thinking (for she had spied him) to hide herself behind the Rock; but she made not haste enough to prevent that barbarous Villain, who rudely seizing upon her, and, by the help of his Companion, having set her up before him upon the Pomel of the Saddle, he carried her away in spight of all the resistance and strugling she could make for Escape: His Companion would have had no pleasant Task to force *Clitie* to the same Posture, if her Resolution to follow the Fortune of her Mistress, discarding the Consideration of her own, had not made her his easy Prey: But Gods! what Fury shot itself into the Soul of *Cæsario*? When hearing the out-cries of his Queen, and his Ear directing his Eye, he spy'd her in the Arms of her cruel Ravisher, who

had

had borrowed all the Wings that Haste could lend, to get Ground of his suspected Pursuers; the whole Strength of his Enemies were now grown feeble to arrest him; for having thrown down one that opposed his Passage, with a Blow that clove him to the Breast, he darted himself among the rest, with such an irresistible Vigour, as he soon cleared the Way to his Pursuit, when (by a fresh Piece of Fortune's Malice) his Horse, no longer able to endure the many Wounds he had receiv'd, fell dead under him, and so suddenly, as falling with his Master's Feet engaged in the Stirrops, he exposed him to the Mercy of his Enemies; two of which spying the casual Advantages, were coming to kill him, which they had easily effected, if the Knight of the Lions (a while before his eager Enemy, resigning hatred to a fitter Season) had not flown to his Defence, and with two Blows laid both his Enemies at his Feet, the one Dead, the other with a deep Wound: And taking one of their Horses by the Reins, just as *Eteocles* had thrown himself down to dif-engage the Prince from his; ' Rise, *Cleomedon*, *said he*, and receive ' this Assistance from thy greatest Enemy, but ' such an Enemy as is unwilling to owe any Thing ' to thy Generosity.

The Son of *Cæsar* at another Time would not have taken this Succour from his declared Foe, without striving to restore the Benefit, or at least tendering an ample Expression of his Resentment, but at that Moment the Loss of his Queen (who to his Eye had appeared and disappeared like Lightning) wholly seiz'd him, and would scarce suffer him to make a fit Reflection upon the generous Act of this gallant Enemy; only in taking the Horse from his Hands, and leaping upon him with more Agility than his Wounds could well

allow

llow of; ' I know not *said he*, how to underftand thee, who in declaring thyfelf my Enemy,
haft render'd me the Office of an intimate Friend :
But I proteft, that as much my Enemy as thou
art, I will ever be ready to pay thee back this
Life which thou haft fo bravely affail'd, and fo
generoufly defended :' Finifhing thefe Words,
and leaping into the Saddle, having now no Enemies capable to ftay him, he hafted after the Ra-
vifher with all the Speed imaginable.

Eteocles, whofe Memory harboured nothing fo
carefully as his Prince's Intereft, after his Example fuddenly re-mounted himfelf, and obferving
the Way he took, followed fo fwiftly, as in a
fhort Time he recovered him.

In the mean Time, the Prince of *Mauritania*
and *Tyridates* had handled the reft of their Enemies fo roughly, as they were reduced to a Defpair of Victory : And when he that fo valiantly
refcued *Cæfario*, was again joined with them, they
made fuch Havock among thofe that remain'd, as
after the Death of all their Companions, three
that were only left, were conftrained to truft their
Safety to their Heels; the gallant Warriors dif-
daining to purfue them, fell to a mutual Admiration of each other's Valour, and the brave unknown,
addreffing himfelf to the Prince of *Mauritania* :
' At firft, *said he*, you did me a Difpleafure that
' made me your Enemy, in hindering the Exe-
' cution of a Revenge fo juft, as, had you known
' the Caufe, you would doubtlefs have favoured
' what you prevented : But you have fince fo nobly
' affifted me againft Enemies, who I think only
' levell'd their Malice at me, as the Memory of
' that overpowers my Refentments; and joining
' with my Wonder at your Valour, devotes me
'   ' to

' to the fearch of Occafions, that may make me
' worthy to become your Friend.

'I am forry, *replied the valiant Moor*, for
' the Difpleafure I have given you, judging by
' what I have fince feen you do, and by the late
' bafe Actions of your Enemy, that he was wor-
' thy of the Punifhment you defigned him; but
' (as the Truth was mafqu'd) I could not refufe
' a Protection which I thought was due to the
' weaker Party. I deem it no mean Happinefs
' to have effected your Refentments by fo poor a
' Piece of Service; and after the Experiment of
' your Valour, I cannot without much Joy re-
' ceive the Profer of your Amity.

This faid, they fhook Hands, and lifted up the
Vifors of their Helmets. If the Stranger was ravifhed with the Beauty and majeftick Air of the
Moor, the two Princes were not lefs furpriz'd at
his high and heroick Mind, both believing, not
without much Reafon, that they never beheld any
that furpaft it; thus they gazed one at another,
their Admiration taking a pretty diftant Precedency of their Words: But the Prince of *Mauritania*
firft breaking Silence, and turning toward *Tyridates*, who was dividing his Aftonifhment betwixt
them: ' It is to you, valiant Man, *faid be*, we
' have the moft confiderable Obligation; to your
' Valour and generous Refolution we owe the
' Wonder, fince naked as you are, you have
' brav'd a Danger capable to difmay Men moft
' fecurely armed, rendering a gallant Succour to
' unknown Perfons.' To thefe Words the brave
Stranger added others that imported the fame Senfe;
which *Tyridates* modeftly receiving, ' I have
' done nothing *faid be*, but what the Incitement
' might juftly challenge; and the little Help I was
' able to contribute, fhew'd fo poor and worthlefs
' in

' in the Presence of your grand Actions, as it me-
' rits no remembrance.

In uttering these Words, he observed their Arms
cover'd with Blood, especially the Stranger's, who
had lost very much in his Combat with *Cesario*,
and not willing to dally in such a Condition, ' I
' see, *said he*, your Wounds express the necessity of
' a sudden Assistance, which I am presently able to
' give, if you refuse not the offer of a poor Lodg-
' ing, about an hundred Paces hence, where your
' Wounds shall be searched, and yourselves serv'd
' with much Affection. But where is *Cleomedon*,
' *continued he, looking round for* Cæsario ?' ' Sir,
'he is gone, *said the Prince of* Mauritania*'s*
' 'Squire, (*who being less eager than the rest,*
' *had better discern'd what pass'd concerning the*
' *Combat*) in pursuit of those Ravishers that car-
' ried away two Ladies, that stood and looked on
' while we were fighting.' ' How ! *cry'd Ty-*
' *ridates*, are the Ladies carried away, that were
' with me when you arrived ?' ' Yea, my Lord,
' *reply'd Emilius*, they were seized on by the
' chief of those Men whom you so lately defeated.'
' Oh Gods ! *said Tyridates*, what an unvaluable
' Loss is this, if it be not speedily recover'd ? how
' passionately could I with these valiant Men in a
' better Condition, that they were able to endea-
' vour the Rescue of one of the most considerable
' Persons upon Earth !' ' Let us go, *said the*
' *Prince of* Mauritania, our Wounds ought not
' to dispense with the Succour of a Person of so
' much Importance.' ' Indeed, *said Tyridates*,
' your Obligation is particular, and possibly I
' know you better than you imagine; but am
' loath to expose you, in this Estate, to any fresh
' Peril, especially that gallant Man, (pointing to

' the unknown) whose Wounds are deeper, and
' more dangerous than your's.

: ' 'Tis true, *said the Stranger*, my Hurts are
' great; but they shall give me leave to go to the
' Sea-side, which is the only Course you can take
' in this Design; for the Pyrate *Zenodorus* (who
' was he that I pursu'd, and doubtless the same that
' bore away the Person whose Loss you regret) has
' carried away the Prey to his Vessels, that rid near
' the Shore, and only there we ought to seek it.

This said, he puts Spurs to his Horse, and led
the way (though not without much Pain) towards that Side of the Coast where he had seen
Zenodorus's Vessels: The Princes eagerly followed; and (being in much the better Estate, quickly left him behind) speeding their Course to that
Part of the Shore which he pointed at; but all,
alas! in vain; for finding no Vessel in the Road,
and coasting a while upon the Sand, without any
Discovery, at last they 'spy'd twoShips afar off,
with full Sails, making off to Sea, which they
presently judg'd to be the same they sought for.
The brave unknown, who was as much interested as *Tyridates*, and possibly not much less than
Cesario, in the pursuit of the Pyrate, fetching
two or three deep Sighs, and casting a sad Look
upon the Prince of *Mauritania*, ' Oh! *said he*,
' how should I hate you, if the Succour you have
' given me, with the knowledge of your Virtue,
' could leave a Possibility for the Passion? Gods!
' *pursued he*; Oh you Gods! what a Loss do I
' sustain by this fatal Combat? What have I
' lost, in a Condition that disables me to give
' myself the least hope of Recovery!

At these Words, he had let himself fall from
his Horse with Weakness, if *Tyridates* had not
hasten'd to sustain him; and the *Mauritanian*
did

did as much on the other Side, protesting his Sorrow for the Injury his Ignorance had done him, and the Share he had took in his Fortune. During this Discourse, *Tyridates* considering that a longer Search would but vainly strengthen their Despair of finding, began to lead them the way to his own House, always keeping near the Stranger, whose loss of Blood, and depth of Wounds, had so enfeebled him, as he was scarce able to keep his Saddle; but they soon reach'd the House, where the Servants of *Tyridates* tender'd the same Offices to the Strangers that were due to the Person of their Prince. They were laid in several Chambers, the House being spacious enough to afford commodious Lodging, and their Wounds visited, which were not found very dangerous, especially the Prince of *Mauritania*'s, who had had only received a Hurt on his left Arm, and another slight one on his Side; the Stranger's were greater both in Number and Condition; but the Surgeon (who was an Officer to *Tyridates*, and an expert Master of his Art) promised an infallible Cure to both.

The Stranger took but little Comfort from this Promise, and appeared so sensibly afflicted, as the Fears of those that serv'd him began to augurate worse Success from his Sadness, than his Wounds. He was no sooner laid, but there enter'd into his Chamber a young Man, whom he presently knew to be his 'Squire; who, having spent a part of that Day in his Search, had at last address'd his Enquiry to that House, where he understood what was happened.

At the sight of his 'Squire, the Master express'd some Signs of Comfort; and having call'd him to his Bed's Side, he entreated the rest to leave him to his Repose. *Tyridates* had received two slight

Wounds

Wounds, one on his right Hand, and the other on his Head; but they were too inconsiderable to confine him to his Bed; and, having caused some Remedies to be applied, he spent his principal Care upon the Service of his Guests, whom he marvellously esteem'd.   At the Evening, understanding that the Prince of *Mauritania* might admit a Visit, he enter'd his Chamber; and being received by the Prince with an Excess of Civility, they spent some time in Terms of Courtesy and Deference; which ended, and *Tyridates* seated by his Bed's Side, before they could methodically change the Subject, he (of *Mauritania*) calling to mind a Word or two the *Parthian* let fall some Hours before, ' I remember you told me, *said*
' *he*, that I was better known to you than I knew
' *of*; make me the Favour, if you please, to let
' me understand what Knowledge you have of
' me, and by what means you gain'd it.'   ' I
' drew it, *reply'd Tyridates*, from some Words I
' over-heard you utter before the arrival of the
' valiant Stranger, against whom you combated;
' your ample mention of the Princess *Cleopatra*,
' and of *Tiberius*, added to what I had heard at
' *Rome* of the Life of that Princess, begat my
' Opinion you were the Prince of *Mauritania*:
' But if at first it was only a single Conjecture,
' the sight of your Visage, with the grand Actions
' you performed in my Presence, have strengthen'd
' it to a Confidence.
This Discourse raised a Blush in the Prince's Cheeks, because it imported him to disguise his Quality; yet willing that his Obligation to *Tyridates* should vanquish the Displeasure, ' I should
' be sorry, *said he*, (as my Affairs are now sta-
' ted) to be known to any other Person than
' yourself; but you have too nobly engaged me
' to

' to a high Esteem of your Worth to allow Dis-
' trust a Being. 'Tis true, I am that unhappy
' Prince of *Mauritania*, whose Misfortunes, if
' you made any stay at *Rome*, have possibly reach-
' ed your Ears ; but because methinks your Face
' too discovers more Marks of Greatness than your
' Equipage, I should gladly learn to whom I am
' reduable, and what he is that I have trusted.'
' If I priz'd my Life, *reply'd Tyridates*, I should
' not have less Cause than you to hide my Name ;
' but, as Fortune has used me, the Preservation of
' it is so inconsiderable, as were my Confidence
' in you less than it is, I should make no Diffi-
' culty to tell you, that I am *Tyridates*, Son of
' *Orodes*, and Brother to *Phraates* King of *Par-
' thia*, persecuted both by my Fortune and Friends,
' and reduced, ever since my greenest Years, to beg
' from Court to Court a Shelter for my Life.' At
this Relation, the Prince of *Mauritania*, a little
lifting himself from his Bed, saluted *Tyridates*
with an Addition to his former Respect. ' I am
' no stranger to your Name, *said he* ; for when
' you quitted *Rome*, you left yourself upon every
' Tongue in so fair a Character, as is not unsuit-
' able to my present Experience of your Person
' and Vertue. I am not sorry to be reduable to a
' Prince of your Birth, nor to find such high
' Worth in him, of whom my Estimation pre-
' ceded my Knowledge.' ' To you, *said Tyri-
' dates*, I owe, with much more Justice, what
' your Expressions have mis-placed upon myself ;
' the Bruit of your beauteous Actions hath pro-
' duced such Effects through the *Roman* Empire,
' as, doubtless, you are not known where your
' Virtue is not admir'd and ador'd.
The Prince modestly retorted this Language,
and they had some while continued a courteous

Con-

Conteſt, full of Deference and Proteſtations of
Amity, they transferred their Diſcourſe upon the
valiant Stranger, who repoſed in the next Chamber; wherein they forgot not to mention his rare
Compoſure, both of Face and Garb; his undaunted Spirit, with thoſe grand Actions they had ſeen
him perform, which kindled an equal Ardor in
both, to be as well acquainted with his Name
and Quality: And as they contriv'd the Means,
they ſpy'd his 'Squire paſs by the Chamber Door,
that ſtood half open, *Tyridates* call'd to him; and
after he had enter'd, and come near the Bed, 'We
'call'd to you, *ſaid he*, to demand ſome News
'of your Maſter, and to entreat, if you may
'grant it, without incurring his Diſpleaſure, the
'Satisfaction of our Deſires to know him, the
'Bravery of his Actions muſt excuſe our Cu-
'rioſity, in containing which, you may deeply
'oblige us.

'My Lord, *reply'd the 'Squire*, had I Permiſ-
'ſion from my Maſter, you ſhould gladly be
'obey'd; but having not yet revoked the Com-
'mand he gave me to conceal his Perſon, I muſt
'be forced to a very unwilling Diſobedience:
'Yet this I may take Commiſſion to ſay, That
'poſſibly I ſerve one of the greateſt Men upon
'Earth; and, young as he his, (if your remote
'Abode be not ſituated where Fame is a Stranger)
'doubtleſs the Noiſe of his Actions had found you
'out; happily when he knows your deſire, he
'will command me to ſatisfy it, and, if you
'pleaſe, I will demand his Leave.

'It is not neceſſary, *ſaid the Prince of* Mauri-
'tania; for, though your Diſcourſe hath much
'augmented our Curioſity, we ſhould be too un-
'civil to preſs any thing that may diſpleaſe him;
'when it ſhall come from his own free Motion,
'we

' we shall joyfully receive it; and, in the mean
' time, content ourselves to know him by those
' Marks of Greatness that shine in his Person,
' and by what he has done in our Presence.

With this Answer the 'Squire departed; and a
while after, *Tyridates* (finding it time to leave him
to his Repose) bad his Guest good-night, and went
to seek that in his own Bed, which was there to
entertain him.

L 4

Hymen's

Hymen's Præludia :

OR,

Love's Master-Piece.

PART V. BOOK I.

ARGUMENT.

Emilius *begins his Master's Life to* Tyridates. *Characters of his Father King* Juba, *whose Power, Pomp, and Life, prove a Sacrifice to* Cæsar's *Fortunes. His Birth and Education at* Rome. *He is struck with* Cleopatra's *Infant-Beauty, as she is shew'd among the Spoil in* Augustus's *Triumph. The rare Example of* Marcellus's *Amity, in resigning his Claim to* Cleopatra, *carries them both to the* German *War. Their brave Behaviour there, and Return.* Tiberius *becomes his Rival. Puts a cunning Trick upon* Coriolanus, *which ensnares him in a jealous Error.*

O

LOVE

OVE never had more Cause, in so little Elbow-room, to employ all his Puissance, than in that House, where *Tyridates* and his two illustrious Guests resided; and scarce could the whole Extent of his Empire shew three nobler Slaves, whom he had fetter'd with more glorious Chains.

The moorish Prince, the brave Stranger, and the *Parthian*, sigh'd at the same time for several Objects; and, as the Earth could not boast any more worthy to light up their amorous Flames, so it would have been difficult to have found, in the Stock of Mankind, three Souls more capable of such Passions, as they had Power to kindle in Hearts least susceptible of Love's Impression. Oh! could the Night (blind as she was) have seen those refin'd Fires, that fed their Lustre in that little Retreat, they would have clear'd her Complexion to a beautiful Day, had they had an equal Commission to shine as well as burn. The Stranger's deep Wounds had so enfeebled his Body, as they seem'd a little to lessen the Violence of those Resentments, wherewith Love and Grief had inspir'd him; those that lighted upon *Tyridates* (which were so favourable as they could scarce be felt) left his Thoughts an entire Liberty to work upon the State of his Love and Fortune; and the Prince of *Mauritania*'s (though something deeper than his) yet not enough to unbusy those sad Considerations, and leave him Leisure to regard his bodily Health, in so cruel an Indisposition of his Mind. All Things that had Power to renew his Anguish, came flocking to his Memory so freshly, as if the whole Time, and all the Accidents of his Life, had still been as young as at the Moment of their

L 5   Birth;

Birth; when, after his officious Thoughts had examined every Good and Ill, that trod their successive Steps in the Course of his Fortunes, that came to hint *Cleopatra*'s Ingratitude, that almost threw him into a Swoon, with the Torments of Grief and Despair.

But Oh! what a Number of bitter Plaints and hollow Sighs did that sad Remembrance tear from his Mouth and Heart! and how fitly did the Blacks of the Night suit with the Mourning which his Soul had put on: To him the darkest Shades were far more welcome and agreeable than the brightest Beams that could spring from the active Treasury of Light; and not well enduring the Day, ever since the Eclipse of those fair Hopes that enlightned his Soul, he found some Comfort in an Obscurity conform'd to that of his Spirit, that help'd him to wrap it in a dull Cloud of heavy Thoughts: And thus having quitted the Care of himself, the Day appeared, before the Repose of his Body could give an Hour's Calm to the Storms of his Mind. He no sooner spy'd the new-born Light shoot itself through the Windows of his Chamber, when saluting it with some Sighs, ‘ How importunate is this bright Intruder! (cry'd ‘ he) how sensibly dost thou aggravate the Vexa- ‘ tions of a Wretch, which should be intomb'd ‘ in an eternal Night? All the Objects thou dost ‘ offer to mine Eyes, serve but to wake a Remem- ‘ brance worse than the cruellest Death. I can ‘ breathe no Air, see no Sun; nor behold a Hea- ‘ ven, common to me and *Cleopatra*, that does ‘ not prompt my Memory with her disloyal ‘ Change. Ah! how much more Happy had I ‘ been, that thou hadst seen me perish in those ‘ Actions, wherein thou didst light me the Way ‘ to Glory; that I had rather taken an eternal ‘ leave

' leave of thee in those Occasions, that the World
' thought worthy of some Remembrance, than to
' suffer such a fatal Preservation, to be trod upon
' by the Malice of injurious Fortune; and, possibly,
' to see my ingrateful *Cleopatra* wrapt in the
' Arms of the subtle *Tiberius*.

' In the Arms of *Tiberius, repeated he?* Ah,
' Son of *Juba!* chase that base Thought from thy
' Soul, and recover the Knowledge of thy Cou-
' rage, that never yet forsook thee in any Acci-
' dent of thy Life, which thou began'st with the
' loss of all thou wert born to; Parents, Crowns,
' nay, the whole Glory of thy House, which at
' the first opening of thine Eyes thou saw'st ex-
' pos'd in thy Person, to the Ignominy of a *Ro-
' man* Triumph: Thou hast carried it through
' Pains and Perils, with Toils of Body and Mind,
' capable to overthrow a common Constancy, and
' at last must end it by Despair; yet such a De-
' spair, as will never leave a Blot upon thy Me-
' mory, nor tell the World thou dost either dege-
' nerate from the *Roman* Education, nor that il-
' lustrious Extraction which thou took'st from so
' many Kings. If thou must die, (as it is requi-
' site, since thy Hopes are perished) if possible,
' thou shalt throw down those with thy Fall that
' caused it; or at least follow thy Father's Steps,
' who took his Repose upon the Point of his own
' Sword, because he scorn'd to ask it elsewhere,
' after the fading of his Glory, and the Fall of
' his Empire.

He had enlarged these Plaints, if his 'Squire,
who over-heard divers of his Sighs, and understood some interrupted Words, had not come to
the Bed's Side, and asked how he felt himself. ' I
' am but too well, *said he*, and with Grief I feel,
' that my Body is not brought low enough to

suit

'suit my Mind.' The Squire was about to reply, when he heard one of *Tyridates*'s Servants at the Door, that came from him to enquire of his Health, and know if a Visit from his Master would not incommode him: *Emilius* was commanded to return him a very civil Answer, which, within a short time after he had carried back, the *Parthian* Prince enter'd the Chamber; and, approaching the Bed's Side, bad him good-morrow. The *Mauritanian* received *Tyridates* with Acknowledgments full of Affection; and after they had spent their first Civilities, having caused him to sit down by his Bed's Side, 'I should deem 'myself highly oblig'd, *said he*, to the Care you 'take of my Life, if every thing (in the Condi- 'tion it now is) that conduces to its Preservation 'were not hateful; however, I hold myself infi- 'nitely bound to your good Intentions, and do 'offer, in requital to that noble Care you take of 'it, all the Remainder that Love and Grief have '.left at my disposal.' 'Your Life is too preci- 'ous, too glorious, *said Tyridates*, to deserve 'the Neglect of any thing that may concern its 'Safety: Report hath made me acquainted with 'some Passages of it, memorable enough to set 'on it a high Value in every Estimation, of 'which I am confident few Persons can be igno- 'rant; and yet I think there are fewer know 'the Particulars of your Love to the Princess '*Cleopatra*: For my part, I understood no more 'of it, than hath already enter'd every vulgar Ear 'in the *Roman* Empire; nor have I gleaned any 'thing from the common Report that could con- 'tent my Desire, to be better instructed in the 'single Passages of your Fortune. I know not if 'my Curiosity be pardonable.

'It

' It is, *said the Prince, interrupting him*; nay
' more, I am not loath to present it with a clear
' Satisfaction, indeed not willing (after the Re-
' ceipt of such generous Favours, with the rare
' Proofs you have given me of your Virtue) to
' debar your Knowledge of the least Particular.
' 'Tis true, you may have learned some Accidents
' of my Life, that are but too well known; but
' 'tis impossible you should understand those of
' the most Importance, unless you receive them
' either from mine or the Mouth of *Emilius*, from
' whom I have nothing concealed.

' It shall be then from *Emilius*, if you please,
' *reply'd Tyridates*, I will take this Satisfaction,
' as well because he has told me you have taken
' little Rest this Night, and therefore it will re-
' quire a good part of this Day to repair your
' loss of Sleep, as because he will give the Rela-
' tion more at large, and possibly more true, than
' your Modesty will condescend to, which, in all
' likelihood, would either silence or disguise some
' of your bravest Actions.

' I have done nothing, *said Coriolanus*, which
' the greatest Modesty might not own and utter;
' but since *Emilius* has more Credit with you than I,
' I'm contented that he shall give you the full Recital
' of my Life, without the least Reserve of any
' Particular.

After this Permission, *Tyridates*, thanking the
Prince, quitted his Chamber, and took *Emilius*
with him, who was willing he should have that
Morning given him to recover his Rest: But be-
fore *Tyridates* would engage his Attention to this
Story, he went to visit the gallant Stranger, for
whom his Care was not less than the Prince of
Mauritania; his Observation of so many Marks of
Grandeur in him, made him regard him with a
high Respect, and a marvellous Esteem; but at the

Cham-

Chamber-Door he met the Surgeon, who diffuaded that Vifit, telling him he had great Hopes of his Cure, but it was not fafe for him to receive and pay the Civilities of any Perfon that Morning, becaufe ftriving to fpeak might impair his prefent Condition, and retard his Recovery.

Tyridates ftopp'd at thefe Words; and after recommending the Continuation of their Care to his Officers, he retired to his Chamber with *Emilius*, and (forcing his Refpect to accept of a Seat) ' Since ' the Prince your Mafter, *faid he*, has given Per- ' miffion, let me defire an entire Relation of his ' Life, without omitting the moft trivial Paffage ' your Memory can hint, or interrupting the Nar- ' ration of fuch things as you may think have al- ' ready reached my Knowledge; for I have taken ' nothing but confufed Notions from publick Ru- ' mour, which often disfigures the Truth of things ' not perfectly known.

' Sir, *faid Emilius*, though I fee myfelf en- ' gaged to a long Narration, I fhall ftrive to pay ' Obedience to your's, and the Prince my Mafter's ' Commands, as well as I am able.' At thefe Words, making a little Paufe, to range with fome Method in his Memory the Things he had firft to utter, he began his Difcourfe in this manner.

The Hiftory of Prince Coriolanus and the Princefs Cleopatra.

NEVER had any Life fo fad a Beginning as my Mafter's, and in fo fmall a Number of Years as compofe his Age, never did Fortune play fo many Tricks with a Prince's Deftiny; yet this I may fay, and Truth can witnefs it, my Mafter owes nothing to her, but has loft all by her: At his Birth fhe took away his Crowns, Parents,

and

and Liberty; she has since endeavour'd, and does still continue to do him Mischief, more sensible than his first Losses; but all the Favours she ever granted him, were still forced from her by his Virtue.

He was born poor, though lawful Heir to two great Kingdoms; born a Slave, though Son to the most potent King in all *Africa*; he saw the Light and his own Shame together, and commenced his Life to appear in an Action, which made *Cleopatra* resign up her's; nor would himself have done less, had his Age been capable to have shew'd himself the Ignominy.

The great King *Juba* (whose Memory still keeps its Beauty without a Blemish) was Monarch of both the *Mauritania's*, and supported himself with a Puissance that struck Terror into his Neighbours, and would have made him consider'd by the whole Earth, as Master of the greatest Part of *Africa*, if his unlucky Choice of the weakest Party had not ruined him, and his Fortune done Homage to that great Man's, for whom Fate had reserv'd the universal Empire. His Dominion was of a grand Extent, his Court pompous and flourishing; and that Authority which the Terror of his warlike Virtue exercised upon his Borderers, render'd himself little less than Sovereign of the third Part of the World. In this Estate he lived with an untroubled Glory; when, after the Defeat of the great and unfortunate *Pompey*, the Fragments of his scattered Forces rally'd themselves again in *Africa*, under the Conduct of *Scipio* and *Cato*: King *Juba*, either out of Friendship to *Pompey*'s Memory, or Jealousy of *Cæsar*'s Greatness, join'd with his Enemies, and help'd to swell their thin Forces with a puissant Army; backed with this considerable Addition, they three

op-

oppofed the Torrent of *Cæfar*'s Fortune, and not only arrefted the Courfe of his Victories, but by fome remarkable Advantages they got at the Beginning of the War, the whole World began to queftion his Succefs.

At laft their malicious Fortunes conducted them to the Plain of *Thapfus*, near to a City of the fame Name; where, prided with a vain Shadow of Profperity, they offer *Cæfar* Battle: Indeed they had much reafon to hope a favourable Event, but the Gods ftruck in his Quarrel, for whom they had defigned the World's Command, and maugre all the *African* Puiffance, made Victory perch herfelf upon *Cæfar*'s Standards; there did King *Juba* and his Companions lofe 50,000 Men, and in one Day faw themfelves and their Hopes ruined beyond repair. This gave them a Refolution, to feek no further than Death for a Remedy; and though they might have hoped a better Deftiny from the Clemency of *Cæfar*, they rather chofe to quit the World, than take their Life as a Gift from the Conqueror's Mercy.

Scipio killed himfelf with his own Sword upon the Spot, *Cato* being fhut up in *Utica*, ftabb'd himfelf, and a While after tore out his own Bowels, to defraud their Care that endeavoured his recovery; and the King of *Mauritania*, with the poor Remnant of his fhattered Forces, took his Flight to one of his neareft Cities, where feeing himfelf hotly purfued by the victorious Army, after he had ftriven in vain to re-affure the Courage of his *Africans*, who had taken too much Fear from the *Roman* Fortune, refolved too to fnatch his Share in the common Fate: And in purfuit of this Intention, having caufed a magnificent Feaft to be made for *Petreius* a *Roman* Captain, who had been of his Party, and was then a Companion

on of his Fortune, at the End of their Repaſt, regarding him with a Viſage that breathed nought but Death, ' Petreius, *ſaid he,* 'tis fit we die to ' preſerve our Liberty; for if we ſtay on Earth ' but a few Days, we ſhall have no Power left, ' to put by the Shame is prepared us; I demand ' no other Proof of thy Affection but Death from ' thy Hands; and, as my Fortune is now ſtated, ' I cannot receive a greater from thy Friendſhip. ' Here, ſtab this Breaſt, *purſued he, preſenting* ' *his naked Boſom,* pierce this Heart, which the ' Arms of our Enemies have unluckily ſpared, ' and make a King fall by thy friendly Hand, ' whoſe Courage ſcorned to bow under the For- ' tune of a puiſſant Enemy.

He mingled theſe Words with ſome others ſo preſſing, that *Petreius* could not refuſe the fatal Courteſy, but without farther delay, ran him through with his own Sword, the King not ſo much as turning his Eye aſide, nor letting fall the leaſt Action unbecoming the Grandeur of his Spirit. *Petreius,* when he had ſeen him breathe his laſt, turned the ſame Point againſt his own Breaſt, and throwing himſelf upon it with all his Force, fell dead at his Feet; thus were the Feſtival Ornaments diſcoloured with royal Blood; and thus did this great King catch up the Shield of Death, to defend himſelf from Ignominy.

A few Days after, the victorious *Cæſar* render-ed himſelf Maſter of both the Realms, and with them of the Queen his Spouſe's Liberty, whom he deſigned for one of the principal Ornaments of his Triumph. She was gone ſome Months with Child, when the King her Husband loſt his Life, and was brought to Bed of the Prince my Ma-ſter, two Days after her Arrival at *Rome*; whither

Cæſar

Cæsar sent her two Months before he made his triumphal Entry.

Thus was my Prince begotten Free, and the Son of a King, but born a Slave: And between his Conception and Birth, happen'd that deplorable Revolution of his Fortune.

Some Days after his Birth, he was carried along, as one of the most remarkable Ornaments of *Cæsar*'s Triumph; Happy in his Misfortune, that as yet he understood not the Shame they made him suffer, being then of an Age incapable of resenting the Loss of his Crowns, his brave Father, or the Death of the Queen his Mother, who resigned her Life a few Days after, she had disclosed the little Heir of her Misfortunes to the World. But there wanted not Persons that took Care of his bringing up; for the great *Cæsar* (from whom the disastrous Fate of his Parents had drawn some Compassion) caus'd him to be brought up at *Rome* in the Garb of a King's Son, and bestowed such a particular Care upon him, that scarce any of his nearest Kindred, in that high swoln Prosperity, was trained to a braver Education: I will yet say further, and believe I shall not injure Truth in affirming, that the Losses of his Estate were in Part repaired by the gallant Education he received among the *Romans*; wherein that tender Age escaping the Impression of the *African* Customs, and the Company of such Persons, which falling far short of the *Roman* Politeness, might have given him a Taste of the *Barbarian*; his excellent Nature contributed such marvellous Assistance to the Care of those, that were ordained to form him, that before his Age could promise it, he became as accomplished in all Requisites of a Prince, as Wish could fancy,

and

and rarely skill'd in every undertaking, to which his vertuous Inclination carried him.

In his earliest Infancy, *Cefar* would often cause him to be brought into his Presence, and observing that something Majestick and Heroical, was already risen with that Morning of his excellent Beauty, he let him get Ground in his Affections, to that Degree, as one Day he broke into an earnest Protestation, That if the little *Juba* (for at his Birth they gave him his Father's Name) seconded those Hopes he had already begun, he would restore him the Crowns of his Anceftors; but he took special Care to mould him to the *Roman* Fafhion, and deface all such unpolifhed Manners, as his Inclinations might poffibly borrow from his *African* Blood. Befides, to fortify the Friendfhip he would have him bear to the Republick, he gave him a *Roman* Name; and becaufe he was brought up in the *Martian* Family, Illuftrious among the *Patricians*, and derived from the famous *Coriolanus*, whofe Valour furvived him in fo glorious a Reputation, he would have the young Prince called by his Name, that the Appellation of *Juba*, which founded Harfh and Barbarous to a *Roman* Ear, might be covered with that of *Coriolanus*.

In all likelihood, the Affection and Bounty of that great Dictator would not here have ftopped, and doubtlefs the Prince had gathered the Fruits of those Promifes, if Death had not robbed him of that Protector, or rather that Father, before he attained to his fourth Year; an Age that hardly rendered him capable to dream of thofe Hopes were given him.

That Man, the Greateft that ever lived; was murdered in the Senate-Houfe, by the ungrateful Confpiracy of thofe, that his own Generofity

and

and Noblenefs had raifed from their Knees; all the World knew itfelf interefled in the Lofs of him, who had made himfelf Mafter of it with his Sword, yet held it in fo gentle a Subjection.

After *Cæfar*'s Death, the little *Coriolanus* (for fo he was always called) wanted no Protection; for the Senate fucceeding *Cæfar* in his Patronage, took up that Care of him which his Death had let fall; and trained him up with the Sons of divers Kings, that were Friends and Allies to *Rome*, without making the leaft Difference in their Expence, or Equipage, though their Fathers had ftill their Crowns in Poffeffion. Divers Children of noble Extraction, and an equal Age, defcended from the Families of *Roman* Knights, were placed in his Service, of which Number I was appointed one, and as I was always brought up near his Perfon, fo his Affection did me the Honour to take me neareft to his Heart. During thofe cruel and difmal Diforders of my Country, that bloody civil War, which Revenge-kindled for *Cæfar*'s Murder, the prodigious Effects of that horrible *Triumvirat*, which overflow'd *Rome* with the Blood of her nobleft Citizens, and that famous Conteft betwixt *Anthony* and *Octavius Cæfar*; the young Prince grew up with a Succefs Miraculous: Never did Eye behold a Youth of thofe Years, handle his Arms with fo great a Grace, or perform any bodily Exercife his Tutors taught him, with a Dexterity comparable to his; his Propenfion led him with fo much Advantage to the Study of Sciences, as he became fo learnedly vers'd in Aftrology and Philofophy, fo critically skilled in all kind of Hiftory, as the World could fcarce afford another to match him; and for Eloquence, that famous Orator that loft his Life in the Heat of the Triumvirat, by the cruel

Com-

Command of *Anthony*, could hardly challenge Preheminence; nor had he Qualities difproportioned to thefe rare Endowments of Body and Mind; fo that the old *Patricians* that took our Examples of high and fublime Virtue, from the ancient *Roman* Difcipline, could find nothing recorded of the *Fabricii*, *Camilli*, and *Scipio's*, which they began not to remark, with Admiration, in the firft Actions of young *Coriolanus*. Befides his prompt Inclination to great Attempts, he conftantly fhew'd fuch a natural Horror of Oppreffion and Injuftice, as it was obferved,. he never cherifh'd a greater Contempt of Danger, nor a more ardent Love of Glory, than Pity of another's Misfortune, and even flighting of his proper Interefts, to give Relief and Comfort to the Miferable. A thoufand Times I have heard him, though fcarce arrived at his thirteenth Year, beg of his Governors in the Heat of a moft preffing Importunity, to lead him to that famous War wag'd between thofe two great Competitors, *Anthony* and *Octavius Cefar*, fince call'd *Auguftus*; and figh at the Recital of thofe great Actions, becaufe he was not permitted to venture for fome of the Glory. Thefe right Marks of a perfect Greatnefs gave him the Hearts and Efteem of all that knew him, and with them purchas'd that of *Auguftus*; for if his firft Inclinations had not been croffed in their Progrefs by another's Intereft, and by fuch Accidents as have fince arriv'd, his Hopes need not have aim'd at lefs Advantage in his Patronage, than they might have done in the great *Julius*, his Uncle, that went before him.; all the noblest *Romans* made Vows in his Favour for this excellent young Prince, who with a fweet, generous, and obliging Behaviour, which he maintained even at the Price of his deareft Interefts,

a charm-a charming Conversation link'd to the lovely Advantage of a most handsome Face and Feature, with that admirable Grace that shined in all his Actions, took into the Affections and Respect of all Persons that were Friends to Virtue: His gallant Deportment in publick Spectacles, drew Admiration both from Senate and People; and before he had fully reached his fourteenth Year, he won the Prize in all those Exercises, wherein Valour or Wit were called to try their Strength; besides other Disputes, wherein his Age might adventure for Repute.

He was scarce fifteen, when *Cæsar*, after the Defeat, and disastrous Fate of *Anthony* and *Cleopatra*, return'd a triumphant Conqueror to *Rome*, where he made himself sole Monarch of the Empire, which that puissant Rival in Ambition had so dangerously disputed. Upon this Occasion, my Prince appeared among those that went out to meet the Emperor, in a gallant Garb; all those that beheld him clad in a Habit, whose Riches lent some Assistance to the Charms of his natural Beauty, mounted upon a brave Horse, which he managed with a matchless Grace and Dexterity, at the Head of a Troop of young Gentlemen much of his own Age, gave him a loud Applause, and cry'd he was not only worthy to be their Commander, but would deserve larger Fortunes, than those to which his Birth intitled him; and the Emperor himself, swoln as he was, at that grand Prosperity and glorious Estate to which he was newly mounted, staid his stately Progress to caress, embrace, and give him such Praises, as the young Prince's Modesty could not accept without Blushes.

The Triumph of *Augustus*, was the proudest that *Rome* ever saw, and it seemed that all the Pomp upon Earth was assembled to make a Master-
piece

piece of Glory for one Man: I will not trouble you with the Description of what I believe you have often received from better Hands, but content myself only to tell you, that the greatest Beauty of the Triumph appeared at the third Day; in the two preceding, *Cesar* only shew'd the Spoils of some barbarous People, and represented his Victory at *Actium*; but at the last he triumphed over *Egypt* and *Cleopatra*. I shall forbear to describe that immense profusion of Riches, and prodigious number of Captives which helped to compose that Show; for my Eyes, as well as those of the people, let all the rest go, to stay themselves upon that stately Chariot, wherein was drawn the lively Portraiture of Queen *Cleopatra*, represented in that posture as she stretched out her arm to the *Asp*, expecting the fatal benefit from his poysonous Tooth; the visage of that Great Queen appeared so full of Majesty, as the pitiful spectacle drew Tears of compassion from the better part of the Spectators; but if the sight of her *Image* tenderly touch'd such hearts as were capable of pity, the living appearance of those Children she had by *Anthony*, which were seated at the feet of their Mother's Effigies, wrought effects no less moving.

The young *Alexander* and his Sister *Cleopatra*, then about ten years of Age, were plac'd upon a seat of an equal height, and their Brother *Ptolomy*, younger by one year than they, a degree under them: Never did mortal Eye converse with any thing so fair as these little Illustrious Captives, which almost unty'd the gaze of all *Rome* from other objects, to fasten them there with extraordinary attention. Their years were not so few to dispense with the apprehension of their own misfortune, which easily made itself

known

known in the fad compofure of their garb, and in
making the Crimfon Rofe only keep the field
in their Faces.

Alexander and Cleopatra were attir'd in the fame
habits of Apollo and Diana, which the unlucky
vanity of their Parents, had formerly caufed them
to appear in ; and had not their prefent condition deftroy'd that belief, they might have paffed in the Spectators opinion for the Divinities
they reprefented ; the Rays that environ'd the
Head of the little Cleopatra, rather feem'd to
proceed from her Eyes, than exterior Drefs ;
and if Shame and Modefty had not directed
their beams downward, fhe would even have
out-fhin'd that Goddefs whofe figure fhe had borrowed. Anthony had been a moft beautiful Prince,
and Cleopatra fuch as Nature would have bungl'd
in their Off-fpring, had fhe made their Features
fall fhort of wonder ; and indeed, this young
Princefs had not only borrowed all that was excellent in both, but furpaffed them in moft apparent Advantages ; fhe had the Queen her Mother's Mouth, with all the bewitching Features
of her Face, but a Complexion beyond comparifon more white and delicate; in the fhine of her
blew Eyes Sweetnefs and Majefty plaid together; her Hair was much brighter than her
Mother's, and as much darker than Anthony's; in
fine, it would then have been a difficult task for
the quainteft invention to find out praifes for her
Shape and Beauty, but time has fince compleated
them to fuch a height of perfection, as it would
pofe the skilfulleft wifh to follow any thing
more accomplifhed. I would fay more upon this
fubject, if your own Eyes had not taken too exact a perufal of thefe rarities, to need my coarfe
defcription. Oh what wonders did my young
                                    Prince

Prince take in at that View! How powerfully
did it wake him out of some melancholly thoughts,
into which he was plunged by that resemblance
of his own Destiny? He had beheld the two first
days Magnificence with an indifferent Eye;
those glittering heaps of Gold and Jewels, the
taking in of Cities, and description of Combats,
represented both by Pencil and Sculpture in the
third day's Triumph, could not wooe him to a
share in the general Acclamation. But he could
not behold the Image of Queen *Cleopatra*, without paying the tribute of Tears to a just compassion, accompany'd with some Sighs, which the
conformity of that Family's downfal with his,
forced from his Breast; and when he cast his
Eyes upon those young Princes, in the same estate
my relation has made them, he thought he had
view'd the beginnings of his own Life, and abandon'd himself to the pity and interest he took in
their condition.

From these first motions of compassion, he succeeded to the admiration of their beauty, and
thence began to enter upon that passion, to which
he has made an entire resignation of his Life; I
was then (as I seldom fail'd to be) near his person, when turning to me, ' Oh, *Emilius, said*
' *he*, what have I seen! did Nature ever make
' an equal to this young Princess, and dost think
' she that is led this day in Triumph, ought not
' one day to Triumph over the most precious li-
' berties? Oh Fortune! (*pursued he a while after*)
' how dost thou play with the destiny of Princes!
' What illustrious companions hast thou given me
' in my bondage!' At these Words he return'd his
Eye, and fastned it with all his thoughts upon that
object, keeping always near the Chariot's side, without the least removal, till the Ceremony was ended.

The Prince was not yet arriv'd to an age capable of strong and violent impressions; and the Princess, who was younger than he by at least four or five years, had not approached to that rare perfection of Beauty, which has since taken her so many Captives; yet *Coriolanus* felt himself struck with an abortive passion, and *Cleopatra*'s Beauty, (though but then in the bloom) staid not for riper Excellencies to begin those Conquests, which she has since perfected with so much ease.

The young Prince began to grow melancholy, to sigh and seek out solitude; and, as he never omitted the caution of hiding his thoughts from me, I knew presently, though my years exceeded not his, where the blow pain'd him. 'Emilius, ' *said he, some days after the Triumph*, didst ever ' see so goodly a creature as this young *Cleopatra*! ' Or rather, can Man's imagination fashion an ' Idea that may pattern Hers! 'Tis true, *said I*, ' the Princess is very handsome. Handsome, *re-* ' *plied he, repulsing me with a little anger*, Say ' rather, that all things else, when they come in ' her presence, are ugly, and that the Gods em- ' ployed all their power to render her the exactest ' piece that ever parted from their hands. Ah! ' how happy will the Man be whom Heaven ' shall think worthy to adore her, and who may ' be permitted to lay down his Life at her Feet, ' and entirely dedicate it to her service! That may ' possibly be yourself, *said I*, and I see you begin ' to aim at that mark, with so direct a disposi- ' tion, that you are most likely to be the happy ' Man you speak of. Doubt not, *reply'd the* ' *Prince*, but my resolution has already devoted ' my Life to the service of that Princess, and that ' no other thought can stay in my breast, but ' such as may shew me how to merit her
' esteem,

' esteem, and promote my design never to be other
' than hers.

'' My Lord, *said I*, in the condition your For-
' tunes are, resolutions of that nature will deserve
' the weighing; and methinks you should not
' dream of any Alliance, but such as may restore
' you to the estate from whence your Family is
' fallen, nor hatch a design of that importance,
' without *Cæsar's* and the *Senate's* approbation,
' upon which apparently depends your destiny.

At these Words the Prince regarded me with an
angry Eye: 'I did not think, *said he*, thou couldst
' have nursed such base thoughts, to advise me to
' do violence upon those beautiful inclinations, by
' any consideration of Fortune: If to scorn *Cleo-*
' *patra* will cut off my pretence to the Crowns she
' has taken from me, it will requite me with a
' glory, upon which that blind *Deity* can exercise
' no power; nor can my desire get up to a nobler
' pitch, than by Courting the Daughter of *An-*
' *thony* and *Cleopatra*, that lately were Masters
' to so many Kings, and held the most conside-
' rable rank in the Universe. Neither *Cæsar* nor
' *Senate* can justly disapprove the design: But
' should they refuse me their protection, if I have
' Virtue on my side, the Gods will never forsake
' me; and possibly my Sword may recover that,
' which my Hopes now tamely expect from their
' condescension.' Such thoughts as these did this
young Amorist already nourish; and if they were
then so stout and generous, time hath since fortified them with such supplies of strength and vigour, as the whole World cannot urge a consideration capable to divert him.

In the mean time *Cleopatra's* Children were
brought up at *Rome*, in an Equipage rather quadrate to their Birth than Fortunes; for the Prin-

cefs *Octavia*, Sifter of *Augustus*, Widow of *Anthony*, and the fame which he repudiated for *Cleopatra*, inftead of preferving an angry refentment againft the memory of her ingrateful Husband, whofe crime was big enough to excufe it; on the contrary, by the fole motion of her own generofity, fhe took home the Children to her Houfe, refign'd up all that Eftate for their maintenance which fhe held of *Anthony*'s, and brought them up with fuch care and tendernefs as if they had been the fruit of her own womb, without putting the leaft inequality betwixt them and thofe fhe had, as well by *Anthony*, which were two Daughters, as by *Marcellus* her firft Husband, by whom fhe had likewife two Daughters and a Son, the brave *Marcellus*, whom doubtlefs you have known to be *Rome*'s darling and delight. The Emperor much applauded his Sifter's goodnefs, which he publickly confirm'd by witnefling a high efteem of that Act; and his Emprefs *Livia*, to fecond his intentions, took the Princefs *Cleopatra* to Court, made her be very carefully educated in the Palace, while the young Princefs remained ftill with the vertuous *Octavia*. In the mean, time my Prince's paffion did daily rife to a greater height in his Soul; and as Nature had given him a hardy confidence, which helped him to enterprize and perform every thing with a fuccefsful grace; fo Love had then left him neither power nor will to keep it longer undifcovered; he had often feen and entertained the young Princefs, in whom, befides an unparallel'd Beauty, he encountred a wit fo vivacious, temper'd with a judgment fo folid, as the World could not boaft the like of another perfon of no greater years; to this charming fweetnefs he had now yielded up his liberty, and cafhier'd all thoughts but fuch as were ferviceable

to

to his amorous Devotion ; he had not yet declar'd his passion while she lived with *Octavia :* though the accostable innocence of her youth seem'd to offer him that liberty : But after the removal to the Court, the increase of hazard hasted the attempt, and one Evening meeting with her in the Empress's Chamber, where the Emperor, with divers of the noblest *Romans,* were likewise present, he aborded her in a gallant fashion, and a graceful garb, only peculiar to himself. ' Fair Princess, *said he aloud,* our Destinies ' carry a near resemblance ; would to Heaven our ' thoughts did so, and that you could as freely ' own the design I have to make myself yours, as ' I have hugg'd the passion that compels me to ' adore you.' These Words were pronounced with an air so hardy, and yet so agreeable, as they got a plausive admiration of all the overhearers ; the young Princess was not then instructed by experience how she ought to receive such language ; yet Innocence did not so blind Apprehension, but that she perceiv'd something in it extraordinary, which made her only blush him an answer ; but the Empress, who had over-heard this Courtship, repeated it aloud to the Emperor, and they both gave it an approbation that augmented the Prince's confidence.

This quickly became the Discourse of the whole Court, and the general opinion voted, that there could not be a pair more fitly coupled than the Son of *Juba,* and the Daughter of *Cleopatra* ; that their Hopes were matches, their Birth and Fortunes equal, and that none could come nearer the graces of young *Cleopatra's* Wit and Beauty, than the noble shape and accomplished qualities of young *Coriolanus.* This discourse, which quickly flew through all *Rome,* marvel-

loufly

loufly favour'd the beginnings of my Prince's paffions, and imbarking himfelf as it were with an
univerfal confent, his hopes were encourag'd to
afpire at a happier fuccefs, than at firft they durft
propofe.

Thus he openly lifted himfelf in the Service
of that Princefs, and employ'd thofe Advantages
which her youth allowed him, freely to infinuate
his affection, and leave impreffions upon her fpirit, which in a riper age would not eafily have
enter'd it; his endeavours wrought fo happily, as,
if he had not yet perfectly taught her how to
love, at leaft he had ufed her to endure the proteftations of his, and oblig'd her to a liking and
efteem of his qualities, that made her to prefer
him before all thofe that came near her. Indeed
the fole merit of my Prince, by thofe rare endowments that garnifh'd his Body and Mind, might
well have wrought that effect; but to thefe he
added an affiduity of refpect and complacence;
which mightily affifted his defert; and prudently confidering that his condition would not always laft in that eftate, and perceiving by fome
marks his obfervation had fhewed him, that the
Princefs, with an accrefcent of years, would raife
her behaviour to a more haughty feverity, than
her youth could yet apprehend requifite, he refolved to prepoffefs her heart as much as poffible,
to level thofe difficulties while time invited, and
ftrive to weaken that Enemy which he knew
would one day combat him.

This conduct is not ordinary in a Perfon of
fixteen years; but at that green Age he had a
grey Difcretion, which brought all Men to their
wonder that remark'd it.

In the mean time, he endeavour'd to delight
her with a thoufand actions of gallantry; and as

he

he had a moſt inventive wit, and an active body
in all ſorts of Exerciſes, he daily made Marches
with young *Romans* of his own Age, either for
Courſes on Horſe-back, or Combats in the Liſt,
beſides divers other agreeable ſpectacles which
were ordinarily preſented in the *Cirque*, in all
which the young Prince behaved himſelf with
ſuch a winning bravery, as it ſenſibly gained the
hearts of all that knew him: But he was not the
only Man deſtiny'd to ſerve that fair Princeſs;
for young as ſhe was, that riſing Sun in her Beauty was already ador'd by the moſt illuſtrious
Romans; two young Princes were ſtruck at
once with her Beauty, and Fortune could not
raiſe him up two mightier Rivals upon Earth;
they were *Marcellus* and *Tiberius*; the former (as
I have told you) Son of the virtuous Princeſs *Octavia*, (Wife to *Anthony*, and Siſter to *Auguſtus*) and
of *Marcellus*, whoſe Widow ſhe was when *Antonius* eſpouſed her; and the other Son to the Empreſs *Livia*, and her firſt Husband *Druſus*. They
were bred up with equal hopes and favour, but
of conditions very different; *Marcellus* had a ſpirit replete with ſweetneſs, freedom, and genero-
ſity, a courage noble and propenſe to great undertakings, and a perſon compleat and becoming
in every Action.

Tiberius with a handſome ſhape indeed, had a
grand courage, but withal, a ſpirit ſo maliciouſly
ſubtile, and known even at that age ſo skill'd in
diſſimulation, as the oldeſt Courtiers were ſcarce
capable of the like. My Maſter was link'd to
Marcellus in the bonds of a ſtrict amity, and the
conformity of their inclinations eaſily taught them
how to love one another; but with *Tiberius* he
liv'd in a faſhion very different, and only contented

ed himfelf to confider him as the *Emperor's* Son-in-Law, without the tye of any particular affection.

One day young *Cleopatra* walking in that ftately Garden that belonged to the Palace, with the Princefs *Julia*, Daughter to the Emperor, a Lady of a florid Beauty, and a lively flowing Wit, whom the Emperor had defign'd for his Nephew young *Marcellus*, to pull the knot of his Alliance ftreighter, and confirm the People (to whom *Marcellus* was infinitely dear) in their hopes, to fee him one day placed upon his Uncle's Throne; thefe two *Princeffes* had walked a while in the great Alley that verg'd upon the River *Tyber*, when they faw my Prince and young *Marcellus*, who had been feeking them, appear at one end of it; though *Marcellus* did but flightly mask his love to *Cleopatra* from his Friends, yet his knowledge of the *Emperour's* intention made him tender in publick a Courtly refpect to *Julia*, though all the fympathy and inclination he had for her, were only perfonated in a bare compliance, which then oblig'd him to proffer his addreffes. The Prince of *Mauritania* was ravifh'd to fee him thus engag'd, becaufe it lent him the liberty of breathing his amorous thoughts to *Cleopatra*; and that fair *Princefs*, whofe efteem was as juft to his worth, as her age would allow, gave him a glad reception, and lending him her hand, they walked at a fit diftance from *Julia* and *Marcellus*: She began but then to enter her twelfth year, and my *Prince* was fomething more than fixteen; but indeed their knowledge had much out-run their age: He entertain'd her a-while with fome difcourfes of divertifement, and in fequel, (hinted by the prefence of the other couple) fucceeded thus to his purpofe: ‘ Would to Heaven, my Prin-‘ cefs, *faid he*, I could promife myfelf as much
‘ inte-

‘ intereſt in your breaſt, as *Marcellus* has in *Ju-*
‘ *lia*'s.   I know not, *anſwer'd the Princeſs,*
‘ what you deſire of me, but I believe *Julia* cannot
‘ think better of *Marçellus*, than I do of you.
‘ 'Tis a greater kindneſs of my Fortune, *reply'd*
‘ *Coriolanus*, than Reaſon could encourage me to
‘ hope ; I cannot be unſatisfied at this Declaration
‘ without injuſtice : But, would you permit me
‘ to unlock my heart with a little more freedom,
‘ 'tis poſſible I might bring you to a knowledge,
‘ that the eſteem you ſpeak of will not ſuffice for
‘ my Felicity.

‘ I thought, *ſaid the Princeſs*, you might have
‘ been contented with it, and that I could not
‘ mention this eſteem, without informing your
‘ underſtanding, how highly I value your good
‘ Qualities.   This favour places me in a conditi-
‘ on which I ought to be proud of, *ſaid the Prince*,
‘ yet let me have leave to tell you, 'tis not enough
‘ to eſtabliſh repoſe in a ſpirit that is dedicated
‘ yours ; for admit the *Gods* had ſtored me with
‘ ſome deſerving Qualities, by the right of thoſe
‘ I might credibly purchaſe a high opinion among
‘ the *Romans*, and yet not engage them to one
‘ ſingle motion of good will ; the buſie noiſe of
‘ ſome Vertue might take me up repute in remo-
‘ teſt Nations ; nay, 'tis poſſible to gain an eſteem
‘ among our Enemies, without changing their in-
‘ clinations : Thus was *Hannibal*'s Vertue as highly
‘ priz'd at *Rome* as at *Carthage*, though in the
‘ former he was mortally hated ; thus the *Gauls*
‘ and *Pompey*'s Partizans conſidered *Julius Cæ-*
‘ *ſar* as the greateſt of Men, and yet he was their
‘ greateſt Enemy.   From thence you infer, *ſaid*
‘ *Cleopatra*, that we may eſteem what we do not
‘ love.   So my reaſon ſays, *ſaid the Prince*, yet
‘ I will not deny, but eſteem is very advantageous

M 5   ‘ to

' to perfons that defire to be loved ; nor that affec-
' tion can hardly enter a well-compofed fpirit, if
' efteem does not lead the way: I will therefore
' receive that efteem with which you reward my
' ardent affection as the beginning of a more ac-
' complifh'd Fortune ; and expect that of time,
' my fervices and your bounty, to which indeed
' my poor ftock of merit can yet plead no claim.
' I am not unwilling, *replied the innocent Prin-*
' *cefs*, to accept your fervices, and I know not
' a perfon whofe carriage and converfe are more
' agreeable than yours. I cannot be fo rude with
' my *Princefs* (*faid Coriolanus, with an action*
' *that exprefs'd a refpective acknowledgment*)
' to demand more at her hands ; I have only this
' to beg of her bounty, that fhe will not fuffer
' time, (which fhall never have power to weaken
' my adoration) to wear out thefe favourable im-
' preffions, nor the knowledge (that will approach
' with increafe of years) of your own admirable
' Beauties, and Divine Qualities, perfuade you to
' regard him with difdain, whom you now judge
' worthy of fo many favours ; nor the encounter
' of refearches, more advantageous for your efta-
' blifhment, prevail with you to prefer perfons
' more happy, or better propt by thofe which
' Fortune has made our Mafters, before fuch as
' fhe has defpoil'd of *Crowns* and *Dignities*.' *Cleo-*
patra young, and as much Infant as fhe was,
was yet fenfibly touched with this difcourfe ; and
regarding my Mafter with an Eye full of fweetnefs, return'd him an anfwer, that proved her
reafon had much got above her age.
' If the malice of Fortune, and the lofs of
' Crowns could render perfons contemptible, the
' Children of *Anthony* and *Cleopatra* would find
' little refpect and confideration among Men ;
' you

' you know our House is fallen as low as yours,
' and were it reared again to its former height,
' neither that age nor knowledge whose approa-
' ches you dread, should hinder me from confi-
' dering that in you, which neither Fortune can
' rob you of, nor the support of our Masters be-
' stow on those, which you excel as well by
' Birth and Virtue, as personal endowments.' The
Prince listned to this well-fram'd language (which
indeed his hopes little expected from so young
an intellect) with transport and wonder, and,
not able to stop the Career of his Joy, with
the consideration of those that were present, he
put one knee to the ground, and fastening his lips
with a little violence to *Cleopatra*'s hand: ' The
' Gods can witness, *said he*, that I never appre-
' hended worth enough in myself to measure
' with this grace my *Divine Princess* has given
' me; but I do here protest in their presence,
' that I will strive to merit it, both by services
' of worth, and such actions as shall either repair
' the ruines of my House, or at least hinder my
' *Princess* from repenting her bounty.

He had enlarg'd his Discourse, if *Marcellus*
(who then preferr'd *Cleopatra*'s converse far before
Julia's) had not oblig'd the *Princess* to break off
the parley, by joining company. If my Prince
had not truly loved *Marcellus*, he would not have
taken that interruption so gently; but his friendship, joined with the late satisfaction his spirit
had taken, helped him to dissemble the displeasure he received, and accost the Princess *Julia*,
with a visage that betray'd not the least mark of
any alteration.

After that day, he oft repeated his passion to
Cleopatra, and confirmed his own hopes by a thousand proofs of her innocent affection.   These beginnings

ginnings prefag'd a happy progrefs, but they met
with checks by the way, for the rivalfhip of
Marcellus did much trouble the ftream of his defign. *Marcellus* was (as I have told you) of a very amiable perfon, and little fhort of my Prince
in any becoming quality, by his advantage in the
Emperor's favour, and People's affection, who
gave him the name of *Rome*'s Darling and Delight; his face, perfon, and excellent parts, with
that clear difcretion that compos'd his Courtfhip
to *Cleopatra*, kindled a juft jealoufie in *Coriolanus*:
Befides, *Marcellus*, as he was *Octavia*'s Son, enjoy'd
the fame liberty with *Cleopatra* and *Anthony*'s
other Children, as if the fame womb had difclof-
ed them; and by that appellation of Brother and
Sifter, both *Octavia*'s Command, and *Cæfar*'s
Will enjoin'd them to call one another. And
which moft preferred this young Prince's hopes,
he poffeft an unreftrained familiarity with the
Princefs, which was not accorded to any other:
But that which ftung my Prince deepeft, was,
that *Marcellus* (being as well the deareft of his
Friends, as the greateft of his Rivals) all the im-
pediments and fears he gave him, were fo incapable of blotting out his amity, as he could not
profecute his re-fearch of *Cleopatra* without regret, fince he could reap no advantage by it, that
would not difturb the repofe, and affront the Fortune of his Friend. A reflection of this nature
in fuch a Soul as my Mafter's, could produce none
but uncommon effects, and the fequel will tell you,
how ftrongly it wrought too in that of *Marcellus*, whofe fentiments, (not to abridge Truth of
her due) were not lefs noble than my Mafter's.
In differs Encounters thefe two Princes mutually
apprehended the difpleafures they gave one another, by a competition which in Souls lefs generous,

rous, would oft have ftrangled Friendfhip; yet in theirs fhe ftood fo firm and entire, as my Prince never glanc'd at *Marcellus*, when he pleaded in his own Love-fuit; nor did *Marcellus* (when he laid his amorous Vows at *Cleopatra*'s Feet) ever let fall a Word in Difapprovement of *Coriolanus*. My Mafter (by what might be judged from Appearance) had more Favour than his Rival, which would have rendered his Joy more perfect, had he carry'd that Advantage from any but *Marcellus*; and he had hugg'd his Happinefs with a clearer Delight; if it had not ftood bent to his Friend's Prejudice. But if *Coriolanus* thus moderated the Refentment of his own Felicity, becaufe it oppos'd his Friends, *Marcellus* indur'd his Advantage with Patience, fince *Coriolanus* reap'd the Profit, nor could his own Misfortune afflict him, without the mixture of fome Comfort, becaufe it conduc'd to his Friend's Succefs.

  ' I defire not (*would* Coriolanus *fay to* Cleopatra)
' you fhould hate *Marcellus*; for, if a Man can me-
' rit it, he is worthy of your Affections: But if it
' be deftin'd for any Mortal, I demand it wholly
' and entire for *Coriolanus*.'   *Marcellus* would almoft fay the fame Things, only he durft not let his Paffion come abroad fo openly as my Mafter's, for fear to difpleafe the Emperor his Uncle, who did him the Honour to defign him his Daughter, helped him to cut out a Difguife for his Affection, and make the borrowed Name of Brother (injoin'd by *Octavia*) ferve to mask that of Lover.

  Thus had they wafted almoft a Year, during which my Prince, doubtlefs more deep ftruck than *Marcellus*, daily gather'd fuch frefh Caufes of Difpleafure from his Friend's Encroachment, as the Melancholly it produced began to ferve itfelf in his Face and Behaviour, though the Caufe was concealed from all the World but myfelf, whom,

by

by a peculiar Preference to the rest, he always
honoured with the Knowledge of his Secrets:
'And why, *said he, one day to me,* should mis-
'chievous Fortune raise me up a Rival of my
'dearest Friend, and such a Friend, whose Re-
'pose I cannot combat, without wounding my
'own? Ah! had it pleased the Gods to inspire
'any other but *Marcellus,* with the Design of
'serving *Cleopatra,* our Swords should decide
'our Titles, and sure I should kill any but *Mar-
'cellus* in so just a Quarrel.' In fine, his Sadness
grew to such an Height, as *Marcellus,* who perceiv'd it with the first, began to be much troubled
at it; and indeed (as one that went a deep Share
in all the Resentments of so dear a Friend) he often demanded the Cause, though his own Suspicion did partly answer him: But *Coriolanus* still
took care to cover the Truth, till all his Friend's
Reasons growing too weak to satisfy *Marcellus's*
Care, at last he was constrained to discharge his
Heart; and one Night, as they lay together, which
they often did, *Marcellus* having often press'd
him upon that Subject, and a thousand times
sworn he could never be capable of any Pleasure,
so long as he saw him drown'd in so deep a Sorrow, and himself ignorant of its Fortune. The
Prince sending one or two Sighs before the Discourse he was to make, 'Brother, *said he,* (*for
'so they always called one another*) the Gods
'can attest, you do force that from me by your
'Friendship, which I ever resolved to wrap in
'silence, though you might easily have read it by
'your own Observation, and so have spared your
'Constraint of a bad Relation: Did you believe
'I could see myself travers'd in a Passion that is
'twined with my vital Thread, by a Friend as
'dear to me as myself, without a mortal Displea-
'sure?

' fure?   Do you think I could defign the Ruin
' of your Content, or abandon the Care of mine
' own Repofe, without a cruel Violence?   You
' know I was *Cleopatra's* eldeft Prifoner, before
' your Eye had marked her out for a Miftrefs ;
' and had my dear *Marcellus* prevented my De-
' fign of ferving her, I fhould fooner have ran
' upon my Death than his Pretences, or expos'd
' him to the Anguifh he has made me refent ;
' nor did I perceive he was my Rival, before I
' was engaged too deep to render what was due
' to our Amity; which (if I may fay it) he him-
' felf has forgotten to pay.   Ah! would to Hea-
' vens our Conteft had been for Crowns, or any
' thing elfe of higher Value, you fhould quickly
' have feen with what a free Heart I would have
' given up my Intereft.   But for *Cleopatra*, my
' dear Brother, 'tis that cannot be obtain'd of an
' enflaved Spirit, that will never recover Strength
' enough to get out of the Abyfs wherein my
' fpightful Fortune has plunged me; I fay, my
' fpightful Fortune, for whatever Glory I acquire
' by *Cleopatra's* Service, and however my Hopes
' may feed high upon Succefs, I fhall never think
' that Fortune propitious, that muft be eftablifh'd
' at the Price of your Repofe; nor have I the
' liberty to court it fo much as with a fingle Wifh,
' fince it can no where be raifed but upon the
' Ruins of your's.

Coriolanus accompany'd thefe Words with many
others of the fame nature; which funk fo fenfibly
to *Marcellus's* Heart, as it was long before he
could recover Strength enough to fhape a Reply ;
at laft, his Words broke their way through his
Refentments, and, embracing my Mafter with an
ardent Affection, ' My dear Brother, *faid he,*
' Heaven is my Witnefs, that when my Eye firft
' told

' told me *Cleopatra* was lovely, I did not believe
' your Youth could have been capable of forming
' a Defign to ferve her ; and if I have fince let
' myfelf flip into the Snare, I render'd my Liber-
' ty to that invincible Puiffance, which no Heart
' can refift ; yet, I confefs, I have finned againft
' our Amity, and fhould prove myfelf unworthy
' of a Place in *Coriolanus*'s Heart, if I do not
' ftrive with my Soul to render the Reparation I
' owe you ; I know my Intentions are good, but
' do a little diftruft my Power : But, however,
' this Night, to clear all Scores, and poffibly be-
' fore we part, I fhall make it appear how dearly
' I prize our Friendfhip.

 Coriolanus would have reply'd to this Difcourfe,
but *Marcellus* oppofed it ; and prefs'd him fo earneftly to give him the Remainder of that Night,
as he was conftrain'd to obey him : They both
paffed it over, without fo much as clofing their
Eyes ; my Mafter often over-hearing the Sighs that
broke away from *Marcellus*, though he ftrove to
imprifon them with all his Power, and ftill cut
them off in the middle, left their Noife fhould
convey them to my Mafter's Ear. The Hour that
he was wont to call them up, was not yet arrived,
when *Marcellus*, turning himfelf to my Prince's
Side, with a vivacious and refolute Action, ' Bro-
' ther, *faid he*, I have combated and conquered
' for you, or rather for myfelf, fince by this
' Victory I am directed in part, how to expiate
' the Crime I have committed : *Cleopatra* now
' is your's, and I ask your Pardon for having fo
' unjuftly difputed her ; our Friendfhip, with the
' Aid of Reafon, has almoft driven her from my
' Heart ; and all that remains unfinifh'd of the
' Cure, I think may fafely be referred to the Sur-
' gery of Time, my Youth, and a fhort Abfence,
          ' which

‘ which is already defigned : I am now enter'd
‘ an Age that alarms me to the Trade of my
‘ Anceftors, and tells me, 'tis time to go feek out
‘ Reputation with my Sword in my Hand. I
‘ will therefore beg the Emperor's Permiffion to
‘ go ferve my Apprenticefhip under the Conful
‘ Vinicius, who marches, within a few Days,
‘ with a puiffant Army into Germany, where I
‘ hope to perfect my Recovery ; not only by the
‘ help of a large Diftance, and a different Em-
‘ ployment, but a ftrong Refolution more exact-
‘ ly to ballance the Emperor's Favour, and turn
‘ all my Thoughts upon the Princefs Julia, who
‘ has already honoured me with more Affection
‘ than I have merited. At my return, I dare pro-
‘ mife, you fhall find me fo perfectly chang'd, as
‘ I fhall conferve no other Thoughts for Cleopa-
‘ tra, but to prize her as a Princefs that deferves
‘ my Friend's Affection ; and both to confirm
‘ and affift her Defigns in your Favour, againft
‘ all fuch Perfons as may plead Pretences to the
‘ Right you have in her.

Thus the noble Marcellus charactered his victorious Friendfhip, and at the clofe of his Difcourfe,
left my Prince fo ravifh'd at his Freedom and Generofity, as it coft him fome time to put a Shape
to his Refentments : Yet at laft he reply'd, but in
fuch Language, as did rather combat than gratu-
late his Friend's Intention ; he was very loath to
be out-done in Generofity, or put his Defires upon
a gentler Rack for his Friend, than he had already done for him. This begat a kind Conteft
betwixt them, which lafted a great Part of the
Day ; and it was fought on both fides againft
themfelves, with fo much Obftinacy, as the Repetition of Particulars would but tire your Attention : At laft, it was but fit that Marcellus (whofe
Paffi-

Paffion was of a later Date, and lefs ardent than
my Mafter's) fhould keep the Lifts, and that my
Prince's Confent fhould quadrate to the Emperor's
Intentions, and People's Defires, by placing his
Friend's Heart in the Princefs *Julia*'s Service ; but
he could not quit him to his *German* Expedition,
without a Refolution to bear him Company. And
befides the Confideration of their Amity, not being lefs tickled than he with defire of Glory, he
concluded to carry his Arms with him under *Vinicius*, and difpofed himfelf for his Departure
with fuch lively Hopes, as helped to charm a part
of his Griefs for leaving *Cleopatra*.

Some Provinces in *Germany*, newly rifen in
Rebellion, had cut in pieces the *Roman* Garrifons ;
and with two mighty Armies, levy'd upon the
Banks of *Danubius*, not only ftruck a Terror into
all the neighbouring Nations ; but, fwoln with
Succefs, began to menace the Empire itfelf. For
this Expedition, *Cæfar* made choice of *Vinicius*, a
fage and experienced Captain, to go in the Head
of the valianteft Legions ; and he was ready to
begin to march, when our two young Princes demanded Leave of the Emperor to go gather the firft
Flowers of their Reputation in the Field. I doubt
not but you know this has been a *Roman* Cuftom ;
and all thofe famous Commanders the World has
talk'd fo much of, whofe Virtue gave *Rome* fo
vaft a Dominion, did firft learn their Alphabet of
War under the antient Captains.

The two young Princes, confirmed in this Defign, threw themfelves at the Emperor's Feet, reprefenting, that now the arrival of their feven-
teenth Year had brought them Strength to charge
through the Incommodities of War, it was time
to begin with fuch Actions, as might inftruct
them to deferve his Affection, and copy the Glory
of

of their Ancestors. This Request was easily obtained of the Emperor, whose generous Spirit highly applauded their brave Resolution.

They presently put Things in order for their parting; but my Master's grand Preparation, was to divide himself from *Cleopatra*; his Passion was already grown to its full Stature, and the Princess still preserv'd him in her Favour, with particular Improvements of Good-will: Yet she began to draw herself within the Guard of a greater Reservation than formerly; and her Increase of Years taught her the Severity to cut off those Liberties by degrees, which her flexible Youth had allow'd him.

The Prince's Fore-sight of this prepared him to endure it with Patience, instructing all his Actions to express a Respect so her so submissive, as pleaded a true Title to what he had gotten in her Heart; yet he could not defend himself from the Stings of Discontent at this Separation, and had not a greedy Desire of Glory been too strong for his Grief, every Eye would have read it too plainly in his Visage.

The parting Day being arrived, he felt a Necessity of all his Courage, to pronounce an untroubled Farewel to his Princess; but he gather'd no slight Satisfaction from his Discovery, by some infallible Tokens, that she was sensibly touched at this Separation, and betray'd a timorous Jealousy of those Dangers to which he was going to expose his Safety.

There are too many Passages challenge a mention in my Recital, to allow me the Leisure of enlarging myself upon the several Discourses they exchanged at this parting; and therefore I shall only content myself to tell you, that my Prince, After he had made fresh Protestations of an eternal Fidelity to the Princess, obtained a Promise from

her fair mouth, to preserve him in her Thoughts
with so vigorous a Care, as should weaken all
the Attempts of Absence against her Resolution,
to prefer him before all Men: But the parting
Words of *Marcellus* were very remarkable; and
after he had vowed at *Cleopatra*'s Feet, that he
despoiled himself (for his Friend's sake) of all those
Pretences, that his Love and Services might have
given him; he spoke such Things in my Prince's
behalf, as (though they did Truth no Injury)
could spring from no other Fountain but a strong
and perfect Amity; yet the sweetest of my Master's Comforts at that parting, was a Permission,
by the Command of *Octavia*, and Consent of the
Empress herself, to write to his Princess.

But I will hold you no longer: The two Princes marched away with a proud Equipage, and
I followed my Master in this Expedition, (as I
did in all the rest that succeeded it (and joining
the Troops that attended them, with the Consul's
gross Body; we left *Italy* behind us, and by large
Marches quickly gained the *Danubius*; we met
no Adventures by the Way that will deserve to
be dwelt upon, and indeed my Relation ought
but slightly to pass away the Morning of my Master's Youth, that it may more speedily arrive at
those weightier Actions of which his Life has
been composed; I will only tell you, that his beginnings were Miraculous, that at his first Encounters he did such Things as ravished the Consul,
amazed the Soldiery; and scarce found Credit at
Rome, though several Letters reported it.

Marcellus also, at the first Essay of his young
Valour, bravely signalized it by Actions worthy
of an eternal Memory; and these two Princes
(instead of Envy and Emulation) did mutually
interess themselves in each other's Glory; *Marcel-*
lus

lus tafted no truer Delight in his own, than in
the Reputation *Coriolanus* had gotten; and *Coriolanus* could not liften to his proper Praifes, with
clearer Satisfaction, than to thofe that cry'd up
Marcellus's Credit: Indeed, 'tis true, my Mafter
had the Luck to perform fome Acts, that made his
Fame found higher than his Friend's; and in the
feveral Encounters were made upon the Banks of
Danubius, before the grand Battle, he rendered
himfelf remarkable by the Effects of a Valour,
which the *Romans* publifhed beyond all Example;
at an Encounter which one of our Legions had
with fome Troops of *Barbarians*, he refcued the
Roman Eagles from a throng of Enemies that had
newly feiz'd them, and brought them back to
Vinicius, with their Wings bathed in the Blood
of his Enemies, who cry'd up that Action with
fuch loud Praifes, as could not be accepted by the
Prince's Modefty: At the Affault of fome revolted
Places that oppofed our Paffage, and were carried
by Storm, he was ever the firft that entred the
Breach; and by the Confeffion of the *Romans*,
their taking it was due to the glorious Example
he gave thofe that fought near him; nor was his
Valour (of which he had given them fo many
Precedents) his only Virtue, for in all thofe Diforders that Victory ufes to drag along with it, he
gave Proofs of a moft unparallel'd Moderation;
treated thofe that fell into his Hands more like
Friends and Allies than Enemies; and at the taking of fuch Places as were won by Affault, he
often obtained many Lives of his Enemies by his
earneft Interceffion, which *Vinicius* had defign'd
for an exemplary Terror to be cut in Pieces. By
fuch Actions as thefe, with the reft of his brave
Demeanour among the Officers and Soldiers, he
had fo gained the Hearts of the whole Army, that
they

they all petition'd *Vinicius* to give him some considerable Command; though it was unheard of in the *Roman* Discipline, to commit any Charge to Persons of his Age: And when *Vinicius* at their Sollicitation, assisted by his own Esteem of their worth, had given him and *Marcellus* a joint Commission to command the Cavalry, all the Officers submitted to them, with a Joy that wanted no Proofs to express itself.

But the *Germans* were not the only Enemies they had to combat; for *Cleopatra's* Remembrance kindled a crueller War, than the *Barbarians* could menace; indeed my Prince had no greater Task than daily to feed and confirm those Thoughts that entirely laid his Life at his Princess's Feet; every Idea that his Fancy could shape, had the Face of Delight, and left a pleasing Impression upon his Spirit; but *Marcellus* fought with a ruder Combatant, and found his Design to banish her his Breast, was not like to gain an easy Conquest; however, he stretched all his Forces to struggle for it, and at last his continued Care carried the Victory: My Master (who in Part perceived the silent Torments that Prince's Generosity inflicted upon himself) did often endeavour to stagger his Resolution, and daily protested, that he had rather have him for a Rival all his Life; nay, would sooner chuse (if necessity required, and possibility consented) to release all his own Pretences, than approve the Violence suffered for his sake.

But the generous *Marcellus* stuck to his Promise with an unshaken Constancy; and then being very young, and daily diverted by his warlike Employment, which he ever followed with a marvellous Ardour, he obtained in Part of himself what he desired; and striving to prefer *Julia* to

his

his Thoughts by the Memory of her Beauty (which indeed might be ranked with the most delicate in the World) by the Favour she had shewn him, and the Emperor's Will, upon whom his Fortunes totally depended, he quickly made a confiderable Progreſs.

In the mean time my Prince wrote often to the Princeſs *Cleopatra*; it would poſe my Memory to repeat all his Letters, I have only in Part retained the Senſe and Words of ſome of the ſhorteſt; and I believe the firſt he wrote little differed from theſe Terms.

Prince *Coriolanus* to the Princeſs *Cleopatra*.

' IT is not to tell you (my divine Princeſs)
' that you are always preſent in my Memo-
' ry; for with greater Truth I may proteſt you
' have the entire Poſſeſſion of my Soul, where,
' in the ſterneſt Dangers, you ever keep your
' Command, and combat *Rome*'s Enemies with
' Arms that are invincible. Ha! my Princeſs,
' who can oppoſe a Heart animated with ſo bright
' an Image! What Enemy will be able to diſ-
' pute the Glory with me that may ſhew me the
' Way to deſerve you? This high Deſign will
' doubtleſs teach me to do ſomething more great,
' than Fortune can promiſe, and my Deſtiny is
' too fair to fear a Defeat by other Enemies, after
' being conquer'd by the divine *Cleopatra*.

This firſt in a ſhort Time was ſucceeded by another, and I think the Words were theſe.

Prince *Coriolanus* to the Princeſs *Cleopatra*.

' I Would ſay Fortune ſmil'd upon me, if the
' Succeſs I have gotten by her Favour, were
' not moderated by an Abſence; to reſiſt which,
' I have

' I have scarce any Courage left me; yet I would
' strive to support it, might I hope a Place in the
' Memory of my adorable Princess; I confess I
' cannot ask it without Rashness, and yet not
' forbear the demand, without neglecting what
' I owe to the Conservation of a Life I have
' given her.

These were the two first he wrote, of which
he received no answer; but a while after, having
done Wonders in another Encounter, which Report quickly carried to *Rome*, the Princess *Octavia* and the Emperor himself enjoin'd her to
write to him, which to satisfy them she did in
these Words.

The Princess *Cleopatra* to Prince *Coriolanus*.

' I Obey the Commands impos'd upon me, to
' write to you without Repugnance; and I
' follow my proper Inclinations, when I assure you
' of the Interest I take in the glorious Success of
' your Arms; the whole World publishes your
' beautiful Actions; *Rome* is an entire Admirer,
' and I a particular Rejoicer at them: The Gods
' grant that Fortune may never forsake you, and
' that you may not so blindly resign your Safety
' to your Courage, as not to be careful of preser-
' ving a Life, that can never be indifferent to those
' you judge worthy of your Remembrance.

My Prince received this Letter from the Princess, with an Excess of Joy, and kissed it a thousand Times, in an amorous Rapture at these precious Marks of her Affection. The Knowledge
it gave him how much she concern'd herself in
his Glory, spurr'd him on to greater Enterprizes,
and carried him to such a sublime Pitch in the
whole Army's Esteem, as it talk'd of nothing
more

more than the Effects of his Valour, nor was he
lefs known (by the Havock he made) in the Enemy's Camp than ours.

After divers Fights in Parties, the two Armies
came to a general Battle, and it was fought fo
bravely on both Sides, upon the Banks of *Danubius*, that the Streams took Increafe and Complexion from the Blood that was fpilt: Young
Coriolanus and his Friend *Marcellus* at the Head
of the Cavalry they commanded, did there difclofe
fuch prodigies of Valour, as till then were not
known among the *Romans*, and gave Proofs of
their Prudence and good Conduct, which no Hopes
could rationally expect from fo immature an Age:
Twice or thrice they rallied, and re-inforc'd their
Troops, which the firft Fury of the *Barbarians*
had put into Diforder, and led them on again fo
courageoufly, as after they had forced their Refiftance by a Valour more than human, they totally
routed the Enemy, and obliged the *Roman* Conful
to publifh at the End of the Day, that the Palm of
Victory was only gather'd by their Virtue.

Marcellus faved the Life of *Vinicius*, mounted
him again, and bravely cut him out a Path to
Safety, through a Throng of his Enemies, in the
middle of which he was fighting on Foot, in manifeft Peril of his Life; and my Mafter, among
other Actions, by which he fignaliz'd himfelf in
that memorable Day, having broken the ftouteft
Squadron that environ'd them, gave death with
his own Hands to the two chief Commanders of
the Enemy's Army; and, by that Action, depriv'd
all the reft of their Courage, which they took from
the Prefence of their Generals.

The Battle did not period the War, for there
yet remained fome fcatter'd Troops to be defeated,
and revolted Places that made fome Refiftance.

Two whole Years were spent in this Expedition;
at the End of which, the two Princes, having
now no more Work for their Swords in *Germany*,
bent their Course with the Consul to *Rome*, laden
with Praises that were never due before to such
young Beginners. My Master daily shorten'd his
way, with all the Joy that could be given him,
by the hope of restoring his Eyes to the sight of
Cleopatra, whom two Years Absence (instead of
effacing) had more lively engraven in his Memory; and, which helped to compleat his Satisfaction, he perceiv'd his dear *Marcellus* was perfectly
cured; and that he had now no further Cause to
fear to be travers'd by such Persons, whose Repose
he was obliged to value.

The Exploits *Vinicius* had done in *Germany* were
so great, that the Senate decreed him the Honour
of Triumph; but he refusing it with a remarkable Modesty, the grandeur of his Services was
acknowledg'd by other Recompences that were
very glorious, and by the Command of the Emperor and Senate, there was made him a most
magnifick Entry, where every thing appeared in
a pompous Dressing; but the greatest Part of the
Romans found nothing so beautiful as our two
young Princes, that marched on both Sides the
Consul, clad in Arms, that were hid in the Splendor of Gold and Jewels, their Head and Shoulders
were shaded with white Feathers, and themselves
mounted on two white Horses, whose beautiful
Pride did marvellously aid the Grace wherewith
their Masters managed them. All those that saw
them pass in that Equipage, and had taken the
Account of the gallant Actions they performed in
War, from the Mouth of Fame, strew'd their Passages with loud Acclamations of Joy, and their Praises throng'd, like themselves, to welcome them.
The

The Emperor receiv'd them with abundance of Careffes; and the Privilege *Marcellus* borrow'd from
his Alliance, gave him no Advantage of my Mafter
in that Reception. They were likewife faluted by
the Emprefs and Princefs *Octavia*, with kind Af-
pects; but when they approached *Cleopatra*, the
fight of her made my Mafter's Eye releafe all other
objects, and his memory efface them; in this two
years abfence he found her marvelloufly chang'd,
her ftature (though fhe was then but fifteen) already reached the common height of Women, her
neck almoft formed to its perfect proportion, and
her Beauty mounted near to that Meridian in which
you have viewed her; but with this advantageous
change, a Royal Majefty fat inthron'd in her face,
and armed her looks with a greater feverity than
appear'd in her precedent years; and my Prince
could not behold her vifage without gathering the
effects of a fear from her flowered Excellencies,
which grew not there before in her budding youth;
yet fhe received him with her obliging Civilities.
He had no fooner accofted her, but without regard
to the illuftrious Spectators, he bent a knee to the
Earth, and ravifhed a kifs from her fair hand,
before fhe could enforce him to rife; by this extraordinary refpect publickly ftripping part of his
amorous defigns to thofe that had not yet difcovered them. In the prefence of fo many witneffes
and perfons that waited to fucceed one another in
his embraces, he then had not the freedom of a
particular converfe with her; but his Eyes were
the Deputies of his Tongue, and elegantly tranf-
lated moft of thofe amorous thoughts into paffionate looks, which his mouth fhould have put into
accents. The whole Court fpoke highly to his
advantage; the general vote publifhed his brave
beginning beyond parallel, and the Emperor him-

felf

self commended him to such a height, as might have topp'd the most irregular ambition; the honours that were rendered him had the approbation of all but *Tiberius*, the only Man that envy'd his Fortune, who (prepossessed by a mortal jealousy against him) was stung to the heart at the praises were given him; *Marcellus* had a great share in the glory, which indeed he justly merited, and the affection which the *Romans* naturally bare him, was marvellously augmented, by that clear proof of his Virtue.

My Master being return'd to his lodging, was visited by a throng of his Friends, and the first news he received, was, that *Tiberius* was enamoured of the Princess *Cleopatra*; my Prince had begun to suspect it before his departure, but during his absence, *Tiberius* had made his re-search so publick, as *Rome* had few persons that ignor'd it: *Coriolanus* resented this intelligence with a sensible displeasure, yet dissembled it to his Friends, with all the power and skill he could use; but when they had left him the liberty to entertain me in private, he passionately declared himself fearful of so puissant a Rival; not that the valour or merit of his Person had any place in his fears, for while those were only in question, he knew himself able to dispute *Cleopatra*; but he dreaded his Mother, the Empress *Livia*, well knowing, the credit she had with the Emperor, had power to cross his designs, if she once approved of her Son's affection: However, he resolved to assault all obstacles that encountred him, and openly to dispute that at the price of his Life, which his reason judg'd to be no Man's due but his own.

He patiently waiteth an occasion to entertain the Princess upon that subject, and (if possible) learn from her mouth the sentiments she had for his

Rival;

Rival; the following day offered him the liberty
to make that trial, and obtaining the permission
to give her a visit in her own lodgings, he enjoyed a large opportunity of exchanging his
thoughts with her without interruption.

Their first discourse may better be imagined
than related, and you may easily judge my Master spent it upon the torments he suffered for her
absence, while the Princess expressed the glad content she took in his return, with the happy and
glorious success of his voyage; yet she contracted
her language and looks with so much moderation
and strict reserve, received the discourse with so
serious a face, as it startled some of his forwardest
hopes, which though he had foreseen, yet he was
not so well fortified against it, as not to read over
her visage with a timorous Eye; yet he met something there that hinted the occasion he desired;
and mingling the respect with his Words, which
that new Majesty imprinted: ' Madam, *said he*,
' if I may be permitted, without offending the ve-
' neration I owe you, to undisguise a part of my
' Sentiments, I must take the liberty to say, that
' the severity that sits upon your brow, does pro-
' mise no happy Augury to my hopes; indeed,
' if it only springs from a right understanding
' of what you are, I have no reason left me to
' complain; and mine shall agree with the judg-
' ments of persons most disinterested, that it is
' but a fit companion of that bright Majesty,
' which we all acknowledge in you, as the Prin-
' cess of the World, in whom it is most justly
' spher'd; but if it parts from another cause, I
' do there behold my condemnation, and read my
' irreparable ruine.

' I did not perceive, *said the Princess* inter-
' rupting *him*, that my behaviour to you had put
N 3 ' on

' on any other fashion than it has formerly worn ;
' and if a small accefs of years, has a little check-
' ed the freedom of my carriage, I cannot think
' the change can either difadvantage your hopes,
' or difquiet your repofe. I did always judge,
' *replied the Prince*, that the childhood of my
' Fortune was too forward to be long-liv'd ; nor
' can I frame a juft complaint, becaufe you cut
' off a part of thofe favours which I never me-
' rited ; but fince all Men are as unworthy as I,
' with your permiffion I will believe, that *Tiberius*
' has not more right to demand them than myfelf.

By thefe Words *Cleopatra* perceived the kind-
lings of my Mafter's jealoufy, and now not doubting but he had heard of the purfuits *Tiberius* had
made in his abfence, fhe refolv'd to keep on the
mask no longer ; and preventing his difcourfe with
a fmile : ' Indeed, I thought, *faid fhe*, you would
' meet with the notice of what has paffed fince
' your departure, and if you ftill owned an in-
' tereft in my affairs, you would not ftay long
' for the knowledge, that *Tiberius* has offered me
' affection. I did believe it neceffary to diffemble
' what I knew of it, nor fhall I make any fcru-
' ple to avow (if my apprehenfion fcap'd mif-
' take) that the refentments *Tiberius* has for me
' are the fame with yours. I With mine, *faid* Co-
' riolanus, *with a hafty interruption*, Ah! *Ma-*
' *dam*, do not wound me with fo deep a difplea-
' fure, to think mine can fuffer comparifon, with-
' out a mortal offence ; I will eafily believe *Tibe-*
' *rius* doth love you, for there is nothing upon
' Earth deferves lefs incredulity ; but that his Paf-
' fion can meafure with mine, is a belief that all
' the ftrength of my fubmiffion and obedience is
' too weak to bow me to. *Tiberius* has excellent
' Qualities, and poffibly a Perfon more confider-
                                              ' able

'able than mine, but our difpofitions are very
'different, and I know our Souls are incapable of
'cherifhing an equal flame; if all the requifites
'of Love were comprized in offering Proteftati-
'ons of fidelity at your feet, or fprufing up the
'Paffion in artificial language, perhaps I might
'juftly claim no advantage; but if to mifprife
'and abandon all thofe things, wherewith am-
'bitious perfons build their felicity, to facrifice
'my Life at your feet; nay, and if poffible, to
'dye it a thoufand times over in your facrifice,
'be to love aright, methinks you fhould find fome
'difference 'twixt the Paffion of *Tiberius*, and that
'of *Coriolanus*.

'Then I will tell you, *faid the Princefs*, to re-
'pair the difpleafure I have given you; that I do
'diftinguifh betwixt you; and if I thought you
'would not take too much advantage of my Words,
'I would add, that you are better placed in my
'opinion than *Tiberius*; not that his affection
'has not put on as fair and fpecious proofs, nor
'that it has almoft fpoke the fame language that
'yours have utter'd; yet with truth I dare affure
'you, that neither his difcourfe nor actions have
'got any hold in my heart; and if I change not
'my humour, I think it will ask a long time
'to make my inclinations look that way.

This free and unreferv'd Declaration of the Princefs gave my Mafter a fatisfaction that drove away
all his fears, and calm'd his difpleafures; which
not being able to diffemble one moment, recovering that gaiety that ufually fparkled in his lively
looks: 'I am made too glorious, *faid he*, by the
'honour you have done me, in thus unmafquing
'your propenfions; and fince they are not dif-
'pos'd of to my Rival, but I am permitted to try
'my title with him by my fervices, I will learn

'to

' to hope from your bounty, and the Divine Fa-
' vour, that he shall not carry the advantage. And
' now, *Madam*, I will freely confess, that I take
' not my greatest fears from his Person, for I do
' much more redoubt the credit of the *Empress*,
' than either the Services or good Qualities of *Ti-*
' *berius*. 'Tis true, *replied Cleopatra*, the Em-
' press did a while since speak in his Favour, but
' she had not as yet much pressed it; for as her
' thoughts are busier in building up the fortunes
' and greatness of her Son, than soothing his af-
' fection; so I think her studies are more direct-
' ly levelled at a power in the *Emperor's Spirit*,
' than in mine. May she have the Gods consent,
' *replied Coriolanus*, to the success of that design,
' for they all know I will neither grudge him the
' Favour of *Augustus*, nor the possession of the *Em-*
' *press*, provided he lets fall his *Title* to my *Prin-*
' *cess*'s Affections.

Cleopatra was going to reply, but was hinder-
ed by the arrival of the Princess *Julia* and *Mar-*
cellus; who, with a great train of other Persons,
then enter'd the Chamber; but the following days
they resumed opportunities of reviving this discourse, which gave my Master a clear discovery,
that he was not only preferred to *Tiberius* in his
Princess's thoughts, but was almost as well seated
there, as his own reason could desire from such a
Person as *Cleopatra*, whose courage was already
mounted to that pitch, that there was not a human consideration capable to abase her Spirit so
much as to one single thought, unworthy of her
former Fortunes.

In the mean time, the two Princes her Brothers
were brought up at *Octavia*'s House, with as much
care as was due to their extractions, and equal to
the Hopes they promised: *Alexander* was of the
same.

same Age with his Sister, *Ptolomy* one year younger ; and both endow'd with a Beauty so excellent, such an amiable gentelness was stamp'd in their behaviour, performing all the Exercises were taught them, with such a graceful dexterity, and disclosing so much grandeur of Courage in all such encounters, as gave them opportunities to shew the marks of it. As all the *Roman* People regarded them with admiration, the *Emperor* highly esteemed, and the Court considered them as the deserving Children of so great a Father, and worthy to inherit a better Destiny : They no sooner reach'd fifteen, but they appeared at all the great Meetings, and despising the childish employments, that commonly busied Persons of their Age, they mingled with those of riper years that addicted themselves to such as were more serious and important.

My Prince who both regarded them as *Cleopatra*'s Brothers, and as Princes that needed no other assistance than their own desert to purchase his esteem, strove to indear them with much affection, and equally engaged himself to their interests and his own ; but he particularly observed something so great and noble in the Mind and Spirit of *Alexander*, as invited him to a perfect amity ; and that Prince (young as he was) so well understood my Master's admirable Qualities, that his affection to him scarce gave *Marcellus* the precedency.

At that time, the inclinations of *Marcellus* began to bend their course to another Centre, and as he still drove on the design of drawing off his thoughts from *Cleopatra*, so he turned his Eyes with less reluctance upon the Beauties of the Princess *Julia*, which he found so full of charms, as it was impossible, after his resolve intirely to put off the other Passion, to regard her long with an indifferent Eye. In effect, that Lady is Mistress of

so

fo delicate a Beauty, as it may fcarce give place
to any of Nature's choiceft Favonrites; and fhe
makes ufe of thofe Advantages with fo nimble an
Ingenuity, as few Perfons in the World come near
her; fhe has a Spirit, hardy, fupple, and pliant
to all forts of Encounters, but very wavering and
dangerous to the Repofe of fuch Perfons as are
taken with her Baits, which had *Marcellus* known
before, I think he would not eafily have engaged
upon thofe Rocks, againft which her inconftant
and artificial Humours have often dafh'd him.

Though doubtlefs you have taken this in bulk
from the Mouth of Report, yet I may learn you
fome particulars in the Recital of my Mafter's Life,
which never yet came at your Ear; and indeed
their Adventures are fo entangled one with another,
as it would be a very difficult Task to fingle them
in my Relation. When *Marcellus* firft undertook
to ferve *Julia* in earneft, he found her Difpofition
fo ready to receive his Addreffes, as (though himfelf had valued his Defert at the higheft) he could
not have gotten fuch large Hopes in fo little Time,
without the Affiftance of a powerful Anticipation;
but this dexterous Wit, no fooner perceived he
had fwallowed the Bait, but fhe began by degrees
to put a Cover upon her former Kindnefs, as much
as to fay, fhe was willing he fhould openly buy
that with fome Pain, which indeed fhe had already
liberally given him, before he was willing to ask it.

Marcellus was not the only Prifoner to *Julia's*
Beauty; for fome of the principal *Romans*, with
divers Kings Sons that were brought up at *Rome*,
and many Kings themfelves, which the neceffity
of their Affairs detained near *Auguftus's* Perfon,
did all figh for her in Secret.

In the mean time, my Mafter and *Tiberius* daily met in *Cleopatra's* Chamber, both openly pro-
feffing

feffing their re-fearch; but the Knowledge they both had of this mutual Competition, would not have been pocketed on either Side, if fome powerful Confiderations had not held their Hands. *Tiberius* was well acquainted with my Mafter's Courage, and my Prince forgot not *Livia*'s Authority and Credit with the Emperor. One Evening they met at her Lodgings, which immediately preceded a Day that *Auguftus* had appointed for publick Spectacles, wherein, befides Gladiators and Combats with wild Beafts in the Amphitheatre, the nobleft *Romans* were to fhew their Addrefs in Courfes on Horfe-back, and divers other Exercifes that fuited their Condition; for thefe my Mafter, *Tiberius*, and *Marcellus*, made their Preparations, and formed Parties to fignalize themfelves before their Princeffes, thus tacitly inftructing the whole City, to expect Things from them worthy of their Magnificence and Gentlenefs.

A Part of the fore-going Night was paft away in the Princefs *Cleopatra*'s Chamber, who had been let Blood that Day, and carried her Arm in a rich Scarf tiffu'd with Gold and Silk, and wrought with admirable Artifice, which the rival Princes had no fooner feen, but they were both ftruck with an equal Ardour, to wear that precious Favour in the next Day's Solemnity. My Prince's Refpect and Moderation imprifon'd his Defires; but *Tiberius* being more hardy, or (to exprefs it better) lefs refpective, was willing to make ufe of that Confidence, which he knew how to practife in the reft of his Actions, and addreffing his Words to my Mafter: ' Think you not, ' *Coriolanus, faid be*, that the Perfon which ' could gain the Princefs's Confent, to let him wear ' this precious Scarf in the Lifts to morrow, ' would not have a grand Advantage of his Com- ' panions,

' panions, and, by a Favour's Encouragement of
' so high a Price, infallibly carry that which the
' Emperor has defigned for the beft deferver?'
' That will be eafily granted, *reply'd my Prince
' coldly*; but as I think it a Grace which few
' Men's Hopes are worthy to afpire at, fo I doubt
' the Princefs will not find out any that are fit for
' fo much Happinefs.' ' And why not, *faid Tibe-*
' *rius*, whatever Price her Favours can amount
' to, can any Reafon forbid Hopes to thofe Cou-
' rages that are hardy enough to enterprize all
' Things for her Service ?' ' Her goodnefs allows
' us to hope for what fhe is pleafed to grant, *re-*
' *ply'd my Mafter*, but Rafh is a fitter Epithet
' than Hardy, for him that will raife a title to it,
' as a Thing that may be merited, when he only
' ought to wait for it from her pure Condefcenfion.
Tiberius was going to reply, when the Princefs,
who had all this Time been filent, regarding him
with a difdainful Look: ' Do not put yourfelf to
' the Trouble, *faid fhe*, of difputing thofe Pre-
' tences any further; my Favours do but weakly
' deferve your Services, and you fhould do well to
' level them at Objects of higher Value, which
' poffibly you may obtain with greater Eafe.
' If ever I took care (*faid Tiberius*) to aim at
' any Thing but you only, let me wear out my
' Life without a Recompence: Yet I cannot de-
' fpair, *continued he with a Smile*, to obtain
' Part of my Defire, and I am now going to ask
' the Gods good Will, that I may have yours to
' accord it.' When he had utter'd thefe Words,
making a low Reverence to the Princefs, he left
her Prefence, with a Face apparently full of Satisfaction.
My Mafter, who had liften'd to this Difcourfe,
not without the ufe of his Patience, ftaid fome

Time with the Princeſs after his Departure, whom
he then entertained with a larger Liberty, and ex-
preſſed an ardent Deſire to appear next Day in the
Field, under her Colours; but he found her in-
diſpoſed to grant that Requeſt; and as ſhe ever
temper'd all her Actions with an admirable Circumſpection, ſhe contented herſelf to afford him
a verbal Aſſurance, that ſhe gave him the Preference above all the Perſons that ſerved her, without conſenting to allow him Advantages, which
ſhe thought would bely that haughty and rigorous
Virtue, of which ſhe had made a ſevere Profeſſion.

The next Day all things were made ready in
the Amphitheatre that the Pomp requir'd, but I
think you do not deſire my Relation ſhould range
on either Side from what concerns my Maſter's
Life; I will therefore contract the Particulars, and
only tell you, that every thing was diſpoſed for
the Celebration of theſe Sports; the People were
ranked according to the cuſtomary Order, the
Emperor placed on one Side, with the moſt conſiderable Perſons of the Senate, and the Empreſs
on the other with all the Princeſſes and nobleſt
Roman Ladies, when my Prince enter'd the Cirque
armed and mounted very gallantly; all his Armour offer'd the Eye a mingled Splendor of Gold
and Jewels, and the Hand of Art had ſo curiouſly
embelliſhed the Materials, as it would long have
kept the Aſſiſtants gazing, if the Grace of him
that bore them had not becken'd their Looks to
a more delightful Attention; his Caſque was ſha-
ded with twenty white Feathers, and through his
Vizor, which was then half up, there appeared
a Face ſo noble and ſo amiably fierce, as all the
Spectators beheld it with Reſpect, and almoſt all
their Hearts voted in his Favour; but the Acclamations of the People could take but little Hold

of

of his Thoughts, and defpifing all forts of other Objects, he fent his Eyes in fearch of the Princefs, whom they found feated at the Emprefs's Feet, by the Princefs *Octavia*'s Side, where fhe fhined like fome great Star, whofe Mafter-Light had half obfcur'd the reft of the celeftial Spangles, attracted the Eyes of *Rome*, and bufied all Mens Thoughts with a juft Wonder at her Beauty; when I faw her in that Eftate, I confefs I was dazled as well as the reft, and pos'd to find any thing ftrange in the Effects, which that marvel of Beauty produc'd in my Mafter's Spirit.

After he had fpent fome Time in gazing upon her, with all the Affections of a Man that had loft his Heart, he was obliged to retire to another Side, and put himfelf in the Head of his Troops after the Example of *Tiberius, Marcellus, Agrippa*, young *Alexander*, and his Brother, who already began to mingle themfelves in thofe Exercifes, with the other Captains, which were then preparing to begin the Sports: Never was any Thing feen more Pompous than *Marcellus*, and his brave Mine had the Help of all the Ornaments and Advantages that the *Roman* Curiofity could invent; nor was *Tiberius* behind him in the Pride of Garb and Equipage; he was jewel'd all over with a marvellous Profufion; his Habit, Cafque, and Armour, were ftarr'd with a thoufand Flames, which dazled all the Spectators Opticks; but, for his moft precious and remarkable Ornament, his Shoulders were covered with that fair Scarf, which my Prince had feen *Cleopatra* wear the Night before, and the fame which gave Occafion to the Difcourfe recited. My Mafter no fooner faw, but he knew it, and that Knowledge fuddenly ftabb'd itfelf through his Heart with a mortal Surprizal, an univerfal Shivering prefently ran through all

his

his Members, and in one Moment overthrew the Force of his Reason; he stood and gaz'd a while, holding his Arms a-cross in the Posture of a Man that was Planet-struck, upon that cruel Object, when the Sound of the Trumpets, which made the Amphitheatre echo, call'd him back to himself, and made him demand a Resolution of his Spirit. The first that presented itself to his incensed Thoughts, was to fly upon *Tiberius*, and snatch away his Life in the Sight of the Emperor and all the *Romans*, and change the Combat which was only design'd to wear the harmless Livery of delight into a crimson Complexion; but these tempestuous Thoughts to which the first Motions of his Fury hurried him, began already to over-blow in his Mind; they were oppos'd with some remains of Reason, but more over-power'd with the Fear of offending *Cleopatra*, than any other Consideration; he had some Thoughts publickly to reproach that Princess, with the Injustice she had done him, but Respect had still Strength enough left to defer the Effect of that Resolution; the last which he clos'd with, was, to retire from those Sports, where he had now neither Force nor Courage to appear like himself, and take fresh Advice of his Thoughts, without the Interruption of so many Spectators.

These deep Cogitations that suspended his Sense and Motion, had swallow'd so much Time, as all the Troops had already chang'd their Places, and begun to join in the Exercise, only his stood still in its Place, attending his Order and Example to move. The young *Alexander*, who was of his Side, had often call'd to him, when taking him gently by the Arm: ' My Lord, *said I*, do you not perceive that ' ours is the only Troop that is not march'd.' This brought him to himself, and regarding him with a Visage wholly chang'd: ' Let us go, *Emilius*, *said*
' he,

'*be*, I can do no more.' At these Words, after he had intreated *Alexander* to take his Place, he crouded through his own Squadron, and leaning upon my Shoulder, retir'd towards one of the Gates.

Tiberius, whose Interest still kept an Eye upon my Master's Actions, perceiv'd him when he parted; and taking Commission from his haughty Pride, newly swoln with this present Prosperity: ' What, ' *Coriolanus, cry'd he*, do you retreat? do you quit ' the Lists?' These Words had like to have put my Master past all Consideration, and provok'd him to a precipitate Assault of that Rival with his Sword in his Hand, who had taken so much Insolence from that Advantage; but a Reserve of Judgment did then hold the Hands of his Passion, and only turning towards him with a furious Look, and a pair of Eyes that flam'd with Rage: '*'Tis not to thee, said he*, ' that I quit the Lists, but to those Marks of thy For- '*tune*, which thou art not worthy to bear; and ' which I shall possibly find a Time to make thee ' resign with thy Life to boot.

I believe *Tiberius* (who had turn'd his Head another Way) did not well understand these last Words, but they were clearly over-heard by divers Persons of his own Party, that might easily carry them to his Ear, and to that Purpose my Master spoke them.

' 'Tis not unlikely, *interrupted Tyridates*, that ' they might be conceal'd by the Discretion of those ' that heard them, lest they should incense the Em- ' peror, with fomenting a Quarrel betwixt Persons ' so considerable as your Master and *Tiberius*.

' I am of the same Belief, *reply'd Emilius*; in the ' mean time, Sir, let me intreat you would not think ' it strange, if I a little amplify some Particulars, ' that are not the most important in my Master's ' Life, tho' not altogether so trivial, but you may ' possibly judge them worthy of your Attention.

Hymen's

Hymen's Præludia :

OR,

Love's Master-Piece.

PART VI. BOOK I.

ARGUMENT.

Coriolanus, *by an Improvement of his jealous Mistake, and the receipt of an angry Answer from* Cleopatra, *falls into a desperate Fever.* Marcellus *unriddles* Tiberius's *Plot; cures the Malady, and reconciles the Lovers.* Julia *loosely deserts* Marcellus; *and displaces her Affection upon* Coriolanus; *her Levity divides the Friends, till* Coriolanus *clears the Suspicion. The Enquiry of their Fate from* Thrasillus, *begets an open Quarrel betwixt him and* Tiberius. *The Emperor interposes, and* Cleopatra *is propos'd as a Prize to him of the two that deserved best in their Military Employments.*

THUS

THUS my Master left the Amphi-theatre, excusing his Departure with some Indisposition to those that de-manded the Reason: Myself was as ignorant as the rest, of the true Cause of it; but when we were arrived at his Chamber, as I was taking off his Arms, I remarked an ex-treme Paleness, and an extraordinary Change in his Visage, which made me timorously demand the Cause of so great and sudden an Alteration. He stood a good while without returning an An-swer, over-whelm'd with so black a Sadness, as it scarce left him the use of Speech; but after I had often redoubled my Sollicitations to know the rea-son, ' Didst thou not see, *said he, with two or* ' *three Sighs*, didst thou not see that Scarf which ' *Tiberius* wore to-day upon his Arms, and couldst ' not perceive it was the same that *Cleopatra* car-' ried her Arm in Yesterday, when thou wert with ' me at her Lodgings? To me she refused the ' slightest and most trivial Favours, though I beg-' ged them with abundance of Submission; and ' to that Insolent has granted what he proudly ' pretended to in my Presence, on purpose to dress ' him up a Triumph over me, while mine own ' Eyes, with all the People's, must stand gazing ' at my Shame. That inconstant Woman has for-' got the Promises she repeated a thousand times ' over, to place me ever in her Esteem before ' him; has forgot herself, on purpose to publish ' her Legerity to the Empire. That *Cleopatra*, ' that Spirit which I believed incapable of the ' Weakness and Imperfections of the Sex, has ' ruin'd me with the Fall from Virtue, and makes ' nothing to give up a Prince as a Prey to De-' spair, that can shew more Desert for her Affecti-

' on,

' on, than he that her Ingratitude and Injustice
' preferr'd before him.'   In the Sequel of this
passionate Discourse, he let loose a Torrent of other
Reproaches; but within one Moment retracted all,
with a sudden Motion of Repentance gets the Mastery of his Resentments, and demands Pardon of
the Princess for the rash Words his Rage had utter'd : Then he turns the Tide of his Choler upon *Tiberius*; and addressing his Speech to him,
with an Action full of Fury, ' Think not, *said*
' *he*, think not, thou insolent Rival, to prevail by
' these Advantages that Fortune has blindly given
' thee ; thou dost hold nothing of me, but of
' her ; and if, by the Fall of my Empires, I am
' fallen to a lower Esteem with *Cleopatra*, than
' the Son of *Livia*, at least, by a Courage more
' noble, a Birth more illustrious, and the Testi-
' monies of a Love more perfect than his, I may
' repair the Defects of that, which giddy Chance
' has only given thee above me : Thou art now
' grown gay with the Spoils of my Repose and
' Glory, and hast proudly deck'd thyself with an
' Ornament due to me only : But fear, *Tiberius*,
' (if thy Fortune will let thee apprehend it) fear,
' that this Present may prove fatal ; thou mayest
' yet be put to buy it at the Price of thy Blood ;
' nor canst thou give dear enough for it, though
' all thy Veins were empty'd for the Payment.
His Passion brought forth a thousand other Complaints, full of the Marks of Transport and Despair.   In this manner he tormented himself the
rest of the Day, till the Evening arrived, and about
the Hour they return'd from the Spectacles, he resolved to write to the Princess : When, after he
had try'd all the Strength of his Reason to tame
the Rage that possess'd him, and reduce himself
to a Condition, employing of the same Respect
                                        which

which he usually expufs'd in his other Letters, at last he made the Paper speak in these Terms.

Prince Coriolanus *to the Princess* Cleopatra.

'IT is not for the unfortunate *Coriolanus* to
'complain of *Cleopatra*: He owes her all,
'and has merited nothing of her; but, if he
'might have leave to assume the Liberty, he
'would make it appear, that, though he be un-
'worthy of her Favours, *Tiberius* has no better
'deserved them. The Grant of so publick an
'Advantage, has openly destroy'd the Promise
'you made me, never to prefer the Son of *Livia*
'before the Prince of *Mauritania*: But since it
'is not permitted me to demand of my Sovereign
'the Effects of her Promises, I will try the Cour-
'tesy of Death, for a Comfort which I can re-
'ceive from none but her, and for which I am
'willing to owe her the entire Obligation.

He had no sooner finished these Words, when (without consulting further with Respect or Reason) he commanded me to carry them to the Princess. I found some Precipitation in this Proceeding; but, as I ever paid him a blind Obedience, I took the Letter and carried it to *Cleopatra*'s Lodgings. She was newly returned from the Amphitheatre, and retir'd alone into her Cabinet much troubled; but when she knew I was there to speak with her, she commanded I should enter: I presently read a part of her Discontent in her Visage, yet she forced it (before I had time to speak) to demand how my Master did. 'In a very sad Estate, 'Madam, *said I*; part of which you will learn 'from the Letter he commanded me to give you.
The Princess, without returning an Answer, took the Letter and read it; but before she had
got

got to the End, I eafily perceived that Choler had drowned the Lilies of her Face in a Flood of Blufhes. That haughty Courage could not fuffer the Liberty he took to reproach her; and feeling her own Innocence, fhe repented her Defign to give him Comfort and Satisfaction, if his Patience could have waited it: And now Defpight began to grow active in her; but fhe commanded herfelf with a Power fo irrefiftible, as hinder'd the Heat of it from breaking out in my Prefence, tho' fhe knew my Mafter honoured me with the Knowledge of his Secrets; and letting fall the Letter upon the Table, with an Action full of cold Neglect, ' Coriolanus has reafon, *faid fhe*, to believe, that ' it is not for him to complain of *Cleopatra*, nor ' demand the Effects of her Promifes; for my ' part, I never made any to him, that could engage me fo deep as he has unjuftly pretended. ' My Favours are neither for *Tiberius* nor him, ' nor fhall ever be granted to any Perfon that ' ufurps the Liberty to upbraid me: I could poffibly juftify myfelf againft his Reproaches, and ' perhaps would have done it too, had he given ' me time; but fince he has prevented the Intention I might have had, with an Act fo unfuitable ' to the Knowledge he fhould have of my Humour, bid him go feek his Comforts where he ' can find them, and let me be quiet.

At thefe Words, (after fhe had made me a Sign to retire) fhe took up a Book, and began to read in it, without turning her Head any more towards me. I went away in a deep Sadnefs, and a grand Confufion, at the bad Succefs of my Meffage; and was no fooner returned to my Mafter, but my Face told him part of the Truth before my Tongue could begin it; yet I had fome defign to fweeten it as much as poffible, but his Impatience would

neither

neither allow me the Time, nor leave me Assurance, forbidding me to disguise any Thing, with a Look so severe and terrible, as I durst not adventure it. Then I punctually recounted to him the Action, and repeated the Language, Word for Word, of *Cleopatra*, which brought him to the saddest Condition that Misfortune could make : I did believe the Unkindness he took at her pretended Change, would have fortified him against the Fear of her Anger, but his Soul found room enough for both the Passions ; and if he were afflicted with a Belief of *Cleopatra's* Discretion, he trembled at the thought of her Anger ; and the very Intelligence of so hasty an Indignation in so moderate a Spirit, confirmed his Opinion of her Inconstancy ; for he could not believe that petty Offence could pass her so suddenly to a cold Indifferency touching his Repose and his Life, unless she had lost that which formerly nourished the Care of it, and receiv'd a new Impression that had effaced the old one ; then did he let fly such Language, and Behaviour, that it was but little conform'd to his ordinary Moderation ; all his Thoughts tended to the Death of *Tiberius :* But he was soon put past the Power of acting those Resolutions ; and whether caused by the Jealousy of his Rival's Fortune, or Apprehension of *Cleopatra's* Anger, he fell that very Evening into a most violent Fever.

He was scarce laid in his Bed, when *Marcellus* (who had been anxious for his Welfare ever since he saw him depart the Cirque so unexpectedly) enter'd the Chamber. I was very glad of his Presence, hoping the Power he had in his Spirit would prove the best Medicine to remit his Disease. Before he approached my Master's Bed, (who yet knew not of his coming) he demanded
of

of me the Account of his Health; and I (knowing my Master never used to hide any thing from him) was willing to give him the naked Truth concerning it, requisite to save the sick Man the Labour, who could not enter upon that Recital, without the Danger of a passionate Transport. *Marcellus* was astonished at the Discourse which I made him touching *Cleopatra*'s Scarf, and the Rage she was in at my Master's Letter; and being indeed his real Friend, he did tenderly interess himself in his Affection; but he was Master of a grand Courage, and that rather disposed him to assist than bewail his Friend: With this Design, approaching his Bed's Side, ' What, *Coriolanus*, ' *said he*, is your Courage fled, as soon as you ' feel the first Blow of Misfortune? Cannot you ' call to mind how bravely it has served you in ' more dangerous Encounters?' ' Ah! my dear ' Marcellus, *reply'd the Prince with a deep Sigh*, ' as my Unhappiness is stated, how vainly would ' my Courage struggle to relieve me? and how ' much more easy is it to brave Death with my ' Sword in my Hand, than thus to support the ' Choler and Inconstancy of *Cleopatra*?' ' I ' know, *said Marcellus*, *Cleopatra*'s Choler will ' not be long-liv'd; and for her Inconstancy, let ' me tell you, your suspicion is built but upon ' slight Appearances.' ' Call you these slight Appearances, *reply'd my Prince*, that I saw with ' my proper Eyes? and could *Tiberius* obtain a ' more considerable Advantage over me, than that ' which glitter'd in the sight of the whole City?' ' *Emilius* has told me all, *said Marcellus*, and I ' confess you have some cause of Discontent; but ' thus to throw yourself down so weakly, is that ' which I cannot pardon, since I can see no solid ' Foundation to prop the Opinion of your Un-
' happiness.

' happiness.' 'Ah! *Marcellus, cry'd my Master,*
' how easy is it for those that swim in a Tide of Pro-
' sperity to sentence a Weakness, which doubtless
' themselves would fall into, if their Fortune once
' grew angry! Do you believe, *pursu'd he, lean-*
' *ing upon his Elbow, and regarding* Marcellus
' *with a passionate Look* ; do you believe, that af-
' ter such visible Marks of *Tiberius's* fortune, and
' my disgrace, I can keep the current of my grief
' within the banks of moderation? And would you
' esteem that a true courage, as you alledge, if it
' should defend me from the sensibility I owe to
' the utter shipwreck of my hopes? No, no, my
' dear *Marcellus,* since I have fastned my Life to
' *Cleopatra's* affection, 'tis but fit it should die
' with it, and I ask no more of the Gods, but
' only to give way to my revenge upon *Tiberius* ;
' I saw that insolent Man deck'd with a precious
' Favour, that I durst not raise my Hopes to ; and
' I remember, after he had proudly demanded it
' in my presence, his Discourse and Action wit-
' nessed that he was sure to obtain it ; that Prin-
' cess, which I believ'd incapable of so black a dis-
' simulation, cunningly cover'd her design to fa-
' vour him ; and since made no difficulty to belye
' the appearances that deceiv'd me, and display to
' every *Roman* Eye the advantages she gave him
' to the prejudice of my Hopes: After so cruel a
' disgrace, one slight complaint, and that too sweet-
' ned with respect, a complaint which the Gods
' never forbad us in our least afflictions, has drawn
' upon me the indignation of that Spirit, which
' (had it not been chang'd) would easily have par-
' don'd the effect of so just a resentment: Nor
' would she have put so much Gall of contempt and
' cruelty in her Words, if she had not design'd
' this Life (which I have intirely given her) for

' a

' a Sacrifice to defpair; And oh that herfelf would
' offer it! or at leaft behold the deplorable end of
' a Life which I will preferve no longer, fince it
' has difpleafed, and is grown indifferent to her.
' At afflictions of this ftamp, my deareft Friend,
' you do but throw away the fruit of your Ge-
' nerofity; and this effect of Friendfhip which
' your admirable Virtue has forc'd from you in my
' favour, is now lavifh'd in vain, fince my pre-
' fent condition will neither permit me to receive
' nor requite it.

. The Prince (who thus let himfelf be carried
down the impetuous ftream of his paffion, would
doubtlefs have inlarged his complaint, if *Marcellus*, who judg'd a difcourfe fo vehement, might
prove a dangerous foe to his health had not interrupted him.

' I do not feek to oppofe your refentment, *faid
' he*, and I am well enough acquainted with the
' caufe that afflicts you, to excufe the effects; but
' I could have wifh'd you had made a clearer dif-
' covery before you leap'd the precipice to thefe ex-
' tremities. I know I can quickly learn the truth,
' and when you have no further caufe to doubt
' of your good or ill Fortune, we fhall fee what
' behaviour will beft become you: 'Tis too late
' this Night to fee the Princefs *Cleopatra*, but to
' morrow I will not fail to vifit her, and as cun-
' ning as fhe his, I dare pawn my promife fhe
' fhall find a hard task to hide her Inclinations
' from my knowledge; in the mean time for my
' fake difpofe yourfelf to reft, and oblige my en-
' deavours to redeem you from this fad condition,
' with the aufpicious Hope of a happy fuccefs.

My Mafter was fo deeply buried in grief, as
he flighted the officious cares of his Friend, and
earneftly oppofed his defign to labour his repofe,

protesting, If his Life were indifferent to *Cleopatra*, he would never try the strength of his own, nor others industry to preserve it. But *Marcellus*, having staid some time with him, made a discreet use of it, insinuating such pressing reasons as, if he did not pacify his Spirit, at least he disposed it, to expect the event of his intended discourse with *Cleopatra*. When *Marcellus* was gone, my Master wasted the rest of the Night with nothing but sighs and sobs, accompanied with disjointed speeches : And though his Fever was very intense, he would not suffer us to call a *Physician*, nor employ any remedies to rescue his health, which himself had abandon'd.

The next day, so soon as the Princess *Cleopatra* might civilly be seen, the officious *Marcellus* went to her lodging, and found her in the same angry mood that possest her the day before, nevertheless she received him with all the civility was due to his condition, to the merit of his Person, and the particular esteem she had always borne him ; she had then no other company with her but one Maid, whom she peculiarly trusted, which offer'd him opportunity to entertain her with liberty enough, and taking a hint from the sadness that over-spread her visage, to fall upon his design : ' If I did not highly value your quiet, *said he*, I ' would borrow some comfort from the encounter ' of a Person, that appears as malecontent as my-' self; but I will always importune the Gods to ' preserve you from such afflictions as I endure.

Though the Princess suspected his drift, yet she was not willing to cross it, and feigning some amazement at his Words: ' If I knew you had a just ' cause for any inward anguish, *said she*, I ever ' esteem'd you at the price of taking my share in ' your afflictions; but I cannot think you have
' now

' now any reason to find fault with your Fortune.
' Yes, I have great cause to complain of her, *re-*
' *ply'd Marcellus*, and if respect would permit me,
' would say, of you too, since you have both
' join'd to destroy me the most generous, and per-
' fecteft Friend that ever breath'd: The unfortu-
' nate *Coriolanus* dies, and I cannot comprehend
' for what offence you have doom'd him; sure
' you can neither doubt the grandeur of his love
' nor respect, and for the qualities of his Person,
' they are so known to all the World, that 'tis
' not likely you alone should ignore them. I
' would say more, (and if you please, you may
' safely give me leave) that you have formerly
' esteem'd him, and time is not two days older,
' since he had cause to be proud of his Fortune;
' but the space of one night has ruined him; and
' then, when he was least prepared for so cruel a
' revolution, he hath seen with his own Eyes the
' indubitable marks of his disaster, and received
' from another's mouth, that brought him your
' intentions, the fatal sentence you pronounced
' against him; yet he does not murmur at you,
' nor complain of his Destiny, since he always
' laid it at your Feet; but if an innocent may have
' leave——

' *Marcellus* would have gone on, when the Princess (who had listened with impatience) hastily
interrupted him: ' 'Tis enough, *Marcellus, said she*,
' I apprehend all you would say for your Friend,
' and possibly I should not so long have suffered
' the same discourse from another Person: I am
' neither ignorant of his birth, nor the qualities
' of his Person; and till now I wanted cause to
' complain of his affection or respect; but since
' he has begun to quit it, and believes he may
' lawfully take commission from my softness, for

' his

' his pretence to the command of my actions, he
' ought not to think it ſtrange, if I deſire to diſ-
' abuſe him, and let him know, that I will never
' reſign that power either to him or any Perſon
' living. See what a Letter he hath ſent me, (con-
' tinued ſhe, taking up my Maſter's Letter, which
' lay open upon the Table) conſider the terms, and
' judge if you pleaſe, whether it holds a proportion
' with that reſpect, for which you would fain re-
' commend him.

   ' When he wrote the Letter, reply'd the diſ-
' creet Marcellus, he deemed himſelf already loſt
' to your thoughts; for he had ſeen Tiberius va-
' pour it with the badge of a happineſs, which
' could never be built but upon his ruine: And at the
' knowledge of ſo viſible and ſo publick an infe-
' licity, would you have him do leſs than put in
' his complaint; which methinks he has done too
' with moderation enough. Had he made uſe,
' reply'd the Princeſs, of that moderation and re-
' ſpect you talk of, he ſhould doubtleſs have re-
' ceived a full ſatisfaction; for as his misfortunes
' had no other foundation but his own opinion,
' ſo that once confuted, he would have been re-
' ſtored to the Eſtate, of which he believed him-
' ſelf unjuſtly deprived: But, inſtead of repairing
' to me, with a due reſpect for my conſtruction
' of the truth, he writes to me in an imperious
' ſtile; upbraids me with promiſes made him,
' and favours given to Tiberius, in terms full of
' pride and inſolence. Do you think he did not
' owe me the deference, at leaſt to inform him-
' ſelf calmly of the truth, before he flew into re-
' proaches ſo audaciouſly againſt a Princeſs, to
' whom by his own confeſſion, he had given ſome
' power in his breaſt, and to whom his choler
' would have been very indifferent, if ſhe had not
                    ' for-

‘ formerly allowed him some Favours, which he
‘ has unworthily abused ?

‘ I confess, *answered Marcellus*, he was a little
‘ inconsiderate; yet, it is true too, that those pas-
‘ sions are faint and feeble, that in such a trial
‘ are compatible with that cold discretion you ex-
‘ pected from him: And I should not have be-
‘ lieved *Coriolanus* had loved with ardour, if
‘ after the knowledge of this disaster, founded up-
‘ on so clear an appearance, he had still kept his
‘ Reason in her Throne. He ought to have un-
‘ derstood me better, *said Cleopatra hastily*, and
‘ rather have given his own Eyes the lye, than
‘ admitted an opinion, and taken the boldness to
‘ declare it too, that has mortally offended me:
‘ he should have left me the liberty of my own
‘ actions, if it be true that he has given me the
‘ command of his; and had he called to mind how
‘ I have led my Life, it would have check'd his
‘ hasty belief, that I had any right to these re-
‘ proaches. I should not, then, have refused to
‘ justify myself to him, as I will now to you;
‘ not for the satisfaction of *Coriolanus*, but *Cleo-*
‘ *patra*; and to stop the course of your opinion,
‘ lest it should condemn me of more kindness
‘ to *Tiberius* than I am guilty of. Know then,
‘ he had not that Scarf of me, that helped to deck
‘ his *Parade* at the publick Sports, but received
‘ it from the Empress his Mother, who yester-
‘ day came into my Chamber when I was dressing,
‘ and finding it lay upon the Table, she fell a
‘ commending the Work, and begged it of me;
‘ I could not tell how to refuse such a Toy, to a
‘ Person of whose bounty I held all that I had;
‘ and I should not have denied it, though my
‘ suspicion had foreseen the request was design'd
‘ with so little Decorum to her Dignity: But con-

O 3 ‘ cealing

' cealing her intention, she carried it herself out
' of my Chamber, and doubtless gave it to her
' Son, who I am confident had obliged her to ask
' it. But when I saw it at the Solemnities appear
' upon his shoulder, I wanted not much of being
' as mad as *Coriolanus* himself; nor could I since
' recover such a temper, as I durst trust myself
' withal, to visit the Empress, for fear the couze-
' nage would have urged my resentments to some
' unbecoming Language. Thus, *Marcellus*, have
' I given you the naked truth, and should not have
' scrupled the same to *Coriolanus*, had he not
' forgot to give me my due, and by his indiscreet
' behaviour redoubled my vexation.

While *Cleopatra* spoke in this manner, and
Marcellus (ravished with joy in his Friend's behalf) heard her with a greedy attention, *Tiberius* entered the Chamber; and as if the Gods had
then voted the conclusion of this adventure, he
still wore the same Scarf upon his Arm, that
had caused so much disorder, which he was resolved to carry there, as long as it would hold the
fastening.

The Princess no sooner spied him, but the object awaked her anger, which *Marcellus* easily
construed by the comment of a blush, that hastily over-flowed her Cheeks; nor could his impatience do less than change his colour at the sight
of those spoils, in a Rival's possession, which had
cost his Friend so much anguish.

Tiberius had no sooner taken a seat, and disposed himself to enter into discourse, when the
impatient Princess (no longer able to keep her
Passion under hatches) regarding him with Eyes
that expressed the contents of her meaning: ' Ti-
' berius *said she, intercepting the first Word be*
' *uttered*, I take it very ill you should carry that
                                    ' about

' about you, by the Artifice and Authority of a
' Person who has power over me, which you could
' not obtain by your own credit; and it was with
' a most sensible displeasure that I saw you make
' your publick *Parade*, with a thing, which
' no consideration should ever have bent me to
' grant you.

Tiberius was deeply surprized at this discourse,
and much ashamed it should happen in the prefence of *Marcellus*, whose affection, he knew, had
knit him to *Coriolanus's* interest; yet his natural
confidence quickly re-affured him, and endeavouring to chain up his resentment, that his respect
to the Princess might still be at liberty: ' I did
' not believe, *said he*, we could have sinn'd in fol-
' lowing the stream of our Fortune and Glory,
' even the same way you have condemned; but
' my desires should have chosen another path,
' had I thought this would have led me to your
' displeasure; but since my unhappiness hath con-
' ducted me hither, I am ready to render as
' great a reparation of the fault as you can claim
' of my obedience.   All I demand, *replied Cleo-*
' *patra*, is, you would presently restore my
' Scarf, and suffer me no longer to languish in
' displeasure, when it is in your power to free me.
' You gave it to a Person, *answer'd Tiberius*,
' from whom I thought you would not have re-
' sumed it in this manner; and since you know
' I had it of the Empress, I hope you will not
' ordain me to put it into any other Hands than
' her's.'   ' When I gave it the Empress, *added*
' *Cleopatra*, I believ'd it was intended for herself,
' and not you; and when she shall desire it again
' for her Service, I will be ready to render it with
' all the Respect I owe her.'   ' Methinks you
' should not place it among my Offences, *said*

O 4   ' *Tibe-*

' *Tiberius*, if I ftrive to preferve what came from
' fo bleffed a Place, and fo good a Hand; nor
' think it ftrange, that I rather chufe to abandon
' my Life, than a Gem that I prize above it, of
' which you have no right to deprive me, fince I
' hold it not of your Bounty.

' You had never received it of the Emprefs,
' *anfwer'd the Princefs*, had you given her the
' leaft Hint how I was like to relifh the Difpofal;
' for I know fhe has too much Noblenefs to pre-
' judice a Princefs for your Satisfaction, that ho-
' nours her as fhe ought: But fince you have de-
' ceived her, as well as me, if you pleafe you
' may render it, or take it ill, if I entreat you to
' fee me no more.

Tiberius was ftruck with a deep Aftonifhment
at thefe laft Words, and at the Inflexibility of the
Princefs, of which his Hopes had promis'd him
the Victory: But, diffembling his Trouble as well
as he was able, ' You treat me extremely ill, *faid*
' *he*, in reducing my Choice to two Evils, the
' leaft of which is as cruel as Death itfelf; but
' if your Refolves ftand firm, to enforce my Elec-
' tion, I had rather refign what the Emprefs has
' given me, than forfeit your fight for ever.' ' You
' will do me a Pleafure, *reply'd the Princefs;*
' and, whether you call it a Prefent or a Reftitu-
' tion, I fhall receive it at your Hands as a fove-
' reign Remedy for my Repofe.' ' 'Tis poffibly
' another's Intereft, as well as your's, *faid* Tibe-
' rius *in Choler*, that thus carries you againft your
' Difpofition to do me Violence: But I obey you,
' *continued he, (taking off the Scarf, and throw-*
' *ing it upon the Table)* becaufe I know no Law
' to difpenfe with my Repugnance; yet you may.
' pleafe to remember, that I am the only Man
' interefted in this harfh Ufage, and I have right
' to

' to complain to the Emprefs of the Injuſtice is
' done me.

At theſe Words he flung out of the Chamber, ſo
tranſported with Choler, as it ſcarce left him Reaſon enough to guide his Foot-ſteps.   Never did
Diſcourſe pleaſe *Marcellus* better than this laſt, at
which he was preſent; he could only have wiſh-
ed, for the more entire Satisfaction of his Friend,
that he had been ambuſh'd in ſome ſecret Place,
to have diſcover'd the Confuſion of *Tiberius*, and
ſeen himſelf reveng'd for the Tortures he had
made him ſuffer.   He could not conceal his Joy
from the Princeſs; and as ſoon as *Tiberius* was
gone, he prepared to expreſs it; when turning
herſelf towards him, and preventing his Words,
' Think not, *ſaid ſhe*, I have taken back my
' Scarf to pleaſe *Coriolanus*, for I could do no
' leſs in behalf of mine own Repute; and your
' Friend has not managed that Credit ſo well,
' which he preſumed he had with me, that I could
' ſtrain my Cares to Complaiſance for his Content.
' Ah! Madam, *reply'd my Maſter's excellent*
' *Friend*, what a vaſt Difference is there (if I
' may adventure to ſay ſo) betwixt your Words
' and Thoughts, and how eaſily your own Know-
' ledge may ſave me the labour of repreſenting
' the Innocence of poor *Coriolanus?* He has com-
' mitted an Over-ſight, which (if rightly ex-
' amin'd) few Men can boaſt they have not fallen
' into the ſame Failing, and for it received a
' Puniſhment which has reduced him to the Ex-
' tremes of his Life. I have left him in an Eſtate
' which, doubtleſs, will plead Pity enough to over-
' throw all the Reſentments your Paſſion can arm
' againſt him; but in ſuch an Eſtate, as bids me
' fear that the Aſſiſtance which my Hopes promiſe
' from your Goodneſs, will arrive too late for his
' Recovery.   O 5   *Cleo-*

Cleopatra, who truly lov'd my Master, grew
tender at this Discourse, which *Marcellus* understood from her Aspect; yet, desirous to dissemble
it, ' Come, I know your Friend, *said she, with*
' *a forced Smile*, cannot be so sick as you would
' make him.' ' He is fallen so low, (*answered*
' *Marcellus, with a sadder Gravity than his Looks*
' *had yet express'd*) as I fear his Life is in the
' Hands of a merciless Danger : And though I
' know it is in your Power to apply the Remedy,
' yet I doubt it will not come time enough to
' heal the Wounds you have given.

He brought forth these Words with so serious
an Emphasis, as the Princess, convinced of the
Truth, and knowing by divers Marks to what
Extremes my Master's Passion was capable to carry
him, she suffer'd his Dangers to soften her Heart;
and turning towards *Marcellus* with a gentle Look,
' My Quarrel to *Coriolanus*, *said she*, is of no
' such Nature to call his Life in question, or pro-
' voke me to refuse him a Remedy, if it may be
' found within my power, and apply'd with the
' Safety of my Honour.

At these Words, *Marcellus* fell upon his Knees
before the Princess; and redoubling the Force of
his Reasons, the length of which persuades me to
leave them out, at last he vanquish'd her, and
wrought so powerfully, as he disposed her to
write him a Letter, which, if I mistake not, spoke
in these Terms.

The Princess Cleopatra *to Prince* Coriolanus.

' MArcellus, who has endeavour'd to excuse
' you, will justify me to you, and wit-
' ness there is more Innocence on my side than
' your's; yet I do not cherish such implacable
' Re-

' Refentments againft you, as not to defire the
' return of your Health: Make hafte to be well
' then as foon as poffible, and your Recovery
' fhall give me as much Joy, as your Impatience
' did Difpleafure.

Marcellus having obtain'd this Letter for my
Mafter, was defirous to take yet a greater Strain
for his Satisfaction, and affay'd by the moft preffing Arguments his Reafon could urge, to gain
him the Scarf which the Princefs had taken from
Tiberius; but he found it impoffible to prevail,
as well upon the Averfion that high Spirit cherifhed to the Grant of fuch Favours, as the Fears
fhe had wifely entertain'd of giving caufe of Complaint to *Tiberius*, which might kindle a Quarrel
betwixt the two Princes.

In the mean time it fell out, that *Marcellus* had
fpoken truer of my Mafter's Malady than he believed; for the Torments that he inflicted upon
himfelf that Night, had enrag'd his Fever to fuch
a height, as the next Day it manifeftly threatned
his Life; yet he perfevered (notwithftanding the
earneft Intreaty of his Friends) in a Refolution to
refufe all Remedies; and the Opinion he had of
Cleopatra's Inconftancy, had made fo cruel an Impreffion in his Spirit, as he fought after nothing but
Death; and certainly had foon found it, if *Marcellus* had not feafonably arrived with the Remedies that were requifite for his Cure. So foon as
he approached his Bed, whence the other Vifitants
were then withdrawn, ' Rife, *Coriolanus*, *faid*
' *he*, you muft be no longer fick, after I have told
' the News I bring you.' At thefe Words of
Marcellus, *Coriolanus* turned his Head that way,
and regarding him with a languifhing Look,
' Ah! *Marcellus*, *faid he*, what Pleafure do you
' take to fport with Mifery?' ' If you call it
　　　　　　　　　　　　　　　　　　' Sport,

'Sport, (reply'd Marcellus, *sitting down upon his*
'*Bed*) I believe you will not think the Game un-
'pleafant; and, before we part, I hope to have
'better Entertainment of your Face than it now
'affords me: All you have to do, is to get up as
'faft as you can, and go and ask *Cleopatra's*
'Pardon for the Offence you committed, or ra-
'ther to pay your Thanks to her Goodnefs, that
'has fo eafily remitted an Injury that merited a
'longer Penance.

My Mafter liften'd to this Language in a Suf-
pence betwixt Joy and Diffidence; but *Marcellus*,
no longer willing to detain his Happinefs wrapt
in Uncertainty, after he had prepared his Attention, began to relate what befel him with *Cleopatra*, and repeated Word for Word all the Difcourfe he had with her. My Mafter abandon'd
himfelf to a painful Joy, when he learned that
Tiberius received not the Favour from *Cleopatra*;
but when the Sequel told him of his unlucky Adventure, with the rigorous Treatment he received
from the Princefs, it feized his Soul with a Ravifh-
ment too deep to be put into Words. But fuddenly returning from thefe Tranfports, to converfe
with fome diftruftful Thoughts that infinuated
there was more Defign than Truth in *Marcellus's*
Words, on purpofe to reconcile him to the Care
of his own Health, he entreated him, with a ferious Look, not to abufe his Credulity, nor raife
him with romantick Hopes to an Eftate, from
whence a Relapfe would threaten more Danger
than the former Malady. 'What Proofs would
'you ask, *faid Marcellus*, to avouch this Truth?
'I would have a Confirmation under *Cleopatra's*
'own Hand.' 'You fhall have it then, *faid*
'*Marcellus*.' And, no longer willing to defer
his Contentment, he delivered him *Cleopatra's*
Letter;

Letter; at the fight of which, with the knowledge of the Character, and the reading of the Words, my Mafter had like to have loft his Senfes; and by an Excefs of Joy, which he was not able to contain, he ftaid a long time motionlefs and mute, as if he had been dazled with his Happinefs.

When he came again to himfelf, he firft ftretched out his Arms, and greedily feiz'd upon *Marcellus*, elegantly expreffing his Refentments in the humble Language of Embraces. From thefe his Joy fucceeds to Words, wherewith he confirmed it, in a Difcourfe fo paffionate, as it drew Tears from *Marcellus*'s Eyes. It would make my Story tedious, to repeat the whole Dialogue of Kindnefs betwixt them. In fine, by the vertue of this delicious Remedy, his Mind was perfectly cured; but his Body was not fo; and the Phyficians that were called prefently after, judged that the Extremity of his Joy had redoubled his Fever : Yet we were encouraged to hope the beft, by my Mafter's ready Difpofition to fuffer the Medicines were prefcribed for him. In effect, he refigned himfelf up to their Difpofal that took care of his Recovery; but his Body could not take example by his Mind, for his Malady vifibly encreafing, in a fhort time it menaced much Danger. The Prince having now no farther Caufe to hate his Life, did all that he was able to gain a Recovery, and reftore himfelf to a Condition of vifiting his Princefs : But his Will found little Obedience in his Body, for the Violence of his Grief, to which he had given himfelf up a willing Prey, had contaminated all his Blood, and his Fever grew at laft to fuch a height, as the Phyficians, with a common Confent, expreffed more Fear than Hope of his Recovery.

All the Perfons of Quality in *Rome* interefted themfelves in this Prince's Difafter; the Emperor

him-

himfelf came often to fee him; and, of the principal Courtiers, there was not a Man but *Tiberius*
(who had the Sting of his laft Affront ftill fticking
in his Memory) that did not render him a Vifit.
Marcellus (who never ftirred from his Pillow, and
did him all the Offices could be hoped from a moft
affectionate Brother) was exceffively afflicted at it;
and the Princefs *Cleopatra* (whatever Violence fhe
did upon herfelf to keep her Griefs at home) could
not totally hide the Difpleafure fhe refented. This
was firft betray'd to my Mafter by a Letter fhe
fent him two Days after the former; in which,
(after he had open'd it with a trembling feeble
Hand) with much Pain, he read thefe Words.

The Princefs Cleopatra *to Prince* Coriolanus.

' **I** Would not have hoped fo little Obedience
' from you, and I thought I had well enough
' exprefs'd my Defires of your Care to engage
' your's upon the fame fcore : If you have any
' Defign to pleafe me, endeavour your Recovery ;
' 'tis the greateft Proof I demand of your Affec-
' tion, and the moft agreeable News I can receive
' for my own Repofe.

These Words had alone been capable to reftore
his Health, if the clear Contentment of his Spirit
could have advanced it. A thoufand times did he
kifs that agreeable Command, and obey'd it with
all the Induftry our Wifhes could ask ; but the
Difeafe had taken too deep a Root, and from
thence Force enough to go on in its Courfe, in
fpight of all the Care we took to arreft it.

The poor Prince defired nothing with fo much
Ardour, as the fight of *Cleopatra* ; and the Princefs
made no fcruple, in that Extremity, to avow, before *Marcellus* and myfelf, the Affection fhe bare
him,

him, profeſſed an equal Deſire to ſee him, and waited for nothing but the Means to do it with decorum.

She durſt not adventure to make the Viſit by herſelf, and the Empreſs (whom ſhe would have accompanied, had ſhe done him that Favour) preſerving ſome Reſentment againſt him, in behalf of *Tiberius*, was contented to underſtand his Condition by the Return of her Meſſages. At laſt *Marcellus* adviſ'd her to go with the Princeſs *Octavia*, who had been once already with him, and he knew would not be ſorry to meet an Occaſion of tendering that Teſt of her Amity to *Coriolanus*: The Children of *Anthony* reſpected *Octavia* as their Mother, and ſhe them with ſuch a Tenderneſs, as fell not ſhort of a Parent's Indulgence: And though the Princeſs *Cleopatra* liv'd at Court with the Empreſs, yet even by her Injunction ſhe daily viſited *Octavia*, ever remembring to pay a ſubmiſſive Reverence to her Perſon.

Octavia was acquainted with my Maſter's Paſſion, which ſhe did not diſapprove, and her Son *Marcellus* no ſooner mention'd his Deſire of her tendering that Office to his Friend, but ſhe readily undertook it, and the next Viſit *Cleopatra* made, ſhe entreated her Company to go ſee the Prince of *Mauritania*. The Princeſs, who knew ſhe might go any Way with her, as her Mother, without the leaſt Fear of Blame, ſince the high Reputation of her Virtue, and the Rank ſhe held as the Siſter of *Cæſar*, and Widow of *Anthony*, might authorize all the Viſits ſhe made in her Company, obey'd her without Repugnance. *Marcellus* by a Pre-intelligence, diſpos'd my Maſter to expect this Happineſs, for fear the Surpriſal of an immoderate Joy ſhould work the ſame Effects it had formerly done, to the Prejudice of his Health;

yet

yet my Master had a hard Task with all the Effects he could make to contain himself, and he no sooner saw the Princess enter the Chamber, but the Sight had like to have made a Rape upon his Sense. *Octavia* came first to the Bed-side, after some Words full of Sweetness, and Majesty, which was as natural to her as Beams to the Sun, protesting the Displeasure she took at the Continuance of his Malady; she was contented her Son, who had feigned a Pretence to speak with her, should lead her to the Window, leaving the Princess alone with him by the Bed-side, and the Maids of her Train at the other End of the Chamber. Tho' *Cleopatra* had prepared herself to see him in that Estate, yet she could not see him there, and hide her Blushes, and she had much ado to make herself Mistress of that scrupulous Nicety, that taught her to criticize too severely upon that Action. However, she sat her down upon the Chair *Octavia* had quitted, while the Prince, whose Confusion had robb'd him of the Strength and Confidence to open his Mouth, strove to express himself at the Eyes, with Regards though wholly languishing, yet full of Fire; *Cleopatra* advancing her Head towards his, that she might not be heard by those on the other Side the Chamber: ' *Coriolanus, said she,* I have reason to complain ' of you, and if you truly lov'd me, you would ' cherish more Care to improve the Interest I take ' in your Recovery: You were told of this by my ' Letters, and I have vanquish'd some Scruples, ' which I would not have combated upon a feeble ' Consideration, to come and confirm it to you ' with my own Mouth; yet I find you still in ' a Condition that shews me no Proofs of the ' Power I have in you.' The Prince, daunted as he was, took Courage from these sweet Words, and

sending

sending some Looks before his Language that spoke more Passion than the former: ' You have Reason
' Madam, *said he*, to condemn the Estate where-
' in you find me, since instead of seeing me in
' this unbecoming Posture, so disproportioned to
' the Respect I owe you, I should be prostrate at
' your Feet, asking Pardon for the Offence I com-
' mitted; this repugnant Body to your Commands,
' has suffered for its disobedience, nor has my
' Soul 'scaped with a milder Punishment; but nei-
' ther one nor the other would ever have been ca-
' pable of expiating the Crime, if your excellent
' Nature had not assisted their Impuissance.' ' Speak
' no more, *reply'd the Princess*, (*not willing he
' should strain his Spirits with too long a Dis-
' course*) speak no more of an Error which I have
' remitted; indeed your easy Belief engaged you
' to some Precipitation, but you have suffered
' more for it than I should have doom'd you to;
' and if I still retain any pique against you, 'tis
' because you struggle too faintly for your Health,
' which is very dear to me, and which I recom-
' mend to your Care. For my sake exile all Thoughts
' that may afflict you, and believe it, I shall ne-
' ver be satisfy'd till your Mind and Body are both
' recover'd:' ' I am so confounded, Madam, *an-
' swered my Master*, with the Favours you heap
' upon me, receiving from your Mouth the Con-
' firmation of your Goodness, in a Place so un-
' worthy to receive you, and where I have so lit-
' tle cause to expect the Grace you have done me,
' as I cannot regret the Loss of that Life which is
' now about to abandon me, but for fear it shou'd
' fail me before------Stay, *said the Princess inter-
' rupting him*, you must not now think of dying,
' while I hold your Life at the same Price with
' mine own. I will have you vanquish your Ma-
' lady,

'lady, I say I will, by the Authority I have over
'you, and the Intelligence I give you, that you
'cannot neglect your Life, without endangering
'mine.

The Princess put her Hand before her Face to
cover a Blush, which got up thither at the first
Alarm of these Words; nevertheless, to confirm
them to *Coriolanus* by Favours that yet she had
not granted, she let the other fall upon his Cheek,
which the Prince taking in his feeble Hand, carry'd
to his Mouth, and with all the Strength was left
him, prest it with an incredible Ravishment.

The Princess, who felt it extreamly hot, and
therefore feared the Countenance of this passionate
Discourse might do him harm, grew willing to
withdraw, and after she had gently retir'd her
Hand: 'I leave you, *said she, rising from her*
'*Seat*, for fear of doing myself any Injury in
'what I demand; remember to obey me, if you
'desire I should love you.' At this last Word
more confused than before, she had not the Confidence to behold him longer, but turning to *Octavia* and *Marcellus*, she told them a farther Stay
might do *Coriolanus* an Injury, and so presently
obliged them to quit the Chamber.

I know not whether I may ascribe my Master's
Cure to that Visit, or whether the Disease was
then come to a Crisis; whatever it was, the next
Morning his Fever was much abated, not many
Days after it wholly left him, and in a few others,
he had gotten Strength enough to quit his Chamber, visit *Cleopatra*, and render his Thanks as he
ought for the Favours she had done him. I have
doubtless given you this Relation in too large a
Stamp, there being still so many great Things that
deserve a Mention in my Master's Story, as I
ought to have passed by those with a slighter touch
that

that were of less Importance; but I staid upon
this Discourse the rather, because I knew it wou'd
draw you *Cleopatra*'s Disposition more lively,
than a Recital of greater Adventures; and by these
petty Marks I have given, you may easily judge
that her Spirit is Lofty and Imperious, but her
Nature Generous and full of Nobleness.

In the mean Time the Empress, by the Complaints *Tiberius* had made of an unkindness in
which herself appeared interested, grew highly
incensed at *Cleopatra*; and probably that Act
might have cost her her Lodgings at Court, if
Marcellus (who above the rest of Mankind was
dear unto the Emperor) had not employ'd all the
Credit he had with him in her Favour.

Cesar, to oblige his Nephew, and serve the
Princess, whom he highly esteem'd, would needs
have the Empress turn that pretended Affront into Raillery; and so the Princess escaped with enduring a petty Reproof, and some sullen Looks,
that lasted but a while from the Empress, who is
very dexterous, cunning, and complaisant in her
Compliance with the Emperor's Humours: But
she could not so easily disguise her Resentments
against my Master; and those of *Tiberius*, much
more violent than hers, did then give a Root to
that Hatred, which has since produc'd such grand
Effects; but as he was the gearest Dissembler
among Men, the Knowledge he had of my Master's Courage, and *Marcellus*'s Credit, who had
openly espous'd his Party, taught him to cloud
the greatest Part of it, and attend till Fortune offered him an Occasion, to let it break out at the
best Advantage.

For a while he forbore the Princess, protesting
he would never see her more; and the Empress
herself, who studied harder for the Establishment
.of

of his Fortune, than the Succefs of his Love, la-
boured to confirm him in that Refolution; but
it could not long hold out againft his Paffion;
and the Choler he conceiv'd againft *Cleopatra* being diffipated, or at leaft over-power'd by a ftronger Paffion, he returned to her more fubmiffive
than formerly, and flex'd himfelf to her Service
with greater Affiduity than ever. 'Tis true, he
did a little change his Fafhion of Life with her,
and difcovering by the laft Encounter, that her
Spirit was too high and abfolute to be eafily managed, he refolved/to feek his Advantages no more
by fo haughty a Carriage, and diligently endeavouring to bring himfelf in Credit by an artificial
Humility, there was never any Part of fubtile
and fupple Infinuation acted, that he did not perfonate before her.

The Princefs, to whom befides thefe Submiffions,
the Greatnefs of his Birth, and the Power of his
Mother, ftrove to render him confiderable, was
conftrained to fuffer his Refearch, and re-admit
him with a fmooth Brow, as fhe had done formerly; in the mean Time, fhe managed both his
and my Mafter's Spirit fo difcreetly, and fo judi-
cioufly fway'd the Authority fhe had over them,
as the Fear to difpleafe her, daily inforc'd them
to fhut their Eyes upon feveral Paffages, that elfe
would foon have kindled a Quarrel, that being the
only bridle that often kept their hatred from coming to Extremes, repreffing their Refentments
with fo abfolute an Empire, as they neither durft
make any Shew or Noife. My Mafter had lefs
Caufe than *Tiberius*, upon whom he had then
a great Advantage; but it was known to none but
himfelf and *Marcellus*; for before the reft of the
World, the Princefs governed herfelf fo prudently,
as it would have pofed the cleareft Eye to pene-
trate

trate her Intentions: Then began Fortune to raise
her Storms against my Master, which my Relation must interweave with *Marcellus*'s Adventures;
for there is so much Connexion betwixt his and
my Prince's, as one of their Lives cannot be faithfully recounted without reciting a Part of the other's.

Marcellus, whose Policy first chain'd him to
the Service of *Julia*, grew insensibly fastened by
Inclinations; and indeed that Princess was arm'd
with an Ability strong enough to subdue the most
disobedient Spirits to Love's Dominion; the Disposition of *Marcellus* was sweet, ingenious, and
susceptible of Impressions; and he no sooner got
the Consent of his own Heart to love *Julia*, but
he began to find out such Charms about her, as
were not only capable to confirm his Resolution,
but impose a Necessity of Progress, in his first
undertook Design; he loved, but he lov'd sincere-
ly, and his Affection insensibly increasing, grew
at last to that Height, as never Heart was deeper
struck than his.   My Master, to whom that
Prince's Secrets were always naked, understood it
with a marvellous Satisfaction, as well for Joy
that this new Passion had clear'd his Fears of the
old, as Desire to see the Fortunes of his Friend
established, by the Conformity of his Will with
the Emperor's, who had design'd him his Daughter,
and daily observed the Proofs he gave of his Affections, with unspeakable Contentment. . Nor
were they unwelcome to *Julia*; and that Princess who had been before-hand with *Marcellus* in
Affection, could not now receive those unfeigned
Oblations of his Vows, without a large increase
of her own; yet in a while she dissembled them
as well as she was able, and desirous to indear the
purchase to *Marcellus*, with a little difficulty, she
plaid the politick Tyrant, and made him suffer.

Mar-

Marcellus complain'd and figh'd away fome time for thefe feigned rigours of *Julia* ; but at laft fhe unmask'd her fentiments, and after fhe had received fome months tribute of fufferings and fervices, fhe fhewed him her acknowledgment and affection at as full a magnitude as he could virtuoufly defire ; nothing was refus'd him that might juftly be demanded of *Auguftus*'s Daughter, and her confeffions were the freer, becaufe fhe knew the *Emperor* not only approved them, but that fhe could not more dearly oblige him than in the perfon of his *Nephew*. He almoft fpent his whole day in her company, and his Life wheel'd away with as much delight as his wifhes could fathom ; for though fome of the chiefeft *Romans*, with divers Kings Sons that were brought up at *Rome* were his *Rivals* ; yet they all fubmitted to his Fortune, and paid fo deep a refpect both to him and the *Emperor*, as they durft not fhock his intentions with the leaft appearance ; the *Senate* and *People*, to whom as I have already told you, *Marcellus* was the *Darling* and *Delight*, were tenderly concern'd in his happinefs, and joyfully hop'd to fee the *Daughter*, and *Throne* of their *Emperor* one day poffeft by the Perfon of the World that was deareft to them ; their hopes were founded upon their likelyhoods, and doubtlefs might arrive at their aim, there being but few Perfons under Heaven, whofe Fortunes would fhew Envy fo fair a mark as thofe of *Marcellus* ; if *Julia*, with one of the rareft Beauties, and the moft vivacious and fubtile Wits, had not the moft wavering and inconftant Heart upon Earth ; of this fhe has given the World fo much experience, as while you refided there, you could not chufe but meet it in many a *Roman* mouth. She began with a perfon, who of all the ftock of Mankind, was fartheft

‘ from

from cause and consent to wrong *Marcellus*. I confess he is Master of so many bewitching qualities, as might well produce the same effects upon a constant Heart; and by this reason I might possibly excuse a part of *Julia*'s first revokings; but they have since been followed by so many others without ground or reason, as all that can be alledged in her defence, is too weak to justify her.

My Master, as the dearest Friend *Marcellus* had, was he, that had the easiest access to her of all the Court; and rendering ther greater respects for *Marcellus*'s sake, than were due from him to the Daughter of *Augustus*; it oblig'd her to requite him with an esteem beyond all the other Princes that were educated in the *Emperor*'s Court: He daily exchang'd long discourses with her, but talked of no other subject but his Friend; and because he was acquainted with most of his thoughts, they still furnished him with matter to entertain the Princess. The love she bare *Marcellus*, made her treat my *Prince* for a time in terms that were reasonable; but at last she ty'd her thoughts too fast to the consideration of his incomparable qualities; and by little and little, from a particular esteem, she proceeded to good will, and from thence was insensily conducted into *Love's Territories*. Had any other Spirit but hers thus suffered it self to be taken, her whole Life would have kept it a secret; and she might have borrowed reasons from the grandeur of her Birth, the *Emperor*'s Command, and *Marcellus* his Services, puissant enough to do violence upon herself, and shut it up in her breast for ever. But her Soul was of another temper, and ever impatient of Constraint and Tyranny; nevertheless, she had yet modesty enough to dissemble it, though not so covertly but if she betray'd not her infidelity to a publick

notice,

notice, she could not so couzen the Advertency of interessed Persons. *Marcellus* was the first that perceived it; for my Master's regards were so fixt to *Cleopatra*, as he had much ado to allow the lightest reflection to any thing else; and finding *Julia's* behaviour much colder towards him than it was accustomed, he often demanded the cause; but the promptitude and artifice of her wit never fail'd in finding pretences to paint the truth; she was loath to break with him, knowing how highly it would displease *Cæsar*, and what she was to expect from his anger; besides, it's possible her breast might still keep some sparks unquenched, that were of his kindling: But the impression of this new image had so alter'd her, as if she had not finished the ruine of all those thoughts that once held him dear, yet she took no delight to see him, and only tasted content in the company of *Coriolanus*.

One Evening *Marcellus* discoursing with her by her Bed-side, (a liberty which the higher Powers had allowed him) and perceiving her thoughtful and melancholly: ' Madam, *said he*, has your ' goodness given me no right to the knowledge ' of those iniquietudes that have lately disturb'd ' you? have not I share enough in your pains and ' pleasures, to be led unto their Fountains? I ' perceive you muse, I hear your sighs, and your ' Face characters an unquiet mind: Is it just, my ' *Divine Princess*, if I have any title to your ' thoughts, I should be longer kept a stranger to ' them? and if any thing perplexes you, where ' will you find a comfort so readily, as in that ' Person of the *World*, that does most participate ' of your Passion?

The earnest sollicitation of *Marcellus* awak'd *Julia* from her dumps, and regarding him with

an

an Air something more affable: 'Do not you
' know, *said she briskly*, that we cannot always
' be of the same humour? and this alteration you
' remark in mine, may it not as well proceed
' from my present *temperament*, as any cause of
' affliction? I will believe what you will have
' me, *reply'd Marcellus*, but either all conjectures
' shoot very wide, or else your *temperament* can-
' not so suddenly bring forth effects so contrary
' to your ordinary humour. Your belief is at li-
' berty, *said Julia, without so much as turning
' her Face to* Marcellus, and since you repose so little
' in me, you may seek for that in your own con-
' jectures, which you cannot find in my Discourse.

   This cold answer froze the very Soul of poor
Marcellus, and beholding the Princess with an Eye
that sent out part of his thoughts before-hand:
' Ah! *Madam, said he*, what have I done? by
' which of my actions have I merited your anger?
' You have done nothing to me, *reply'd the Prin-
' cess*, but at present I find you a little too pres-
' sing; and since you are melancholly as well as
' I, pray take it not ill if I change your company
' for a person's whose mirth may divert my sadness.

   She spake these Words just as she saw my Master enter the Chamber, where he had not trod
many steps, when rising from *Marcellus*, with a
Face that had changed in a moment the Scene of
Sadness into Gaiety, she advanced towards *Coriolanus*, and offering her hand with a free kind of
action, she led him to the other end of the Chamber, and there discours'd away the Evening with
him, without so much as a single reflection upon
the estate wherein she left the griev'd *Marcellus*.

   That Prince was sensibly afflicted at her Words,
but cruelly galled with that he observed in the Sequel of her carriage; and though he was not yet

poyſoned with a ſuſpicion of my Maſter, yet this unkind uſage ſtung him to the heart, and diſtruſting his own ſtrength to keep a Mask upon his grief, after he had ſtaid ſome time alone by the Princeſs Bed-ſide, he went out of the Chamber, without engaging in any further Diſcourſe. After this, *Julia* plaid him divers tricks of the ſame nature, which ſhew'd *Marcellus*, and my Maſter himſelf, how to level their thoughts at the truth: Yet the ſuſpicion was nothing ſo ſtrong on my *Prince*'s ſide, and whatever cauſe he had to think well of himſelf, he knew not how to imagine ſhe would abandon ſuch a perſon as *Marcellus*, for a Man that loved her not, nor could he eaſily admit this belief, and it would long have been getting credit with him, if *Julia*, after ſhe had a thouſand times brought her thoughts into her actions, had not ſhewed them naked in the following Diſcourſe.

One Evening, my Maſter having waſted a part of the Night in her Chamber with *Agrippa*, *Mecenas*, and divers other perſons of both Sexes; after the *Princeſs* had bid good Night to the company, and all were gone, *Julia* cauſ'd *Coriolanus*, who was got as far as the Anti-chamber, to be called back again; telling him ſhe had forgot to acquaint him with an affair that deſerv'd his notice. *Coriolanus* received this command with a due reſpect, and coming back into the Chamber, *Julia*, who was already retired to her Bed's-ſide, beckened him thither, and cauſed him to ſit down by her, which when he had obeyed, after ſhe had darted ſome glances at my Maſter, capable to enflame the moſt frozen heart: ' I know very ' well, *ſaid ſhe*, I do now offer you violence, ' and that all the moments are tedious to you, that ' you waſte in my company, when the Princeſs ' *Cleopatra* is not there. I acknowledge, *reply'd* ' *my*

' my *Master*, that my Heart lies at that Princess's
' feet, where the power of Love has placed and
' faften'd it; yet that entire prepoffeffion of my
' Soul cannot fhut up my Eyes upon what I owe
' to the Princefs *Julia*, and the moft preffing and
' paffionate thoughts fhall fufpend their violence,
' while I have the honour to be near her perfon.
' This is a flattery, *anfwer'd Julia*, that I cannot
' pardon, and I only defire you would anfwer my
' queftion without Artifice : Does Report fpeak
' truth, that you are fo enflaved to paffion for
' *Cleopatra*, as it has ftruck you blind to all other
' objects and confiderations, and centered your
' thoughts in her fo ftrongly, as nothing elfe has
' power to remove them ? Whoever fpread that
' rumour, *faid Coriolanus*, fpoke my thoughts
' as clearly as if he had been in my breaft to copy
' them; for it is moft certain, the World has not
' a perfon fo free, that is more abfolutely his own,
' than I am the Princefs *Cleopatra*'s.
   ' I expected this confeffion from you, *reply'd Ju-*
' *lia*, fince it is but the fame you have publickly
' avowed, and hitherto you have done it with reafon;
' but, as I demand a little better fhare in your fecrets
' than another, fo I expect you fhould tell me truly,
' whether you be fo ftrongly chained to *Cleopatra*,
' as no confideration can untye or divert you : I
' know well your condition is glorious in ferving fo
' fair a Princefs; but fhould the will of the Gods of-
' fer you a right to greater advantages, would you
' fo doat upon your former Paffion, as not to open
' your Eyes upon a fairer & Fortune.
   ' I cannot tell how to frame belief, *reply'd Co-*
' *riolanus*, that there can be a nobler Fortune found,
' than what refults from the glory of ferving *Cleo-*
' *patra*; and could others (by the help of a greater
' blindnefs than mine) acknowledge fuch a pof-
      ' fibility,

' fibility, I fhould never be drawn to own their
' thoughts, nor hatch one fingle defire in my whole
' life for a more happy condition, than to pafs
' it entirely at the feet of my adorable Princefs.
' Imagine, *faid Julia*, you were beloved by a
' Princefs equal in Beauty to *Cleopatra*, and infi-
' nitely before her in all things elfe, whofe high
' birth might give her precedency of the whole
' Sex, and reftore you to the fame eftate which
' your Parents loft, or perhaps raife you to another
' more fublime, would you defpife her for *Cleo-*
' *patra?* I fhould have little reafon, *anfwer'd*
' *my Mafter*, to mifprife fuch a perfon as you
' have reprefented, nor could my infenfibility of
' that favour be ftrained to a contempt; but might
' fhe tempt me yet with fairer offers, they could
' never make me halt in my fidelity to my *Cleo-*
' *patra*. What if *Julia, added the Princefs*, (*van-*
' *quifhing the fhame that oppos'd the liberty of*
' *her language*) What if *Julia* herfelf fhould love
' you, would you difdain her for *Cleopatra?*
   Thefe Words at the fame time almoft wrought
the fame effect upon the Prince and Princefs, and
if the confufion fhe took from her own Words,
made *Julia* bend her looks downward, *Coriola-*
nus was fo abafh'd at a difcourfe, which indeed he
had little reafon to expect from fuch a Perfon as
Julia, as it was long before he durft raife his to
her Face. In fine, that he might not increafe his
Confufion by his filence, ' Madam, *faid he*, there
' is no need of an Anfwer to this Difcourfe, no
' neceffity of declaring my Sentiments, in a Reply
' to Raillery.' ' But admit, *faid Julia*, what you
' call Raillery fhould prove Reality, how would
' you take it? and what Entertainment would
' your Breaft give to *Cæfar's* Daughter, had fhe
' a mind to banifh *Anthony's* from thence?
                                        Corio-

Coriolanus, seeing himself press'd in that manner, was resolved rather to take Advice of his Conscience and Virtue, than lean to a Complaisance which he could not approve; and after he had taken some Moments to contrive a fit Answer, ‘ Madam, *said he at last*, though I have little ‘ reason to explain myself, or exchange my seri- ‘ ous Thoughts for Mockery, yet I must tell you, ‘ since you have commanded me, that should that ‘ Fortune befal me you mentioned, I were the ‘ most unfortunate of all Men; since I am forbid- ‘ den to enjoy it, not only by the Fidelity I owe ‘ *Cleopatra*, but the Amity I preserve for *Mar-* ‘ *cellus*, who only merits the entire Affection of ‘ the Princess *Julia*, and from whom I would ‘ not take it, though it were offered me in the ‘ pompous Dress of all the Grandeur and Felicity ‘ the Gods can bestow.

‘ Thus did my Master unlock his Thoughts, which touched *Julia* so sensibly, as it was long before she could recover her Speech; but at last her Anger forced a Passage for Words; and regarding my Master with a scornful Air, ‘ You ‘ construed my Discourse aright, *said she*, when ‘ you apprehended it Raillery; it was so, *Corio-* ‘ *lanus*, and believe it; and the Affections of *Julia* ‘ shall never oblige you to crack your Amity to ‘ *Marcellus*, nor your Love to *Cleopatra*: I was ‘ only desirous to try the Temper of your Heart, ‘ and now I have seen how well it guards the Fi- ‘ delity you owe your Friend and Mistress, it ‘ shall heighten my Esteem of your Merits.

She brought forth these Words with a Constraint, that my Master easily observed; and tho' she strove to hide it, by entering a Discourse upon other Subjects, yet she followed it in so much Disorder and Confusion, as perceiving it would

P 3

ask

ask some time to undistemper her Reason, she bad *Coriolanus* good-night.

My Master went away better instructed than he desired in *Julia's* Inclinations; and though by her last Words, which Despight had utter'd, she seemed to retract what before she had too easily offered, yet he was not so ignorant as not to discover the Truth. He since did me the Honour to tell me, that he never resented any thing in his Life with so much Anxiety, sadly reflecting upon his own Impuissance to satisfy the Princess's Desires; but much more upon *Marcellus's* Interests, whom he now perceived so lightly forsaken, and foresaw how cruelly he was used by *Julia's* Levity: Nevertheless, he was unwilling to acquaint his Friend with this unwelcome News, and there resolved to stay till *Julia's* Humour should change, or *Marcellus* learn it from some other Mouth; nor would his Discretion give him leave to let *Cleopatra* know of it, as well to conceal the Shame of *Cæsar's* Daughter, and his Friend's Mistress, as to forbear a Discourse that might betray the least Appearance of Vanity.

In the mean time, he carefully fled all Occasions of meeting *Julia* alone; and that Princess perceived it, with a Despight that might well have banish'd him her Breast, had her Power been proportion'd to her Anger; but she had Force enough to hide her Flames for a time, and treat my Master with a more reserved Carriage than was usual. However, he abated her no Respect, but still paid her his Civilities in as specious a manner as her Quality could challenge, only he was careful to escape both her Entertainment and her Sight, when the Place was void of Witness.

Julia for a time feigned herself very well satisfied; and meeting him one Day in a Gallery that

be-

belonged to *Livia*'s Lodgings, notwithstanding he
was accompany'd with two or three of his Friends,
' Coriolanus, *said she, passing by him*, there is
' seldom Safety in Presumption; you lately pass'd
' a serious Construction upon what was meant in
' jest; pray disabuse yourself, and be not so light-
' ly seduced by an erroneous Opinion.' My Master would have replied, had she given him time;
but she passed by him so swiftly, as he had not
the leisure to shape an Answer; and he was a
little troubled at the manner of these Words, tho'
he found some Cause of Satisfaction in them.

Thus *Julia* persevered in her Behaviour for
some Days, still treating my Master with a cold
Indifference; and her Spirit wanting Resolution to
endure too much Violence, her Inclinations got
the Victory of her Anger, and she began to speak
at the Eyes in such Accents, as soon gave *Coriola-*
nus Intelligence her Resentments were dissipated:
but as before he stopp'd his Ears at her Words, so
now he shut his Eyes at her Glances, and compose'd all his Actions with so much Caution towards her, as, if her Spirit were not hardy beyond
Example, she could never have had the Confidence
to bring her Affection again into the Scene. She
repented of all she had said to revoke the first Declaration; and, desirous to repair that Breach,
meeting him one Day at Court, she drew him to
a Window; and when Respect had drawn those
that stood near to a greater Distance, advancing
her Head towards him in a languishing manner,
speaking so low as none could over-hear her,
' Coriolanus, *said she*, think it no more a Mocke-
' ry, when you are told that *Julia* loves you;
' for, believe it, 'tis a perfect Truth.

My Master was surpriz'd at these Words, yet
not so deeply, as to be unfurnished of a ready An-

swer:

fwer: ‘ Madam, *said he*, I am now grown fo
‘ well acquainted with your Intentions, as I can-
‘ not be any more miftaken ; and fince this Sport
‘ does divert you, I fhould be loath to oppofe
‘ the Pleafure you take in purfuing it.

Julia was forry fhe had lent my Mafter Weapons to defend himfelf againft her ; and having
now no time to explain herfelf further, fhe only
try’d to perfuade him with a fiery Blufh, that her
Words were ferious, and that fhe had difplay’d
her naked Thoughts, but with too much Truth.
However, the Prince concludes to perfonate an
Ignorance, arms her own Difcourfe againft herfelf, and ftill feigns an Interpretation of her Words
and Actions as the Effects of Raillery. In the
mean time, (as it became him, as well in reference
to her Birth, as *Marcellus*’s Affection) he ftill
treated her with his ufual Deference ; and becaufe
in that Point he deemed it not fit to difoblige her,
he could not fo cunningly evade her Company ;
but fhe often engaged him in long Difcourfes, and
then ufed fo little skill in concealing her Affection,
as few Perfons frequented their Company that had
not already difcovered it.

Marcellus, as the moft interefted, took the Impreffion deeper than all the reft ; and receiving
daily Symptoms from *Julia*’s Deportment, that
no longer permitted him to doubt her Inconftancy, the Blindnefs of his Paffion made him ftumble
upon a Jealoufy, that *Julia* not only loved *Coriolanus*, but was again beloved by him. This Belief had no fooner got Credit with him, but it
produced Effects that had like to have dragged
him to his Tomb: And when he called to mind
thofe rare Proofs he had given *Coriolanus* of his
Amity, he could not reflect upon the Ingratitude
(of which his Thoughts had now pronounced him
guilty)

guilty) without falling into a mortal Agony. His cruel Jealousy, for some Days, made him fly the sight of that unfaithful Friend, and seek out Solitude in the most untrodden Places, discoursing his Woes to himself, in the saddest Fashion that Grief could invent.

My Master, who could never endure to be long out of his sight, sought him on all sides; and understanding one Day that he was retired alone, into those Alleys of the Palace Garden that verge upon the *Tiber*, he follow'd him thither without a Companion, and at last found him laid upon one of the Seats of an Arbour, in the most unfrequented Part of the Garden. At my Master's Approach, he suddenly started up, and discovered such a wild troubled Look, as my Prince, no longer able to suffer him in that Condition, ' Mar-
' cellus, *said he*, what strange Change is this?
' What Sadness is it that sits lowring on your
' Brow? And why do you fly from the Person
' of the World that loves you dearest?' At these Words, *Marcellus* only nodded his Head twice, without returning an Answer, keeping his Eyes still fixed upon the Earth in so sad a Posture, as it put my Master into a grand Confusion. *Coriolanus*, deeply touched at his Behaviour, took him in his Arms, and earnestly press'd him no longer to hide the Cause of his Affliction: But *Marcellus*, after he had staid a while in his first Posture, gave a sudden Leap out of his Arms; and when he was gotten some five or six Paces from him, he drew his Sword; and presenting the Pomel to my Master, ' *Coriolanus*, *said he*, since
' thou art proved the most disloyal Friend that
' ever infected the World, and hast so cruelly be-
' lied my Opinion of thy Virtue, here finish thy
' Crime by my Death, and pierce the Heart of

' thy

' thy unfortunate Friend, that so unluckily trusted
' thy dissembled Amity; thou hast done that al-
' ready that may clear all thy Scruples of consent-
' ing to this; and believe it, this last Piece of
' Cruelty will merit a gentler Censure than the
' former.' *Marcellus* spake in this manner, and
my Master (however his Discourse and Action
surpriz'd him) yet recover'd himself so readily,
as his Face scarce confessed the least Astonishment;
and, regarding *Marcellus* with a cold and composed Look, ' Since I am that base and faithless
' Friend, *said be*, that has so perfidiously be-
' tray'd your Confidence and Amity, why do you
' offer me the wrong End of your Sword, and
' not rather sheathe it in my Breast? 'Tis the
' Heart of a Traytor that ought to feel the Point,
' and not of a deceived and guiltless Friend.

While the Prince of *Mauritania* spoke this, he
held his Arms a-cross upon his Breast, and beheld
Marcellus with a mind so assured, as it would
have been easy for a Person less dimm'd with Passion, to have read in his Looks the Contents of
his Innocence: But *Marcellus*, distracted with
cruel Jealousy, could not be so soon disabused; yet
he grew so tender at the Discourse and Countenance of his Friend, as instead of pursuing his
passionate Obstinacy, he set some Tears (the Marks
of Weakness) at liberty, which presently over-
flowed his Visage; and letting himself fall upon
one of the Seats behind him, ' Ah! *Coriolanus*,
' cry'd be, was I to expect my Ruin of you? did
' I not offer fairly to our Friendship in quitting
' *Cleopatra*, without releasing *Julia* too? I had
' never bent my Aims that way, but to abandon
' that to you, which I loved above myself; my
' Inclinations have since voted my Design to please
' you; and the Gods, to reward my good Inten-
                                           ' tions,

' tions, have given an After-birth of Sweetneſs in
' that Affection, where my Hopes looked no far-
' ther than a Toil for your Repoſe : And when
' by the help of Time, and my Service, I had
' gained ſome Intereſt in the Heart of that incon-
' ſtant Princeſs, you have carried her from me,
' with a Cruelty that ſuits not with yourſelf, and
' reduced me (with *Cleopatra* and *Julia*) to ren-
' der up my Life, which muſt now become a ſud-
' den Sacrifice to Deſpair.

Marcellus had enlarged himſelf upon this Subject, if his Sighs had not cut off the Paſſage of his
Words ; and my Maſter, who had not heard him
all this Time without letting in a Grief to his
Soul, little ſhort of his, after he had wiped away
ſome Tears, which he had no Power to bridle,
' Marcellus, *ſaid he*, the Eſtate you are in will
' ſcarce give me leave to upbraid you with the
' Injury you do me, and the unjuſt Opinion which
' has poſſeſs'd you, may ſpeak your Excuſe for
' the Outrage you have offered me ; but I am
' comforted in this, that every thing pleads my
' Juſtification : Admit I could grow faint in my
' Friendſhip to *Marcellus*, yet ſtill I love *Cleopatra*
' too well to change her for *Julia* ; and, ſay my
' Heart could draw off from *Cleopatra*, yet my
' *Marcellus* is too powerful there for me to affront
' his Pretences ; and now you force me to avow,
' what Reſpect and Diſcretion devoted to ſilence ; if
' there be ſome Levity in *Julia*'s Spirit, the Gods can
' witneſs, that inſtead of indulging it, I have ſtill
' carefully render'd what Amity requir'd, even when
' Civility and good Manners forbad it : However,
' I perceive, my dear *Marcellus*, in two Things
' I am extreamly unfortunate ; firſt, that your
' Friendſhip was not ſtrong enough to defend me
' from the Cruelty and Injuſtice of your ſuſpici-
' on :

'on: And then, that I wanted Occasion to evi-
'dence mine in such clear Proofs as yours was
'stamped in, for in quenching for my sake, the
'Affection that *Cleopatra* kindled, you inflicted
'Rigour upon yourself to strangle the Passion;
'but in flying the Sight of *Julia* for the Love of
'you, I do no more than quit a Person to whom
'('bating your Interests) I scarce carry a single
'good Will; would to Heavens (could I do it
'without betraying my Fidelity to *Cleopatra*) that
'I had now as much Affection for the Daughter
'of *Augustus*, as you had for *Anthony*'s, I would
'find out a better Way than I can now make use
'of, in quitting a Person that I do not love, to
'witness my Amity not inferior to yours; all that
'I can now do for your Quiet, and my Devoir,
'is to abandon not the Love, (for that would be
'impossible to me, and unprofitable to you) but
'the Sight of *Cleopatra*, and since I cannot be
'near her without hurting you, to remove my-
'self beyond the Reach of *Julia*'s Eye, I am con-
'tent to leave that Princess whose absence will
'not be a milder Misery than what you offer'd.

While my Master spoke in this Manner, tho'
Marcellus could not be cur'd of the Grief that tormented him, yet he felt some Ease by the dissi-
pation of his Jealousy, and reflecting at the same
Time upon the free and faithful Disposition of his
Friend, the cold Composure of his late Actions
to *Julia*, much short of the wonted Deference
he usually paid her, and the strong Passion he
kept for *Cleopatra*, which daily broke into clearer
Proofs, he entertained a Belief he might be innocent, and suffering himself by these Appearances,
with the Help of that Affection he bare him, to
be insensibly perswaded, he repented his Suspicion,
and throwing his Arms about his Neck, with a
passio-

paſſionate and tender Action: ' Pardon, dear Bro-
' ther, *ſaid he*, forgive the Offence you have re-
' ceived from a Spirit diſcompos'd with its own
' Misfortune, and reduced by Deſpair, to inter-
' pret all Things in the worſt Senſe: Indeed I
' ought to have underſtood you better, but you ſee,
' that with the Knowledge of my Friends I have
' loſt mine own, and as my Condition is now
' ſtated, I am ſcarce Maſter of a reaſonable Mo-
' tion: I doubt not but your Friendſhip is able to
' give Proofs of a greater Difficulty, but I will
' never conſent to accept thoſe you offer, and will
' rather ſuffer all Things than condeſcend, that
' you ſhould abſent yourſelf from *Cleopatra*, be-
' cauſe you fly *Julia*; no, let the Gods keep my
' Repoſe, if nothing will redeem it but yours, and
' let me rather be an eternal Mark of *Julia*'s Diſ-
' dain, than recover her Affection by your Diſ-
' pleaſure.

' I ſhall never be diſpleaſed, *reply'd the Son of*
' *Juba*, by ſuffering any Thing for my Friend,
' nor will my Miſery be ſo great as your Imagi-
' nation ſhapes it, ſince in leaving *Cleopatra*, I
' ſhall travel at the ſame Time, for your Happi-
' neſs and mine own Glory; beſides, 'tis not fit
' that a Prince deſcended from ſo long a Succeſſi-
' on of Kings, ſhould waſte the Beauty of his
' Age at *Rome*, in the Employment of ſimple Ci-
' tizens; and ſince, of all I ſhould have heired
' from my Anceſtors, there is nothing left but a
' Sword, 'tis but fit it ſhould ſhew me the Way
' to overtake that departed Glory, and thoſe Dig-
' nities that once dwelt in our Family. I know
' well, that I ought not to hope a Recovery by
' Force, of thoſe Crowns that the *Roman* Arms
' have raviſhed from us, they are poſſeſſed by a
' Puiſſance that others are too feeble to encounter,

' and

' dition of a private Man at *Rome*, and yet love
' *Cleopatra*, are Things incompatible.

  ' I do not wholly oppose your Design, *reply'd*
' *the Princess*, to pursue that Path of Glory to
' your Establishment which you have already be-
' gun to tread so hopefully; and though your Pre-
' sence be as dear to me as you ought to desire,
' yet I can resolve to lose it for a Time, in Hope
' to see your Virtue remount the Throne of your
' Ancestors; not that the Loss of your Crowns can
' render your Person less considerable than if they
' encircled your Brow; that blind Deity has handled
' us as rudely as you, and humbled our Family
' too low, to leave us any Cause of misprizing
' those Princes that she has plunder'd; but since
' nothing can look big enough to daunt your
' Courage, and that inspires you to trace the Steps
' of your Predecessors; the Knowledge I have that
' you are born to great Undertakings, shall van-
' quish that Repugnance; which indeed dissuades
' my Consent to this Separation; and if the De-
' stinies do not oppose you, you ought to expect
' all from your Valour; but *Coriolanus*, though
' this Reason be strong enough to take you from
' us, you must confess it is not the Cause that
' drives you away, and that some other Conside-
' ration precipitates your Departure.

  ' The Respect which I have always chain'd to
' your Will, *answered the Prince*, does not per-
' mit me to disguise the Truth, and though Dis-
' cretion and Modesty dispute against it, they are
' too weak to confute my Obedience. It is true,
' Madam, since you are pleased I should avow it,
' I do owe a little Voyage to my Friend's Repose,
' and being infortunate enough to injure him, I
' am going for a Time to fly those Occasions,
' and seek others, that may render me worthy
' to

' to be own'd by you.' ' I apprehend enough,
' *added the Princess with a Smile*, and I think I
' shall not make you blush, when I tell you, you
' are loved by *Julia*.' ' I cannot believe it Love,
' *modestly answered the Prince*, but rather the
' Malice of mine and *Marcellus*'s Fortune, that
' was willing to conduct the Addresses of that wa-
' vering Spirit, while she sought Occasions of In-
' constancy, rather to me than any other.' ' I
' suspected it before, *reply'd the Princess*, by di-
' vers remarkable Conjectures, but was loath to let
' you know so much, for fear of disturbing the
' Satisfaction you receive in the Affection and Re-
' search of so fair a Princess.' Indeed it is so great,
' *coldly answer'd Coriolanus*, as I am too weak
' to support the Weight of it, and for that Rea-
' son will fly as far as the Earth has Limits, if it
' be otherwise impossible to defend myself from it.

. ' You are cruel, *Coriolanus*, reply'd the Prin-
' *cess with a graceful and majestick Action*, and
' if you thus contemptuously treat fair Ladies, and
' such as are of *Julia*'s lofty Quality, what may
' those hope from you to whom Nature and For-
' tune have been penurious?' ' She that I adore,
' *reply'd my Prince*, has received of Nature all
' that she was capable of giving, nor can Fortune
' substract any thing from that, which still keeps
' her placed in the first Rank of Mortals.

' I am well pleas'd, *said the fair Princess*, that
' your Blindness has betray'd you to this Opini-
' on, and though I am not the same you speak
' me, I am very willing to appear so in your Eyes
' and Judgment.

She pronounc'd these Words with an Air so
sweet, and a Fashion so obliging, as the Prince
was lost in a delightful Ravishment, and pressing
her Hand, which he held with an Action full of
Ardour

Ardour and Transport: 'Oh Friendship! *said he,*
' Oh Honour! What Enemies are you grown to
' my Repose? How sweetly might I pass my en-
' tire Life at the Feet of my adorable Princess, if
' you would consent to it.

He had said more, and their Discourse had
lasted longer, if the Arrival of the two young
Princes, *Alexander* and *Ptolomy* had not interrupted it, who, after they had saluted the rest of
the Company, they approach'd the Princess their
Sister, and *Coriolanus,* whom they loved exceedingly; divers noble *Romans,* which came thither
in their Company, also mingled themselves in the
Troop, and the Walk continued and ended, without offering my Master an Occasion of reviving
his Discourse with *Cleopatra.*

The next Day there befel him an Accident, that
gave a Report loud enough through *Rome,* to arrive at your Ears, when you resided there, which
as it hastened his Voyage some Days sooner than
he intended, so it gave him the Means to undertake it with more Glory than he expected. There
was then at *Rome* a Mathematician call'd *Thrasillus,* who by his sublime Skill in judicial Astro-
logy, had acquir'd a Reputation that highly advanced his Credit, and made his Acquaintance be
courted by the principal *Romans.* ' Alas ! *cry'd*
' Tyridates, *interrupting* Emilius, that Name is
' but too well known unto me, and I have hither-
' to found his Prediction of my Fortune so credi-
' ted by a Succession of Accidents, and have now
' so little Reason to expect an End unsuitable to
' the former Events, as it must ever have a Place
' in my Memory.' This *Thrasillus, reply'd Emi-
' lius,* whose Science you experimented, had a
' particular Access to *Tiberius,* whose Thoughts,
' (eternally ty'd to his Love and Ambition) made
' him

' him ranſack this Man's Knowledge for a Flat-
' tery of his future Hopes.

That Day I ſpoke of, he being in the Palace
Gallery, where the nobleſt *Romans* uſually walk'd,
attending the Emperor's Riſing, my Maſter and
Tiberius met there together, followed by a Throng
of the moſt conſiderable Perſons in the Empire;
though their mutual Jealouſy had extinguiſh'd all
the ſparks of Friendſhip, which might otherwiſe
have been kindled betwixt them, eſpecially in the
malicious Spirit of *Tiberius:* Their Enmity was
not yet come to a Declaration, and if the reſpect
which my Prince carried in *Livia*, kept a part
of his under hatches, *Tiberius*, who is a perfect
Maſter in the Art of Diſſimulation, conceal'd his
hatred for other conſiderations, often ſpoke to
Coriolanus, and treated him with as affable looks
as his cunning could put on; but at that encounter,
approaching to him: ' Come, *ſaid he*, ſhall we
' know our Deſtinies, from the mouth of *Thra-*
' *ſillus?*' Then beckening the *Artiſt* to come nearer, and preſenting my Prince unto him: ' What
' think you *Thraſillus, ſaid he*, of the Prince of
' *Mauritania's* Fortune and mine? Shall our in-
' clinations thrive in the deſign they are levell'd at?'
Thraſillus had often ſeen my Prince, knew his Age,
the Conſtellation that ruled at his Nativity, and
had conſulted all other circumſtances from whence
he uſually raiſed his conjectures; but he had ſtu-
died *Tiberius's* with more circumſpection, and
often told him many things that concern'd his
Deſtiny; to my Maſter he had never ſpoken, having receiv'd but little encouragement from his
curioſity; but then after he had ſpent ſome time
in peruſing the two Princes: ' If my *Science* de-
' ceives me not, *ſaid he*, you ſhall both be great,
' and both ſatisfied, the one in his *Love*, and the
' other

' other in his *Ambition:* And becaufe you defire
' not a more particular knowledge, I will affure
' you upon my Life, that one of you fhall one
' day be poffeffor of the Perfon you both love;
' and the other fhall fee himfelf feated on the tal-
' left Throne in the Univerfe.

This Difcourfe of *Thrafillus,* to whofe prefages
the conformity of Events had acquired him a great
deal of credit, was followed by a loud acclamation from the whole company; and the two
Princes, to whom it was addreffed, ftood and
gazed a while upon each other without uttering
a Word; at laft my Mafter, after he had ferioufly
ballanc'd *Thrafillus's* Words: ' For the enjoyment
' of what I love, *faid he,* I fhould eafily quit the
' Empire of the World; and on condition fhe
' may be mine, I fhall bear no grudge to my com-
' petitor's Fortunes.' This language was amorous
and modeft, but the reply of *Tiberius* was not fo;
and though he had power enough upon himfelf
not to be carried away with the Tide of a vain Prefumption: ' I pretend, *faid he,* to the poffeffion
' of *Cleopatra,* nor do I renounce my claim to
' the Empire, fince the World has not another
' Man, that is born with a better Title to both.'
This Difcourfe lighted up an indignation in my
Mafter's Spirit, as well for his own intereft, which
receiv'd an open affront in what referred to *Cleopatra,* as *Marcellus's* right, who by the univerfal
Vote of the *Romans,* the intention of *Cefar,* and
the fuffering of Equity it felf, might pretend with
more juftice to the *Imperial Diadem* than *Tiberius,*
and by all thefe was placed before him: Befides,
he could never ftudy the Science of diffembling,
though then for divers confiderations, he ftruggled
with himfelf to confine a part of his refentments,
and darting a difdainful look at *Tiberius:* ' I
' know

‘ know not, *said he*, to what you may be born,
‘ but I hope that neither *Cleopatra* nor the Em-
‘ pire shall be any part of your Portion. And who
‘ shall dispute it? *reply'd Tiberius, fired with*
‘ *rage*, can juster pretences, and better supported
‘ than mine, be shewn by a despoiled, *African?*
‘ For the Empire, *answered my Prince, Rome*
‘ has enough more worthy than thy self to com-
‘ mand it; and for *Cleopatra*, that *African* will
‘ dispute her with thee; who, wholly despoiled
‘ as he is, is yet the Son of a puissant King, and
‘ not of a paltry Citizen, as thou art, and from
‘ whom Fortune has taken nothing that could
‘ make him lose those advantages he had of thee
‘ both in Birth and Virtue.

At these Words they both laid hands upon the
guards of their Swords; and though the respect that
was due to the place might have restrained them
to more moderation; yet that consideration had
not then been capable to stop their hands, if the
whole company had not suddenly thrown themselves betwixt them, and so cut off a farther passage
to their fury.

The noise of this divided the whole Court in
two factions; and if the authority of the Empress
his Mother, added to the large Alliances he had
in *Rome*, gain'd *Tiberius* a puissant Party, the credit of *Marcellus*, and the Friends which his Virtue had acquired, made my Master's full as formidable; which may seem strange, if the glorious
rank and garb be considered, which *Tiberius* did
then, and doth still appear in: Yet, 'tis true, my
Prince, as much a stranger and despoiled as he was,
saw himself in a condition to hold up his head
against the Son of *Livia*, the *Drusi, Sulpitii, Me-*
telli, with divers other Families that ranged themselves on *Tiberius* Party: And with *Marcellus*, the
gene-

generous *Agrippa*, the Children of *Anthony*, the *Fabii*, *Cato's*, with all that were brave and honeft among the *Romans*, had their Swords ready to ftrike in *Coriolanus's* quarrel. Yet this number of divided Friends ferved for no more than to make known the *Competitor's* Credit: For the fame day the Emperor being advertis'd of the quarrel, and having learned the truth from the mouth of *Agrippa* and *Mecenas*, one of which was my Mafter's declared Friend, and the other had high thoughts of his Virtue, he fent them to try if he could make them Friends.

This favour was not ordinary; but befides that he was willing to do honour to the Son of his Wife, and a Prince of the Birth and Virtue of *Coriolanus*, he deemed his authority requifite to hinder the animofity of two fuch important men from proceeding to extremities ; indeed, the follicitations of *Livia*, (who made the boldnefs of *Coriolanus*, and the little refpect he expreft to the Wife of *Cæfar*, found high in his Ears) might have drawn his judgment away in *Tiberius's* behalf, if, befides the credit of *Marcellus* and *Agrippa*, who had much power with *Auguftus*, the carriage of *Coriolanus*, that feemed to fecond the Emperor's intentions in repreffing boldnefs, and condemning his fawcy pretences to the Empire, had commended his caufe to *Auguftus*, and difpos'd him to treat them with an impartial equality.

They both prefented themfelves before him, each with a proud train at his heels; and the Emperor, after he had heard them apart, fharply reproved *Tiberius* for the knowledge he had given of his ambitious afpirings to the Empire, and my Prince, for the contemptuous mifprifal of his Birth, whofe Mother himfelf had taken to his Bed, he commanded them to embrace each other.

My

My Mafter gracefully difpos'd himfelf to obey
him: But before they interchang'd that Ceremony,
bravely addreffing to *Cefar*, with a boldnefs full
of Majefty: 'Sir, *faid be*, I accept your command
' with a due refpect, and to witnefs my refig-
' nation to your Majefty's will, I will propofe a
' means (if it may be allow'd) to cut up the root
' of any further quarrel betwixt *Tiberius* and my-
' felf: We both love *Cleopatra*, and fo long as
' our competition lives, we fhall find a task too
' difficult to keep Life in our amity: If Juftice
' doth appoint that Princefs, as a treafure to re-
' ward the fervices of one of us, decree it, my
' Lord, that by thofe fhe may only be difputed,
' and not by indirect courfes, to which it would
' be injurious to ftake fuch a prize as *Cleopa-
' tra*; I am going, Sir, as I did at my firft ac-
' quaintance with the Camp, to carry my Life
' and my Sword into the *Roman* Army, and if
' it may pleafe Grand *Cefar* to give me an em-
' ployment, wherein I may fignalize myfelf for
' the glory of his Empire, I may poffibly make
' it known, that though I am born an *African*
' Prince, I have neither lefs Fidelity nor Valour
' than the Native *Romans.* Let *Tiberius* do the
' fame, and fince to the intereft of his Love he
' may link the fervice of his Country, let him
' court fome dangers for occafions to merit *Cleo-
' patra*: Suffer not your favour, Great *Cefar*, to
' be partially fwayed, but let him have the glo-
' rious Prize that fhews the moft Valour for it;
' I am willing to refign her, with my Life to
' boot, if in this Warlike decifion *Tiberius* carries
' the advantage; and I hope from your Juftice,
' that what Fortune has already given, fhall not
' be accounted in the purchafe of a Jewel which he
' only ought to buy with his blood and fervices.

My

My Master had scarce ended these Words, when
Tiberius, with as fierce a confidence in his *looks*
as *Coriolanus* could shew, thus pursued his request :
' I glady consent, *said he*, to the proposition *Co-*
' *riolanus* has made, and if it pleases the Emperor,
' that our Valour shall only try our Titles to *Cleo-*
' *patra*, I shall that way advance my claim by
' fairer pretences than ever ; I will go as well as
' he into the Armies that combat for the Empire,
' and if the Emperor judges me worthy of a Com-
' mand, I hope my behaviour in his service shall
' render it apparent, that I want no courage to
' merit such a recompence as *Cleopatra*.

The Discourse of these two young Princes,
which had attracted the attention of all the assistants, marvellously pleased *Augustus*, and at the
same moment he openly protested his approbation
of their brave design, and promised by his consent,
that *Cleopatra* should never be given but to him
of the two, that in *Rome*'s service could shew best
proofs of their Military Virtue.

My Master receiv'd this Declaration of the Emperor with an excess of joy ; and *Tiberius*, who really
is very courageous, exprest as great a satisfaction.

From that very day the Emperor grew studious
to find out employments for them both, and by
good fortune an occasion offered it self as favour-
ably as they both could wish.

Terentius Varro, and *Tilius Corisius*, with a
puissant Army made War against the *Austrians*
and *Cantabrians*, who were risen in Rebellion
against the Empire in prodigious numbers. But
the Soldiers, no longer able to endure the insup-
portable humour of *Varro*, the Emperor was constrain'd to call him home, and *Corisius* made incapable by his personal defects of the sole Command of that War, the Emperor was oblig'd to send a
Captain,

Captain in *Varro*'s place, who, till then, by means of *Coristus*'s infirmities, had suftain'd the whole weight of Care in the conduct of that Expedition.

On the other fide, War being kindled in *Pannonia* and *Dalmatia*, and the Captain that commanded the *Romans* Army having been kill'd in an encounter; the *Legions* had fent to demand a new General of *Cæfar*, which yet he had not nominated.

These two employments, after the method of fome deliberation, were given to the two *Rival Princes*, with hopes of fuccefs that were yet equally divided betwixt them.

My Mafter had Commiffion to march in *Varro's* place againft the *Auftrians* and *Cantabrians*; and *Tiberius*, who indeed, though very young, had already given many fignals of his gallantry, was defign'd to command the Army in *Pannonia*.

These two *Princes*, highly fatisfied with their employments, equally prepar'd for their departure, and vanquifh'd by the help of their mutual Emulation the grief they took to part with *Cleopatra*.

Marcellus, boiling as well as they with a defire of glory, took example by them to demand a Military employment; but the Emperor told him it was his abfolute will be fhould ftay near his Perfon, yet flattered him with the hope of an important expedition which he had in his thoughts; and my Mafter's earneft entreaty that he would ftay a while with *Julia*, and endeavour to recover her fickened flames, wrought upon him fo fuccefsfully, as at laft he was contented that *Rome* fhould yet be his refidence.

I need not fpeak of the preparations thefe two young Generals made for their Voyage, nor trouble you with *Julia*'s difcontent for my Mafter's feparation, who in every place that he met her, and when he took his leave, ftill evaded particular

VOL. I. Q cular

cular Difcourfes with a grand Circumfpection ;
and the hafte I make to pafs to the Narrative of
weightier Affairs, only permits me to tell you,
that the day of their departure being arriv'd, after they had received the Emperor's *Orders*, the
two *Princes* took leave of *Cleopatra* apart ; I know
not what Language was exchanged betwixt her and
Tiberius, but my Mafter's fhewed the marks of a
moft ardent paffion, and *Cleopatra*'s of an affection,
which gave *Coriolanus* caufe enough to be contented.

  ' It is not Madam, *faid be, after fome preced-*
' *ing Difcourfes*, it is not your affection that calls
' my courage to this difpute with *Tiberius* ; That
' keeps to a greater height of value for either to
' afpire at, at the charge of all our blood ; nor
' can it be bought but with fuch fervices as are pe-
' culiarly paid to yourfelf, and not thofe that are
' laid out for the Empire's interefts ; no, 'tis the
' favour of *Auguftus*, that by glorious actions I
' muft pluck from *Tiberius*, if it be poffible ; and
' fince your fortune has fubmitted you in fuch a
' fort to his power, as after purchafe of your con-
' fent, my hopes muft ftill wait upon his to com-
' pleat my happinefs ; give me leave, if you pleafe,
' by lavifhing my Life for his interefts, to oblige
' him to confider my fervices as well as *Livia*'s
' follicitations. Yes, *Coriolanus, reply'd the Prin-*
' *cefs*, you have my confent, and to confirm you
' that you have it, know, you need not difpute
' my affection with your Rival in the rough ar-
' gument of Arms ; be affured the advantage fhall
' ever ftay on your fide ; and though fortune fhould
' crown the Creft of *Tiberius* with the Palmy
' wreaths of moft glorious Victories, fhe fhall
' never have a power to give him any part of my
' inclinations ; you have already too great a fhare
' in them to leave him the fpark of any hope
               ' alive,

‘ alive, and I cannot now aſſume the liberty of
‘ expreſſing that to you with any *Decorum*, which
‘ I did not fix in my breaſt before I had weighed it.

I will trace their amorous Dialogue no further,
for fear the length of it ſhould diſoblige your patience; at laſt, after he had breath'd a thouſand
Vows at her feet of an eternal Fidelity, and received a confirmation from her own mouth of
thoſe dear hopes ſhe had given him; my Prince
receiv'd her Adieu with a conſolation that help'd
to ſweeten the regret of his abſence; and about
an hour after mounted on Horſe-back, with a
great number of Friends, who brought him many days journies on the way; but at laſt, having
parted from thoſe that went not the Expedition,
we march'd with the reſt through *Gallia Nar-
bonenſis*, and thoſe other Provinces that lay in our
way to *Auſtria* and *Cantabria*.

Hymen's

Hymen's Præludia :

OR,

Love's Master-Piece.

PART VII. BOOK I.

ARGUMENT.

The gallant Acts, and gallant Victories of Coriolanus *in the* Austrian War. Tiberius *luckily
finishes that in* Dalmatia, *returns before his
Rival, and by* Livia's *means gains the Emperor
to a partial Arbitration. The news of this
hastily calls home* Coriolanus. *His haughty
Language to* Cæsar *procures his Banishment.
The fantastick vicissitudes of* Julia's *kindness
and inconstancy to* Marcellus. Coriolanus *chal-
lenges* Tiberius *in the Temple, and the next
day runs him through in the Streets.*

THUS

THUS *Emilius* recounted his Ma-
ster's Life to Prince *Tyridates*, who
heard him with a marvellous attention, when there came one and
told him that *Coriolanus*, after some
hours quiet repose, was newly awak-
ed. *Tyridates*, whose generosity was deeply concerned in the care of such a qualified *Guest*, though
he flamed with desire to learn the Sequel of his
Adventures, he then preferred *Society* before his
Story; judging it time to dine, and enjoined by
Civility to keep him company, he was willing for
a while to defer the continuation of *Emilius*'s recital.

They went together to his Chamber, and the
Son of *Juba* no sooner saw *Tyridates*, but receiving him with an obliging action, full of bewitch-
ng sweetness: ' You come, *said he*, from trifling
some hours upon a mean divertisement, and you
' have had your desires, to be acquainted with things
' so little worthy of your Attention, as I fear you
' are justly displeased with my complacence to your
' Curiosity. I have yet understood no more, *re-*
' *ply'd Tyridates*, than the Morning Actions of
' your Life; and though those of the latter edition,
' which I confusedly took from the mouth of
' *Rumour*, be doubtless the greater and more im-
' portant; those beautiful beginnings have so tied
' me to your Virtue, in the chains of love and
' wonder, as I can now no more regard you without
' the extraordinary motions of affection and re-
' spect. Your affection is too dangerous, *answer'd*
' *the Moorish Prince*, to be otherwise received
' than as the greatest bliss that Fortune can offer
' me, but I rather owe it your generous dispositi-
' on, than the recital of a few trivial actions, in-
' capable to merit it. That excessive modesty of
Q 3 ' yours,

' yours, *reply'd Tyridates*, has confirmed my de-
' fign, to accept no part of the Story from your
' own mouth, for I fee you will debafe the Gran-
' deur of your Actions, as I fhall draw nothing
' from you but what will fall infinitely fhort of truth.

While thus they inlarged their Civilities, their
Dinner came in, during which they entertain'd
each other with Difcourfes as agreeable as their
melancholly Hearts could allow.

The valiant unknown, was ferved in his Chamber with other meats, for the depth of his wounds
oblig'd him to another fort of nourifhment; he
was very hardly difpos'd to fuffer the application
of any remedy, and the reafon he had to afflict
himfelf, returning to his memory, left him fo little regard of Life, as the care of his recovery was
only acted by *Tyridates* and his 'Squire.

Indeed, the Prince of *Parthia* omitted no endeavours that could have been contributed to his
proper fafety; and by the brave things he had
feen him do, and that Majeftick mind which was
able to fink an impreffion of refpect in all the
Souls that beheld him, he had received an opinion
of him as a Perfon wholly extraordinary.

Dinner was no fooner ended, but he was at his
Chamber door to enquire of his health, and underftanding from the Chirurgeons, he might now
fafely be fpoken to, he entered the Chamber, and
approaching the Bed, gave him the *Bon-jour*.
The Stranger inforced his griefs to return what he
thought was due to his Benefactor, and regarding
him with Eyes that in fpight of their fickly Eclipfe
fparkled fomething more fierce and martial than
was to be found in the reft of mankind: ' You
' mif-employ your pity, *said he*, upon a man that
' has neither Fortune nor Life enough left to ac-
' knowledge it; but the Gods will pay you in my
' behalf,

' behalf, and supply by their bounty the impuissance
' of a wretch on whom you have so nobly, and
' yet so ineffectually placed yours.' This discourse
(the pulse of a most violent grief) touched the Soul
of *Tyridates* with a fresh compassion, and desirous
to sweeten the sorrows of that valiant Man, as well
as his own would permit him : ' I should be real-
' ly happy, *said he*, in a power as well to recon-
' cile your Spirit with repose, as your Body with
' health ; but the Gods, from whom you bid me
' expect a reward for such trivial Offices, will
' employ their puissance (to which nothing is
' difficult) in restoring what they have taken from
' you, and if you trust their Goodness, you will
' doubtless receive all the assistance requisite for
' your consolation.

In reason the Stranger ow'd a reply to this Language, and doubtless in another reason would have
paid it ; but his thoughts were then in pursuit of
another subject, and after he had spent some moments in a deep study : ' Have you yet learn'd no
' news, *said he*, of the cruel Pyrate that fled
' yesterday from my just pursuit ? Know you not
' whether the persons that were in his power, were
' delivered by some Divine or Human assistance ?
' We have heard nothing of that, *answer'd Ty-*
' *ridates*, and believe he saved himself with his
' Prey in those Vessels we saw last Night put off
' to Sea. Gods ! *cry'd the Stranger*, *with an*
' *action full of transport*, Gods ! who have suf-
' fered me to find nothing among Men but cruelty
' and ingratitude ; shall I ever meet the refusal of
' succour at your hands, and must I be eternally
' expos'd to oppression and injustice ? Have you
' favour'd me in those occasions that would con-
' tribute to my glory, to cross me in all those that
' should serve my repose ? And in fine, shall these

Q 4   ' advan-

' advantages you have given me, serve for nothing
' but to dress my Misfortune, and gag my ruine ?
He stopp'd at these Words, which he mingled with
deep sighs, and after he had staid some time in the
posture of a Man possest with furious resolutions :
' Do, pitiless Fortune, *pursued he*, Do, cruel Ene-
' my, all the mischief that thy blind power can
' fasten upon my Destiny ; I do here lay myself
' open to thy cruel persecution, and defy thy ma-
' lice to trample upon a Courage, which yet thou
' hast but vainly combated with.

He paus'd at these Words, and *Tyridates* perceiving he had much ado to stop there, out of fear
that his presence might put him to some constraint, and the Chirurgeons opinion that a pursuit of his passionate discourse might injure his
health, after he had intreated him to take some
repose, and follow their advice to whose care his
health was committed, and seek, if possible, for
comfort in that grand Courage, whereof he had
given so many glorious proofs in so short a time,
he took his leave for the rest of the day.

From that Chamber he return'd to *Coriolanus*,
to whom he gave an account of his Visit, repeated the Words, and described the passion of the
Stranger : At this the Son of *Juba* shrugg'd up his
shoulders, and lifted up his Eyes, when after he
had been some moments silent : ' Oh valiant
' Stranger ! *cry'd he*, if thy Soul be seized with
' a violent grief, how well has Fortune pattern'd
' our condition : Yet thy Calamities must swell to
' a strange bulk to measure thy Calamities with
' mine ; when you shall know my last Adventures,
' *continued he, turning to Tyridates*, you will
' doubtless deplore my Misfortune, and possibly
' believe that the miseries of others are trifles in
' comparison of mine. To keep you no longer in
' doubt

' doubt of this, *Emilius* is ready to finifh his Story,
'' fince you had rather have it from his mouth
'' than mine. For that, *faid Tyridates*, I fhall
' take a time when Civility forbids me to enjoy
' your company; though 'tis confeft I defire with
' fome violence to learn the fucceffion of thofe
' beautiful Actions, whereof the beginnings were
' fo charming, but I fhall refer it to thofe hours
' which will not permit me to fee you without im-
' portunity. I cannot fuffer the conftraint your
' Courtefy offers, *faid Coriolanus*, to a Perfon
' who has no neceffity to require it, do not difob-
' lige yourfelf for my Divertifement, my thoughts
' do furnifh me with an ample entertainment, and
' let me have leave to tell you, that in the fad
' eftate to which Love and Fortune has reduced
' me, if your company was not marvelloufly be-
' witching, it would not be fupportable.

By thefe Words *Coriolanus* obliged *Tyridates* to
leave him, and that Prince taking *Emilius* along
to his Chamber, made him fit down in the fame
place where they pafs'd away the morning, and
the faithful 'Squire knowing his Intention, after he
had prepared his Difcourfe with fome Moments
of Silence, he purfued the Story in this Manner.

The Continuation of the Hiftory of Coriolanus and Cleopatra.

WE marched out of *Rome* to *Auftria*, with the
Encouragement of many aufpicious Prefages
for the War, and all thofe to whom the Frequen-
tation of my Mafter's Company had given any
Knowledge of his Virtue, entertain'd very pregnant Hopes of his Succefs in that Expedition:
Though he could take no Employment that over-
topp'd his illuftrious Birth, he had fome Reafon to

Q 5   think

think it ftrange, that a Prince born of a barbarous
King, Enemy to the People of *Rome*, not exceeding the Age of twenty one, fhould command a
Roman Army, at a Time when *Rome* abounded
with fo many famous Captains of her own, that
were capable of Conduct: I fay to command; for
indeed though *Tilius Corifius* remained with fome
Shadow of Authority in thofe Provinces, his want
of Experience, with the Infirmities of his Perfon,
had render'd him fo inconfiderable to the Soldiers,
as though my Prince ftill did him the Honour to
receive his Advice in all Affairs, the abfolute Power was folely in his Hands, and the entire Glory
of all thofe memorable Events in that Expedition,
by the general Vote was alloted to him only. He
was receiv'd by the Legions with loud Acclamations; and befides that, the Opinion of his former
Exploits, had gained him the Hearts of Part of
the Captains; the bounteous Diftribution of Nature's Favour, fignally ftamp'd in his Face, Language, and Actions, quickly procured him the
Affection and Refpect of all thofe to whom his
Virtue was yet undifcover'd.

The Commiffion he receiv'd from the Emperor
was generally approv'd; the Soldiers, Officers,
and *Corifius* himfelf, (to whom *Varro*'s violent
Humour had been intolerable) accepted this young
Companion in Command without a Murmur;
and, though he was Lieutenant to a *Roman* Army,
he held it an Honour, that the Son of a King, a
thoufand Times more confiderable by his Merits
than Birth, was apparently contented to fhare the
Dignity with him, only referving all the Trouble
and Danger to himfelf. 'Tis then to my Prince
alone you may pleafe to attribute the Honour of
all that was done in that War: And though the
Orders were often fubfcribed with *Corifius*'s Name
as

as well as his, I am able to affirm, as a conſtant
Witneſs, that never forſook him, he had no more
hand in any Part of the Action, than if he had
then been at *Rome*, only amuſing himſelf with
political Maxims how to govern the Provinces,
and preſerve the Cities in Obedience, that we had
reduc'd; while my Maſter, at the Head of his
Army, did the Buſineſs of the War, making new
Brooks of barbarous Blood run thro' *Campania*.

The Enemies had two renowned Captains
among them; he that led the *Auſtrians* was call'd
Sillo, and *Theopiſtus* commanded the *Cantabrians*: They had many flying Bodies beſides, rang'd
under ſeveral Lieutenants, which were placed as
Neceſſity adviſed, in divers Parts of the Provinces, where they might beſt diſtreſs the *Romans*;
their Cities were univerſally up in Arms, fortified
with ſtrong Garriſons, and furniſh'd with abundance of Victuals; all their Streights and Paſſes
upon Rivers defended with ſo much Strength and
Caution, as it appeared no petty Enterprize, no
contemptible Task to tame this warlike People.

Yet the Threats of theſe Difficulties, inſtead of
diſcouraging, enflamed the Heart of the fierce young
Prince, with an eager Deſire of forcing from
thoſe fair Occaſions an Improvement of his Glory; and joining to his admirable Valour an incredible Prudence, if compared with his Years,
he began to act in that War, both by Conduct and
Execution, like another *Hannibal*, or a *Julius
Ceſar*; never did any thing appear ſo beautiful,
as my brave Prince in the Functions of his Charge,
and when his Head was in a Caſque, that noble
and warlike Mind was ſo highly advantaged by
the Grace he uſed in his Command, as his Enemies themſelves had not Power to behold him
without Affection. The firſt Time he preſented
himſelf

himself to their View was upon the Bank of a little River, where *Theopistus* appeared in Person at the Head of above 30,000 Combatants; the River was narrow, but scarce fordable, which kept the Armies from joining, and forc'd them for a long Time to fight at a Distance, with no other Weapons than Arrows, 'till my Master, knowing the Advantage of the *Romans* consisted in a closer Combat, and not in those wooden Showers, whereby the *Barbarians* might happily dispute the Victory with Danger to his Party, after he had sought the fittest Place, he spurred his Horse into the Water, and like another *Alexander*, at the Passage of *Granicus*, both by Words and Example encouraged a Part of his Cavalry to keep him Company in the Danger; and thus sometimes fording, sometimes swimming their Horses, they gained the opposite Bank.

The *Cantabrians* amazed at so prodigious a Daring, had not Courage enough left them to stand the Encounter; and my Master taking Advantage of the Disorder, wherein Fear and Wonder had shuffled them, gave his Enemies a hot Charge, and his own Soldiers Time to pass the River with greater Facility than before, which still came up with such fresh Supplies to his Succour, as at last he totally routed their Army, and carried so entire a Victory, as more than 15,000 *Barbarians* were left dead upon the Spot.

The first Loss struck such a Terrour into the Enemy, as made them manage their Quarrel with more Caution.

A few Days after, they thought they had gotten an Occasion to revenge the last Slaughter by our total Ruine; and indeed they put us in great Danger; for my Prince, sitting down with his Army before a Town called *Tilloe*, built upon a
Marsh,

Marſh, and made by its Situation almoſt inacceſſible, the Enemies two Generals having rallied and rais'd all the Forces they could make, came up with an admirable Diligence in two great Bodies, incamped themſelves at our Backs, and ſhut us up between the City, the Marſh, and their two Armies, leaving no Paſſage free, unleſs we could cut out the Way through one of their groſs Bodies.

My Maſter preſently perceived what an Error his Ignorance in the Country had made him incur; but loath to give his Soldiers Time to perceive their Diſadvantage, and receive a Terror that might give the Enemies the Victory; to ſave his Men, he reſolved to raiſe the Siege: And judging the Deſign more fit for the Favourite of Darkneſs than Light, having caus'd the Troops and Legions to be ready to march about Midnight; and giving all neceſſary Orders to the Officers, he ſent two or three hundred Men to give an Alarm at *Theopiſtus*'s Quarters; and when the Enemies believ'd the Danger bent itſelf that Way, he ſuddenly broke with all his Forces upon *Sillo*'s Army, threw down all that ſtood in his Way; and by his Example we charg'd ſo vigorouſly, as aſſiſted by our ſudden Surprizal, and the Fire we threw about into all the Quarters of their Camp, and the Night's Darkneſs, which increaſed the Terror, we put them to ſuch a general Rout, as after we had killed about 10,000 *Barbarians*, we paſſed through their Camp upon the Neck of the reſt, which were left covered with Carkaſſes and Blood, and made good our Retreat ſcarce with the Loſs of 600 Men, to the top of a Mountain, where we incamped before Day, whoſe new-born Light made us quickly underſtand ourſelves in a Condition to preſent them Battle.

This

This brave Piece of Service pass'd for a Miracle among the *Barbarians*, and so fearfully astonished them, as instead of marching in Battle against us, they rose up with their Army, and directing their March through the City, they went and encamped on the other Side the Marsh.

A few Days after, my Master re-inforcing his Numbers with the Supplies of 8000 Foot, and 4000 Horse, which *Corisius* had sent him, he re-attack'd the City so vigorously, as in spight of the Enemy's Army that lay at the Gates on the other Side, and fortified it with Numbers necessary for Defence, within six Days time we carried it by Storm, and marched toward the Enemy with so much Courage and Confidence, as it took away their's, and obliged them to a timorous Retreat into such Places, whose Situation hinder'd us from forcing them to fight. I contract the Recital of these Things in as narrow a Volume as possible, for should I tie my Relation to every particular, it would cost more Time than I have now to lay out upon the whole Discourse.

While these Things pass'd at the Camp, Fame daily carried Intelligence of my Master's grand Actions to every *Roman* Ear, which brought as much Joy to *Marcellus* and the rest of his Friends, as Despight to *Livia*, and the whole Faction of *Tiberius*; the Princess *Cleopatra*, who claim'd a more peculiar Interest in his Glory than the rest, forgot not to acknowledge her particular Satisfaction, and to that Purpose she answer'd all his Letters; but my Memory, too weak to retain them, I only preserved some of the shortest, and especially that which she wrote upon Intelligence of his Victory I last related: I believe the Words differ'd not much from these.

The

The Princess *Cleopatra*, to the valiant *Juba*
Coriolanus Prince of *Mauritania*.

'TO gain great Battles against the valiantest
'People in *Europe*, to force Cities defended
'by an Army that out-number'd your's, and ren-
'der the Nights themselves famous by your Victo-
'ries, are Actions conformed to my Wishes, and
'worthy of your Courage; but thus every Mo-
'ment to lavish such precious Blood; so oft to
'expose a Life so dear unto me, to the Mercies
'of Danger, when Necessity does not bind you,
'are Actions contrary to your Obedience, and
'the Care you ought to take of my Repose; yet
'I incline to pardon, when I remember you com-
'bat for my Conquest, as well as your own Glo-
'ry, and that you owe Part of those Advantages
'your Valour will give of your Rival, to the
'Thought that you fight for *Cleopatra*.

These clear Proofs of *Cleopatra*'s Affection
swelled my Master's Courage to a greater Height,
and daily carried him to the Enterprize of braver
Exploits, for which Fortune offer'd him fair Opportunities, and the Gods seem'd willing for his
Glory, that our Enemies, by the Arrival of a great
Recruit, should be once more able to face us in
the Field, and trusting to the Number of their
Men, which far exceeded our's, they descended
into the Plain of *Gangaris*, and presented us Battle.

Coriolanus, though much the weaker in Number, joyfully accepted the *Austrians* Defiance, and
ranging his Army with a dexterous Prudence, he
marched against the *Barbarians*, not as to a doubt-
ful Combat, but a certain Victory.

I remember he was that Day cover'd with a
Coat of Steel, so exceedingly bright, as the Splendor of it mingled with the Rays of the Jewels that
en-

enriched his Arms, and both receiv'd the Sun-Beams, formed a Flame which seemed to inviron him; besides, there appeared another in several Flashes at his Eyes, that darted their fierce Glory with such extraordinary Ardour, as it was even difficult for his Friends to behold them without betraying some kind of Fear; he wore no Casque to cover his Face, but only a little *Morion* after the *Greek* Fashion, shaded with twenty white Feathers, under which his Visage appeared that whole Day naked to the View, and his long curl'd Hair which descended upon his Shoulders in gross Annulets, seemed to borrow Brightness from his warlike Ardour. He was mounted upon a white Horse, dapled with black Spots, which at once expressed both Pride and Beauty, and in his right Hand held two Darts, which he brandish'd against his Enemies in a menacing Fashion.

Thus, and more fair than I am able to describe him, after he had made an Harangue to his Troops, with an Eloquence that few alive could match, he led them on to the Combat; and at his first Blow, in the view of all his Army, gave Death to *Sillo*, General of the *Austrians*, a Man of an extraordinary Force and Stature; who, after my Prince's Example, marching at the Head of his Forces, was pierced through and through with one of his Javelins, and fell without a Soul at his Horse's Feet.

Coriolanus accompany'd that brave Act with a thousand others; which, in spight of the Throng into which he rush'd with a precipitate Fury, were remark'd by Thousands; and so courageously animated his Soldiers, both by his Voice and Example, as, after a well disputed Combat, Victory declared for us, and remain'd so entirely our's, as more than 35,000 *Barbarians* died upon the Place, their

their whole Baggage was taken, and all those that escaped the Fury of our Soldiers, scarce found their Safety in the wild Shelter of the Forests and Mountains.

This Victory, which by the *Romans* Judgment, to whom the News was quickly carried, might have challenged a Comparison with the most memorable of those that helped to establish their Empire, gave a great Stagger to this War, but it was not capable to end it : And though it was long before the *Barbarians* could recover a Condition of fighting again, yet they had a great Number of strong Cities, not one of which would render without Resistance ; so that it cost us no less than a whole Year's Time to reduce them. During which, we had divers Combats upon Parties with the Enemy's scatter'd Troops, which they sent to set upon us on all Sides. At last we received Intelligence, that they had made one great Effort for all ; and having drawn all the Forces together they could make, they were marching towards us, for the last Decision of their Liberty.

But while my Master thus bravely busied himself in the Service of the *Roman* Empire, (and besides the purchase of a Glory that carried his Name to the remotest Limits of it, with the Applause of the People, Senate, and Emperor) flew at a proud Height in *Cleopatra*'s Favour, which he still received, confirmed by daily Proofs. The Malice of his Fortune would have it, that *Tiberius* should light upon no worse Success in *Germany*, than he had in *Spain*. 'Tis true, he had the Advantage to command the valianter Legions, and deal with Enemies of far less Strength and Courage than our's ; whatever it was, (for my Master's Interests cannot bribe me to debate the just Value of his Enemy's Glory) he defeated the *Pan-*

nonians

nonians and *Dalmatians* in two signal Battles, took five or six of their chief Cities, and reduced them to so feeble a Condition, as wanting those great Resources that so often crested the *Austrians* and *Cantabrians*, they were constrained to beg their Peace of *Tiberius*, and receive those Conditions it pleased the Conqueror to impose; which the cruel Disposition of *Tiberius* (ever inflexible to Pity or Pardon) render'd very rigorous; and though indeed he did signalize himself in that Expedition by divers Pieces of personal Valour, he was much censured for spilling of Blood, without a just Necessity, and breaking the Articles in his Capitulation. However, in eight Months time, with great Advantages to the Empire, he finished that War; and returned to *Rome*, cover'd with Laurels in so pompous an Estate, as the Triumphs of *Cæsar*, *Pompey*, and *Paulus Emilius* did scarce shew more Magnificence.

His Actions, to mention them without Partiality, were certainly far short of my Master's, as the Story's Sequel will inform you; but the Success not less conducing to *Cæsar*'s Service, which the Empress, with her whole Party, cry'd up with loud Praises, and strew'd the Court with such a Noise of his Atchievements, as if all other Men's Glory ought to suffer an Eclipse when his was mentioned. *Cæsar* made him a Reception, not unworthy of the Service he had render'd him, nor the Place that he held near his Person by his Mother's Authority; and the Princess *Cleopatra*, that she might not be construed an Enemy to the State, by betraying any Trouble for his Prosperity, by Advice of those whom her own discreet Choice had given Authority over her, received him with a smooth Brow.

Tiberius -

Tiberius left out nothing in his Language or Behaviour, that might prove a Bait for her Affection, and try'd all the Strength of his Power with the Empress, in disposing her to sway *Cæsar's* Judgment on his side.

Livia, as she had formerly done, did for a time resist his Intreaty, eagerly desirous to address his Aims at the Princess *Julia*, whose Possession would put him in a fair Path to the Empire, a Design that especially toil'd her working Thoughts. All the Persuasions she could urge, were employ'd upon her Son to change the Object of his Passion, endeavouring to make him feel the Stings of Emulation against *Marcellus*; who, by the Enjoyment of *Julia*, would strengthen his Pretences to the Sovereign Authority, and doubtless carry the Imperial Crown by the double Advantage of Nephew and Son-in-law to the Emperor.

Tiberius was the most aspiring Man upon Earth; yet then more amorous than ambitious, which arm'd him with an obstinate Defence against *Livia's* Importunities; and after he had assur'd her they were all in vain, he press'd so hard for her Assistance, protesting his Repose and his Life depended on it. As that indulgent Mother to the Passions of her Son, gave over her Persuasions, and began to set her Subtleties a-work to content him, losing no Occasion to sollicite *Augustus* in his behalf, and practising all those Charms upon him, which she knew had greatest Influence to persuade his Preference of *Tiberius's* Services to those of *Coriolanus*.

The Emperor long resisting her Persecutions, and remembering what was due, as well to his royal Word as the Friendship of *Marcellus*, (who publickly propp'd my Master's Interests) and my Prince's Services, who was then struggling with

Death

Death and Danger for the Glory of his Empire ;
he shut his Ears to the sly Insinuations of *Livia*,
which incessantly tormented him. This Perseverance lasted some Months ; during which, he often protested to determine the Difference betwixt
the two Competitors with an impassionate Equity,
and decide the Prize of their Actions by such a
general Judgment, as neither should have cause to
suspect Partiality. But, in fine, what could not
Love do upon a Soul when he had once disarm'd
it ? And what might not *Livia* hope from him,
who for her sake had violated the sacred Laws of
Marriage, and (beyond all Precedent) had ravished her great with Child from her Husband's Arms ?
Well, that subtile Spirit ply'd him so perpetually,
as his easy Soul, at last consenting to believe that
Coriolanus's Mouth might be stopp'd with Re-
wards more important than *Cleopatra*, to please
the importunate *Livia*, he declared against him,
and promised to pronounce his Judgment to her
Son's Advantage.

Of this the whole Court had present notice,
and it quickly flew to the Ears of *Marcellus* and
Cleopatra. The Princess receiv'd this News with
a most violent Displeasure, yet supported it with
more Moderation than *Marcellus*, who burst into
a loud and haughty Passion at the Injury was
offered his Friend, vigorously disputed his Interests in the Emperor's Presence ; and went so far
with *Tiberius* upon that Subject, meeting with
him at the Door of the Capitol, and exchanging
some warm Words, they drew their Swords one
at another. This Quarrel might have raised dangerous Disorders in *Rome*, if *Cæsar*'s Authority
had not stepp'd between, and forced them to a mutual Embrace, charging *Marcellus* to keep his Resentments to himself.

My

My Mafter had Advice of his Misfortune that
fame Day that he fought the laft Battle with the
Auftrians and *Cantabrians*, and was giving Orders at the Head of his Army, when two Letters
were brought him, one from *Marcellus*, and the
other from *Cleopatra*. Whatever his Employment
could then alledge to difpenfe with their prefent
Perufal, was all over-borne by the Paffion he preferved for thofe two Perfons ; and, opening the
Letters, he found thefe Words in that of *Marcellus*,
which he firft read.

Marcellus *to* Juba Coriolanus *Prince of* Mauritania.

' I Would ftay till you receive the troublefome
' News I fend you from fome other Hand,
' were it not dangerous to retard the Intelligence ;
' the Emperor declares for *Tiberius*, if your Prefence
' does not fcatter thofe Advantages that *Livia*'s
' Perfuafions have gained upon our's : Come away,
' my dear Brother, if it be poffible, and attend all
' things from the Affection of a Friend, who
' would not have told you this Mifchief, but with
' a purpofe to ferve you againft it, at the Price of
' his Fortunes, his Blood, and his Life.

This was *Marcellus*'s Letter ; and *Cleopatra*
fpoke thus.

The Princefs Cleopatra *to Prince* Coriolanus.

' YEfterday I underftood from the Princefs
' *Octavia*, that *Auguftus* intends me for
' *Tiberius*. The previous Difcovery of my In-
' tentions will tell you how I relifh the Defign :
' However, I know his Authority, as big as it
' is, fhall never change my Inclinations. Your
' fudden Return will poffibly befriend you more
' than

' than all the Power we can stir in your Favour ;
' and, if you apprehend me right, no Considera-
' tion will be able to defer your coming.

My Master, as I told you, received and read
these Letters, just as he was at the Point of giving
the last Signal for the Battle ; and his Eye had no
sooner arrived at the Period, when, stopping the
forwardest with a loud Cry, and commanding
their Stay till the Signal was given, he remained
in a confused Perplexity, with his Thoughts at a
loss what Resolution he should take. His Resentments of this Injury no sooner took fire in his
Soul, but it presently flew into such a Flame of Anger, as the first Thought that presented itself was
to give away the Victory, and punish the Ingratitude of *Augustus*, by the Loss of his Army, and
the Ruin of his Affairs, in a Country where his
Valour had establish'd them. Then distasting the
Treason in that Design, and passing thence to another that clash'd not so much with his Generosity, he took up a Thought to abandon the *Roman*
Troops, carry over his Sword to the Enemy's Party, and raise them by that to the same Height
from whence he had thrown them.

While this Irresolution kept him buried in a
profound Study, some of the Commanders that
were nearest his Person, had asked him divers
Questions touching their Employment, without
gaining the least Word of Answer from his Mouth.
At last, awaking from his deep Cogitations, he
lifted up his Head, which all this Time he had
hung down as low as his Saddle Bow ; and turning his Eyes round, wherein Choler was lively
represented, ' Let us go, *said he*, whither our
' Duty calls us, and prefer our Honour before
' such Resentments as cannot be justified by the
' Event of this Day ; we may possibly reverse
' *Cæfar's*

' *Cæsar*'s Intention, or at least find out a Death
' to guard us from the Injustice is offered.

Finishing these Words, after he had sent all the
Commanders to their several Charges, he first
gave the last Signal, and was the first that flew in
among his Enemies. I shall forbear the Particulars of this Battle, which was the most cruel and
bloodiest of all the rest; only after the Dispute
had hotly held a part of the Day, there fell to our
Lot so intire a Victory, as of more than 50,000
Barbarians that faced us in the Morning, scarce
the Tenth of that Number were alive at Night.
The General *Theopistus* was there slain, with all the
most considerable Persons of his Party, and thus
this Root of Rebellion was cut up without the
Hope of Resource; for this miserable People, a
few Days after, submitted to all the Conditions
were thought fit to impose.

They would have been very gentle, could my
Master have staid his Authority in those Parts,
but the next Day after the Battle, conceiving his
Duty amply discharged, he went to find out *Corisius*, whom he had left lame of the Gout in a
neighbouring City, where after he had passed him
an Account of the State of Affairs as he left them,
remitting the whole Power into his Hands, he
took his leave of him, and a few Days after parted with the same Equipage that followed him
to the Army, endeavouring by great Days Journeys to reach the imperial City.

I will not repeat the passionate Complaints which
broke from the Sense of his Wrongs in that Voyage; Grief and Anger took their Turns in his
Words and Actions, and sometimes the latter
transported him to such rash Language, and loud
Threats, as his Friends till then had never observ'd,
and indeed were very unsuitable to his ordinary

Mode-

Moderation; whatever Diligence we ufed in the Voyage, we arriv'd not at *Rome* till three Days after the News of our laft Victory, which we found had taken up a glorious Welcome, and exprefs'd itfelf in all the Varieties of Joy to receive us; Bonfires and Sacrifices made the Streets flame, and the Altars fmoak, at a more confpicuous Expence, than was ufually beftow'd upon the Conqueft of larger Territories; and for a more confpicuous Mark of Glory, the Emperor having now no more Enemies in the World to trouble the Tranquillity of his Dominion, in Sign of an univerfal Peace, had caufed the Temple of *Janus* to be fhut, which always ftood open in Time of War, and was never feen clofed fince the Reign of *Numa Pompilius.*

Had Notice been given before of my Mafter's Coming, his Reception had been little fhort of a triumphal Entry; and certainly had he defired the Triumph itfelf, it would have been granted him; but becaufe he left his Charge, and came back without *Auguftus*'s Orders, he thought it not fit to give Advice of his Arrival, yet could not hinder the firft that faw him pafs from breaking out into loud Acclamations, and the Noife of his Return ran fo fwiftly from Mouth to Mouth, as in a few Moments it was divulged through the whole City.

The END *of the* FIRST VOLUME.